Praise for *Mind to Matter*

"If you've been wondering whether your thoughts really do affect your life, this marvelous book will make you a believer. From the level of the atom to the level of our bodies to the level of the galaxies, Dawson Church's painstaking research shows that mind is profoundly creative. Synthesizing hundreds of studies in the fields of biology, physics, and psychology, he shows that moment by moment, the energy fields of our brains are literally creating reality. These insights can have a radical effect on your health and prosperity, and I highly recommend you apply them in your life."

— John Gray, #1 *New York Times* best-selling author
of *Men Are from Mars, Women Are from Venus*

"We have entered an era of healing in which the influence of consciousness in health and illness is being validated as never before. For a view of these crucial insights, researcher Dawson Church's Mind to Matter *is invaluable."*

— Larry Dossey, M.D., author of *One Mind: How Our Individual Mind Is Part of a Greater Consciousness and Why It Matters*

"Dawson Church's careful scientific work shows that the Law of Attraction isn't just a metaphysical proposition—it's a scientific reality. Drawing from hundreds of studies, and illustrated with inspiring real-life stories, it demystifies the intricate mechanisms by which thoughts become things. As the boundaries of what you believe is possible for your life are stretched by Dawson's work, they may never snap back to their old shape."

— Marci Shimoff, #1 *New York Times* best-selling
author of *Happy for No Reason*

"I love this book. It constantly fascinated me with delicious facts and so many captivating stories. And it is wonderful to see science catching up with what the shamans and sages have always known!"

— Donna Eden, author of *Energy Medicine*

"Mind to Matter *challenges the core principles of modern medicine and conventional science. Dawson Church makes a compelling case that the mind/body link is more profound than we ever suspected, and that science must expand its paradigm to include forces like consciousness, resonance, and energy. Profusely illustrated, the book includes an impressive compendium of research citations, from classic papers to recent breakthroughs. Many practical examples and exercises provide tools to work on our own personal transformation and, if the book's thesis of interconnection is correct, our social transformation as well. I highly recommend this book."*

— Eric Leskowitz, M.D., Department of Psychiatry,
Harvard Medical School

"Dawson Church has been a pioneer in the field of healing for decades, his research far ahead of its time. His book Mind to Matter *is perfectly timed for an era in which people are opening up to the science and research behind energy techniques. Dawson offers a brilliant and insightful guide to how our thoughts create our reality. Packed with fascinating history from the dawn of evolution to the latest brain research, his work is a blueprint for both experts and non-professionals looking for effective healing strategies. Dawson succinctly shows us not just that these methods work, but the empirical basis for how they work. If you have ever wanted to learn the science of manifestation and how your thoughts affect your material world, this book is a must-read. It will change your thoughts, and applying these principles every day will in turn change your reality. The question is—what will you create after you read it?"*

— Peta Stapleton, Ph.D., School of Psychology,
Bond University, Australia

"Many in our culture are shifting from powerless victims to powerful co-creators. Yet as this evolutionary impulse toward greater power emerges, we are coming face to face with what happens when power is abused. As we face global crises of unpredictable proportions, we need heart-based creators of deep integrity in touch with their power now more than ever. What would be possible in our lives and on our planet if we connected our power with our hearts? What does science have to say about such manifesting power? Mind to Matter explores this edge of how our power to participate in the co-creation of reality functions from the scientific perspective. It also calls us out on how to avoid overstating our human power, as so many 'law of attraction' books mistakenly promise. As our power grows, we are called to acknowledge with humility the paradoxical nature of how powerful we are as creators, yet how uncontrollable the great Mystery really is. May those who read this book step fully into their power, their hearts, and their integrity, and may the world be blessed by how this book affects you."

— Lissa Rankin, M.D., *New York Times* best-selling author of *Mind Over Medicine*

MIND
TO
MATTER

ALSO BY DAWSON CHURCH

BOOKS

*The Genie in Your Genes: Epigenetic Medicine
and the New Biology of Intention**

*Soul Medicine: Awakening Your Inner Blueprint
for Abundant Health and Energy**

*The EFT (Emotional Freedom Techniques) Manual**

*EFT for Weight Loss**

*EFT for PTSD**

*EFT for Love Relationships**

*EFT for Fibromyalgia and Chronic Fatigue**

*EFT for Back Pain**

EFT for Golf

Psychological Trauma: Healing Its Roots in Body, Brain and Memory

*The Clinical EFT Handbook Volume 1 (co-editor)**

*The Clinical EFT Handbook Volume 2 (co-editor)**

*Communing with the Spirit of Your Unborn Child**

Facing Death, Finding Love

*Available from Hay House
Please visit:

Hay House USA: www.hayhouse.com®
Hay House Australia: www.hayhouse.com.au
Hay House UK: www.hayhouse.co.uk
Hay House India: www.hayhouse.co.in

MIND
TO
MATTER

THE ASTONISHING
SCIENCE OF HOW
YOUR BRAIN CREATES
MATERIAL REALITY

DAWSON CHURCH

HAY HOUSE, INC.
Carlsbad, California • New York City
London • Sydney • New Delhi

Published in the United States by: Hay House, Inc.: www.hayhouse.com® • **Published in Australia by:** Hay House Australia Pty. Ltd.: www.hayhouse.com.au • **Published in the United Kingdom by:** Hay House UK, Ltd.: www.hayhouse.co.uk • **Published in India by:** Hay House Publishers India: www.hayhouse.co.in

Cover design: Victoria Valentine • *Interior design:* Riann Bender
Indexer: Joan Shapiro

Library of Congress has cataloged the earlier edition as follows:

Names: Church, Dawson, 1956- author.
Title: Mind to matter : the astonishing science of how your brain creates
    material reality / Dawson Church, Ph.D.
Description: Carlsbad, California : Hay House, [2018] | Includes
    bibliographical references and index.
Identifiers: LCCN 2017060615 | ISBN 9781401955236 (hardcover : alk. paper)
Subjects: LCSH: Neuropsychology. | Brain. | Cognition. | Mind and reality.
Classification: LCC QP360 .C4848 2018 | DDC 612.8--dc23 LC record available at
https://lccn.loc.gov/2017060615

Tradepaper ISBN: 978-1-4019-5525-0
E-book ISBN: 978-1-4019-5524-3
Audiobook ISBN: 978-1-4019-5526-7

10 9 8 7 6 5 4 3 2 1

1st edition, June 2018
2nd edition, August 2019

Printed in the United States of America

CONTENTS

FOREWORD

Science has become the contemporary language of mysticism. In my experience from teaching audiences around the world, the moment terminology related to religion, ancient traditions, secular cultures, or even new age idealisms is spoken in public, audiences become divided. Yet science unifies—and thus creates community.

Thus, when some of the principles of quantum physics (how mind and matter are related) and electromagnetism are combined with the latest discoveries in neuroscience and neuroendocrinology (the study of how the brain regulates the hormone system of the body), then a little *psychoneuroimmunology* (the study of how the brain, nervous system, and the immune system impact each other—*that's the mind-body connection*) is added and finally the last findings in epigenetics (the study of how the environment affects gene expression) are included in the equation, you can demystify the mystical. In doing so, you will also uncover the mystery of the self and unravel the true nature of reality.

All these new areas of research point the finger toward possibility. They prove we are not hardwired to be a certain way for the rest of our lives, and we are not doomed by our genes—rather, we're marvels of adaptability and change.

Each time you learn something new, unique possibilities you were not previously aware of open up before you, and as a result you are changed. This is called knowledge, and knowledge causes you to no longer see things the way *they* are, but the way *you* are. This is the process of learning, and the more you learn, the more you make new synaptic connections in your brain. And as you'll learn in this wonderful book, recent studies show that just an hour of focused concentration on any one subject doubles the number of connections in your brain related to that subject. The same research tells us that if you don't repeat, review, or think about what you've learned, those circuits prune apart within hours or days. Thus, if learning is making new synaptic connections, remembering is maintaining those connections.

In the research I've conducted with literally thousands and thousands of people all over the world, I now know that once a person understands an idea, a concept, or new information—and they can turn to the person next to them and explain that information—they are firing and wiring certain circuits in their brain. These circuits add new stitches into the three-dimensional tapestry of their brain matter, allowing them to successfully wire the circuits necessary to initiate that new knowledge into a new experience. In other words, once you can remember and discuss the new model of understanding, you are beginning to install the neurological hardware in preparation for an experience.

The more you know what you're doing and why, the easier the *how* gets. That's why this is a time in history when it's not enough to simply *know*—it's a time to *know how*. It makes sense, then, that your next job is to initiate the knowledge by applying, personalizing, or demonstrating what you've philosophically and theoretically learned. This means you're going to have to make new and different choices—and get your body involved. And when you can align your behaviors with your intentions, make your actions equal to your thoughts, or get your mind and body working together, you are going to have a new experience.

So if you are given the proper instructions on what to do, and you follow the directions and perform it properly, you are going to create a new experience. Once you embrace a new experience, the new event will add to (and further enhance) the intellectual circuitry in your brain. This is called experience, and experience enriches the circuitry in the brain. The moment those circuits organize into new networks in the brain, the brain makes a chemical. That chemical is called a feeling or an emotion. That means the instant you feel freedom, abundance, gratitude, wholeness, or joy from that novel event, now you're teaching your body chemically to understand what your mind has intellectually understood.

It's fair to say, then, that knowledge is for the mind and experience is for the body. Now you are beginning to *embody the truth* of that philosophy. In doing so, you're rewriting your biological program and signaling new genes in new ways. That's because new information is coming from the environment. As we know from epigenetics, if the environment signals new genes, and the end product of an experience in the environ-ment is an emotion, you are literally signaling the new genes in new ways. And since all genes make proteins and proteins are responsible for the structure and function of your body (the expression of proteins is the expression of life), you are literally changing your genetic destiny. This suggests that it's quite possible your body can be healed.

If you can create an experience once, you should be able to do it again. If you can reproduce any experience repeatedly, eventually you will neurochemically condition your mind and body to begin to work as one. When you've done something so many times that the body knows how to do it as well as the mind, it becomes automatic, natural, and effortless—in other words, a skill or a habit. Once you've achieved that level, you no longer have to consciously think about doing it. That's when the skill or habit becomes the subconscious state of being. Now it's innate and you're beginning to *master that philosophy*. You have become that knowledge.

This is how common people around the world are beginning to do the uncommon. In doing so they are transitioning from philosopher to initiate to master; from knowledge to experience to wisdom; from mind to body to soul; from thinking to doing to being; and from learning with their head to practicing it by hand and knowing it by heart. The beauty of it is, we all have the biological and neurological machinery to do this.

The side effect of your repeated efforts will not only change who you are, but it should begin to create possibilities in your life that reflect your efforts. Why else would you do it? What do I mean when I say pos-sibilities? I'm talking about healing from diseases or imbalances of the body as well as the mind; creating a better life by consciously directing energy and attention into a new future—the manifestation of new jobs, new relationships, new opportunities, and new adventures—equal to our ability to imagine it; and initiating mystical experiences that literally transcend language.

It makes sense that when the synchronicities, coincidences, and new opportunities appear in your life, you'll pay attention to what you have been doing and it should inspire you to do it again. That's how you go from being the victim in your life to being the creator of your life.

And that's what this powerful book is all about. *Mind to Matter* is your personal guide to prove to yourself how powerful you truly are when you organize your thoughts and feelings into coherent states. It was written for you to not just intellectually understand the content but to consistently use the practices and apply them to your life so that you reap the rewards of your efforts.

It's no short order to create a scientific model of understanding that suggests that our subjective mind (our thoughts) can influence our objective world (our life), never mind write a book about it. Finding the research alone is a task in and of itself. And yet, my dear friend and colleague Dawson Church has taken this task on in this fantastically well-written book.

I'd like to tell you a bit about Dawson Church. I met Dawson at a conference in Philadelphia, Pennsylvania, in 2006. The moment we met, there was an instant connection. I quickly realized when we first were introduced that this was going to be a long and healthy friendship. The energy from the exchange of ideas between us felt like a thunderstorm. And every time we talked about something we both believed to be true, it was like lightning struck. We were both changed from our first interaction. Since then, we have worked together on several different projects. Not only has Dawson published several of his own well-researched studies on energy psychology, but he has been part of my research team that has been busy quantitatively measuring the effects of meditation on the brain and the body. He has impeccably led several of our studies and he has become the voice of reason in our research.

Dawson is one of those people I can e-mail or call and ask, *How long does it take for trauma to consolidate in the brain as a long-term memory?* And he will—without hesitation—tell me the exact time it takes, the best reference, the particular research studies as well as the scientists who conducted those studies. It's as if he were giving me directions to the local supermarket. When I discovered this, that's when I realized I was not working with an average scientist, I was in the presence of a super mind. Dawson is brilliant, charismatic, loving, and full of life. He and I share a passion—to understand and to know more about who we really are and what is possible for human beings, especially during these present times of change.

I loved reading this book because it provided answers to some of my own personal questions about the relationship between mind and the material world as well as the connection between energy and matter. I learned new concepts and it helped me see the world differently. I was changed from my time reading it. It is my hope that not only will it change you and help you to see the world differently, but it will also inspire you to apply the principles so that you embody the truth of what is possible for you in your life. If science is the new language of mysticism, then you are learning from a contemporary mystic—my dear friend Dawson Church. He wants you to become your own mystic too and to prove to yourself that your thoughts matter—they literally become matter.

Dr. Joseph Dispenza
New York Times best-selling author
of *You Are the Placebo: Making Your Mind Matter*

INTRODUCTION

Metaphysics Meets Science

Thoughts become things. This is manifestly true. I am sitting on a chair right now. It began as a thought in someone's mind—every detail of it. The frame, the fabric, the curves, the color.

Thoughts become things. This is manifestly untrue. I will never be a quarterback for the National Football League, no matter how earnestly I think about it. I will never be 16 years old again. I will never pilot the starship *Enterprise.*

Between the ways in which thoughts become things and the ways in which thoughts can never become things there is a wide middle ground.

This book explores that middle ground.

Why? We want to be able to create to the outermost limits of our thought, expanding our lives to the limits of our potential. We want to be as happy, healthy, wealthy, wise, fulfilled, creative, and loved as possible. We also don't want to chase pipe dreams, thoughts that are never going to become things.

When we apply the rigorous standards of science to the inquiry, that middle ground turns out to be enormous. Research shows us that with thought, used deliberately, we can create things beyond the ordinary.

The idea that thoughts are things has become a meme in popular culture. It's held as a firm proposition in metaphysics, and some spiritual teachers ascribe infinite powers to the mind. Yet there are clearly limits to human creative abilities; I cannot manifest an aircraft carrier simply by thinking about one. I cannot become Indonesian, jump over Mount Everest, or turn lead into gold.

New discoveries in epigenetics, neuroscience, electromagnetism, psychology, cymatics, public health, and quantum physics, however, are showing that thoughts can be profoundly creative. The page or device on which you now read these words began as a thought. So did democracy, the bikini, space travel, immunization, money, the four-minute mile, and the assembly line.

THE SCIENTIST VERSUS THE MYSTIC

Science and metaphysics are generally considered to be polar opposites. Science is experimental, practical, rigorous, empirical, materialistic, objective, and intellectual. Metaphysics is spiritual, experiential, abstract, mystical, ephemeral, internal, irreplicable, imprecise, subjective, otherworldly, impractical, and impossible to prove. Science studies the world of matter while metaphysics seeks to transcend it.

I have never perceived science and metaphysics as separate and have delighted in being both a mystic and a scientific researcher. When I bring the rigor of science to the questions of consciousness, each illuminates the other.

This book examines the science behind the creative powers of the mind. It reviews the studies that show, step-by-step, exactly how our minds create material form. As each piece of the puzzle falls into place, the science turns out to be even more astonishing than the metaphysics.

This book is also full of case histories—real, up close, authentic personal accounts of people who had an experience of mind-into-matter. Drawn from the worlds of medicine, psychology, sports, business, and scientific discovery, these stories run the gamut from profound to inspiring to heart-wrenching. They show us that thoughts can become things in ways that stretch the fabric of our space-time reality.

Keys in the Ocean

In 2004, I faced a tight deadline to finish my book *The Genie in Your Genes*. The material, on how our emotions turn genes on and off in our bodies, was fascinating. But finding the time to research and write an emotionally engaging yet scientifically impeccable text—amid the demands of my busy life as a single dad, the owner of two businesses, and a doctoral candidate—was a challenge.

I decided to flee to Hawaii for two weeks for a writing intensive. I booked a room at the Prince Kuhio condo complex, a funky 1950s relic on the beach in Poipu, Kauai. I rented a Jeep Wrangler so I would have a rugged four-wheel-drive vehicle to reach more remote beaches and a place to store my snorkeling gear. That way I could swim each day as well as apply myself to completing the project.

One bright, sunny day, I went for a swim at a gorgeous spot called Lawai Beach. Five hundred feet long, with a turtle colony in a reef 300 feet from shore and a healthy population of tropical fish, it was one of my favorite places. I grabbed my snorkeling gear out of the Jeep, locked up, pocketed the keys, and jumped in the water. An hour later, after swimming all over the bay, wet and happy, I rinsed my goggles and flippers to put them back in the car.

When I reached into my pocket for the keys, it was empty.

Could I have dropped them on the path from the car to the beach? I retraced my steps, looking over every inch of ground. I sifted through the sand between the road and my entry point to the water. Nothing.

The only possible conclusion was that my keys had fallen out of my pocket somewhere in the bay. Not only did the key ring hold the car keys, I'd clipped the apartment keys to it as well. I was now locked out of both the car and the condo.

I decided not to panic. I centered my consciousness in my heart, and I imagined the keys gently drifting back to me. Then I dove into the water and started swimming with a purpose. I was determined to find those keys.

The bay covered about 150 square yards or meters, and the coral on the bottom was 6 to 12 feet down. It twisted into thousands of colorful crannies, and finding something as tiny as a key ring seemed impossible.

I worked my way systematically back and forth across the bay, searching each yard intently. My head told me I was on a fool's errand, but I kept my heart soft and receptive. Each time my thinking brain began to panic, I refocused my consciousness in my heart area. I certainly intended to find the keys, but I didn't let my thoughts take me out of the state of flow.

I had searched for an hour without success, and it was getting dark. The visibility was dropping as the sun set, and I couldn't see clearly down to the coral anymore. I decided to abandon my quest and swim back to shore.

Though most of the other bathers had left and the day was ending, I saw a father and three sons snorkeling nearby. They were diving to the bottom and coming up in turns.

My intuition gave me a nudge. I swam up to them and asked, "Did you guys find anything on the bottom?" The youngest boy held up my keys.

THE CHAIN OF EVIDENCE FROM MIND TO MATTER

My skeptic's mind tells me there is a logical explanation for every piece of the key event. I just happened to swim around looking for the keys for the exact length of time it took the boy to find them. I just happened to turn toward the shore at the same moment the family began diving. They just happened to start diving at the spot where my keys had fallen to the bottom. The boy just happened to notice a tiny key ring 12 feet down in an enormous bay after the sky was already dark. It was all a matter of random chance.

But after decades of hundreds of similar experiences, my skeptic's mind has to think again. How can so many highly unlikely things come together at once to produce a desired result?

They led to a quest to determine if there is any scientific link between thoughts and things. As a researcher who has conducted many clinical trials, the editor of a peer-reviewed journal called *Energy Psychology,* and a science blogger for the *Huffington Post,* I read all or part of more than a thousand scientific studies per year. I started to see a pattern. There are multiple links in the chain between thought and thing, and I realized that science could explain many of them. I wondered if anyone had ever connected all the dots to see just how strong the evidence was. Where was the chain strongest, and where were links missing?

If I were to treat the idea of mind creating matter as a scientific rather than a metaphysical hypothesis, would it hold up? I began seeking out research that addressed this question and interviewing some of the brightest minds in the field.

With mounting excitement, I realized that much of the evidence was hiding in plain sight, like pearls scattered in the sand. But no one had strung the facts together in a necklace before. Most of the research is new, and pieces of it are astonishing.

The first pearls I began to pick up from the sand were the easy ones. Research on the human body has been going on since medieval alchemists dissected cadavers. But recently, technology has given scientists unprecedented insight into how our bodies work at the level of cells and molecules.

Nobel Prize–winning physician Eric Kandel showed that when we pass signals through a neural bundle in our brains, that bundle grows rapidly. The number of connections can *double* in *just one hour* of repeated stimulation. Our brains are rewiring themselves along the pathways of our neural activity in real time.

As the thoughts and feelings of our consciousness are carried through our neural network, they trigger the expression of genes. These in turn trigger the synthesis of proteins in our cells. These cellular events produce electrical and magnetic fields that can be measured by sophisticated medical imaging devices such as EEG and MRI.

THE 11-DIMENSIONAL UNIVERSE

The next set of pearls was more challenging. The world of quantum physics is so strange that it confounds our conventional experience of space and time. String theory posits that what we perceive as physical matter is actually composed of strings of energy. What we measure as heavy molecules are fast-moving energy strings, while what we experience as light molecules are energy strings that are vibrating more slowly. The closer science looks at matter, the more it looks like pure energy.

String theory requires a universe with 11 dimensions, not just the 4 required by classical physics. How do our 4-dimensional brains contemplate 11 dimensions? Physicist Niels Bohr said, "If quantum mechanics hasn't profoundly shocked you, you haven't understood it yet."

Then came the pearls that connect consciousness with energy. Energy is entwined with consciousness on both a personal and a cosmic scale. Albert Einstein said: "A human being is a part of the whole, called by us 'Universe,' a part limited in time and space. He experiences himself, his thoughts and feeling as something separated from the rest—a kind of optical delusion of his consciousness." When we begin to "free ourselves from this prison," as Einstein phrased it, then we expand our consciousness to "embrace all living creatures and the whole of nature." Our consciousness interacts with the energy of the universe.

CONSCIOUSNESS AND NONLOCAL MIND

Physician Larry Dossey calls this expansive consciousness that embraces the whole of nature "nonlocal mind." While we live our lives in our local minds and ordinary reality, we're unconscious participants in the larger consciousness of nonlocal mind. Moments of synchronicity like finding my keys remind me of the presence of nonlocal mind. Dossey presents compelling evidence for the existence of nonlocal mind and inspires us with the potential of living our local lives in synchrony with it.

That's a choice we can make in consciousness. Nobel Prize–winning physicist Eugene Wigner says that "the very study of the external world led to the scientific conclusion that the content of the consciousness is an ultimate reality." Though there are many definitions of consciousness, the one I prefer is the simplest: simply being aware.

The way we use that consciousness—the way we direct our awareness—produces profound and immediate changes in the atoms and molecules of our bodies. Science also shows us that our consciousness affects the material reality around us. As our consciousness changes, so changes the world.

Writing this book, I began to string the pearls together, study by study. Additional evidence began showing up in my life in the same synchronous manner in which my lost keys had appeared. When I looked at all the pearls strung together in sequence, I realized that science can explain every link in the chain from thought to thing.

THE DANCE OF CREATION

I am excited to share each one of these links with you. Through story and analogy, through experiment and research, through case histories and anecdotes, we'll trace every part of the process by which your mind creates the material world around you.

You'll discover that you are a potent creator, and that your thoughts lead to things. You'll learn how to use your mind deliberately, as a creative tool, to think nurturing thoughts. You'll understand how you can nudge material reality effortlessly toward your desires. You'll grasp just how powerful you really are and how capable you are of creating change by simply changing your mind.

You'll also discover how the process works on a grand scale, from the molecule to the cell to the body to the family to the community to the country to the species to the planet to the universe. We'll investigate the dance of creation happening at the scale of nonlocal universal consciousness and how your local mind participates in that dance.

This perspective lifts our awareness from the confines of our ordinary reality into a vast field of potential. As we align our individual local minds with the consciousness of the universal nonlocal mind, the beauty of the material reality we create surpasses anything our limited local minds can even dream of.

PUTTING THESE IDEAS INTO PRACTICE

At the end of each chapter, you'll find a list of practical exercises for implementing the ideas of the chapter in your own life. You'll also find a link to an online Extended Play version of the chapter, with resources to expand your experience. These resources include videos, audios, links, lists, case histories, and previews of ideas explored in following chapters. I encourage you to enrich your transformational journey with the activities in the Extended Play version.

The Extended Play version of this chapter includes:

- Audio interview with Daniel Siegel, M.D., author of *Mind: A Journey to the Heart of Being Human*

- Centering in Your Heart exercise

- Additional case histories and references

To access the Extended Play version, visit:
MindToMatter.club/Intro

CHAPTER 1

How Our Brains Shape the World

Mrs. Hughes was short, red-faced, and round. Her hair had a life of its own, throwing off incandescent wisps like solar flares escaping from the grip of the sun's gravity. The bobby pins with which she attempted to confine it were unequal to the task. Her face alternated between pinched disapproval and resigned boredom. As her students suffered through her high school biology classes, she managed to stamp out every trace of curiosity and wonder in us.

I remember looking at line drawings of the human brain in the biology textbooks provided by Mrs. Hughes. The whole structure was fixed and unchanging, just like another organ such as a liver or a heart. In the 1970s, the science Mrs. Hughes taught "knew" that the brain grew until we were roughly 17 years old. After it had filled our skulls, it remained static for a lifetime, faithfully coordinating the many processes of life through its network of neurons.

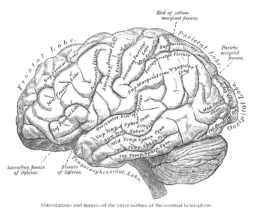

Traditional illustration of the brain.

MIND AS AN EPIPHENOMENON
OF COMPLEX BRAINS

We also had some idea what the mind was. As evolution produced more and more complex brains, going from the simple ganglia of nematode worms to the massive prefrontal cortex that crowns the human head, mind arose. To scientists of Mrs. Hughes's day, *mind* was an "epiphenomenon" of the brain's increasing complexity. Humans could write poetry, record history, make music, and perform calculus because of the power of the mind residing in the brain locked inside the bony circumference of the skull.

As they say in *The Big Short*, "It ain't what you don't know that gets you into trouble. It's what you know for sure that just ain't so." Most of what science knew, as recorded in the biology textbooks of Mrs. Hughes's day, like the static brain, just ain't so.

Our brains are on the boil. Frenetic cellular activity cycles through the brain constantly, creating and destroying molecules and cells, whether we are awake or asleep (Stoll & Müller, 1999).

Even the structure of neurons is constantly changing. Microtubules are the scaffolding that gives cells their rigidity, similar to the way girders shape a building. The microtubules in the brain's nerve cells have a shelf life of just 10 minutes between creation and destruction (Kim & Coulombe, 2010). That's how quickly our brains are changing.

Microtubules are the rigid skeletal structures giving cells their shape.

In this seething mass of activity, selected neural circuits are enhanced. The ones that grow are the ones we use. Pass an information signal repeatedly through a neural bundle and the bundle starts to enlarge. Just as the arms of a bodybuilder get bigger as he practices lifting heavier weights, our neural circuits grow when we exercise them.

THE SPEED OF NEURAL CHANGE

Studies published in the 1990s stunned neuroscientists with findings that even people in their 80s rapidly add capacity to frequently used neural circuits. On November 5, 1998, the headline "news of the week" in the most prestigious research journal, *Science*, read: "New Leads to Brain Neuron Regeneration" (Barinaga, 1998).

The speed of the process caused an earthquake in the world of our scientific knowledge. When the neurons in a neural bundle are stimulated repeatedly, the number of synaptic connections can double in just an hour (Kandel, 1998). If your house acted like your body, it would notice which lights you were turning on, and every hour it would double the amount of electrical conduit going to that light circuit.

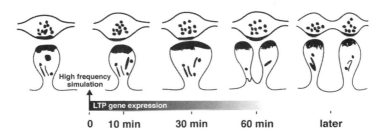

**Within an hour of repeat stimulation,
the number of synaptic connections in a neural pathway doubles.**

To obtain the raw materials to rewire the rooms in which you turned on the lights the most, your smart home would strip wiring from other sources. Our bodies do the same. Within three weeks of inactivity in an existing neural signaling pathway, the body starts to disassemble it in order to reuse those building blocks for active circuits (Kandel, 1998).

INCREASING THE MASS OF THE BRAIN'S MOST USED REGIONS

This process of neural plasticity is evident when we learn new mechanical or intellectual skills. Take an adult education class in Russian at your community college; by the end of the first hour, you've already learned a few words. By the end of a year of practice, you've built up those neural bundles enough to speak simple Russian sentences without conscious effort.

Or you might decide that chess is a mental challenge that will keep your mind sharp into old age and start playing. At first, you're terrible; you can't remember whether it's the castle or the knight that moves diagonally. But after a few games, you move the pieces around purposefully and even develop plans for long-term strategies.

Youngster engrossed in a chess match.

Maybe you decide you'd like to manage your money better. You take a look at your retirement plan statements and notice that under the tender loving care of your fund manager, they've been growing at 2 percent a year. Someone's getting rich here, but it's certainly not you. You think you might do better on your own, so you take an online course in stock market investing. At first, even the language seems baffling. What's a covered call? How is return on investment (ROI) different from return on equity (ROE)?

Your first few trades might not make money. But after looking at charts and reading investment news for a few months, you gain confidence and discover that you're getting better at the money game.

Whether you're learning a new language, mastering a new hobby, navigating a new relationship, grappling with a new job, or starting a meditation practice, your brain's process of building and unbuilding is at work. You're adding capacity to the neural circuits you're using the most actively, while old ones wither away, a process called pruning.

Eventually, whole regions of the brain that are being actively used start to gain mass. With MRI scans, researchers are able to measure the volume of each part of a living human brain. They find that people who use their memory actively, like London cabbies who navigate a tangle of ancient streets, have a larger volume of tissue in the hippocampus, a part of the brain responsible for memory and learning. Dancers develop more mass in the part of the brain that manages proprioception, the holographic understanding of the body's location in space.

Your mind is constantly making decisions, such as whether to enroll in that Russian class or join the chess club. What the mind does then determines which brain circuits are engaged. The neural pathways in the brain that the mind's choices stimulate are the ones that grow. In this way, the mind literally creates the brain.

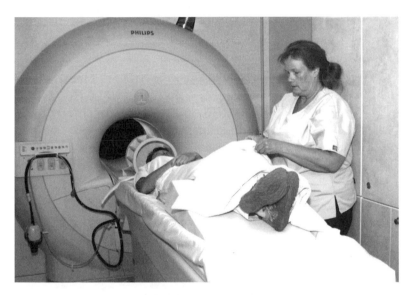

Patient in an MRI machine.

Mindfulness Changes the Brain of a Skeptical TV Journalist

Graham Phillips, Ph.D., is an Australian astrophysicist and TV journalist. Skeptical about feel-good techniques like meditation, he decided to put meditation to the test (Phillips, 2016). In his words, "I'd never really contemplated whether meditation could do anything for me. But the more I hear about the research, the more keen I am to see whether it has any effect. So I'm going to try it myself for two months. . . . For me, to take meditation seriously, I need some hard evidence that it's changing my brain for the better."

Before he began, he was evaluated by a team at Monash University led by biological psychology professor Neil Bailey, Ph.D., and clinical psychologist Richard Chambers, Ph.D. They put him through a battery of tests to evaluate his memory, reaction time, and ability to focus. They also used an MRI to measure the volume of each region of his brain, especially those responsible for memory and learning, motor control, and emotional regulation.

After just two weeks of practicing mindfulness meditation, Phillips felt less stressed and more able to handle the challenges of his job and life. He reported that he "notices stress but doesn't get sucked into it."

Eight weeks later, he returned to Monash for testing. Bailey and Chambers put Phillips through the same battery of tests again. They found that he was better at behavioral tasks, even though he showed diminished brain activity. The researchers noted that his brain had become more energy efficient. It showed an overall decrease in neural activity, doing a better job but exerting less energy. His memory tests also improved.

His reaction time to unexpected events had been cut by almost half a second. Phillips imagined the benefits, such as a quicker reaction time if a pedestrian steps out in front of him when he's driving on a busy street.

One of the brain regions the researchers measured was the hippocampus. They looked especially at the dentate gyrus, the part of the hippocampus responsible for regulating emotion in other parts of the brain. It exerts control over the default mode network, the part of the brain that's active when we aren't engaged in a task. They found that the volume of nerve cells in the dentate gyrus had *increased by 22.8 percent.*

That's an enormous change. Such brain reconfiguration is occasionally seen in young people whose brains are still growing, but it is rarely seen in adults. The change in Phillips's brain indicated a dramatically increased ability to regulate emotions. Psychological tests showed that Phillips's cognitive abilities had increased by several orders of magnitude as well.

There are many studies showing that meditation changes the structure of the brain. A review of the research on mindfulness-style meditation was published in the prestigious journal *Nature Reviews Neuroscience*. It found 21 studies in which participants were placed inside MRI machines to measure the volume of each part of their brain before and after meditation, just like Graham Phillips.

This accumulation of a large body of evidence identified neural growth in "multiple brain regions . . . suggesting that the effects of meditation might involve large-scale brain networks." The review found increases in the volume of "brain regions involved in attention control (the anterior cingulate cortex and the striatum), emotional regulation (multiple prefrontal regions, limbic regions and the striatum) and self-awareness (the insula, medial prefrontal cortex and posterior cingulate cortex and precuneus)" (Tang, Hölzel, & Posner, 2015).

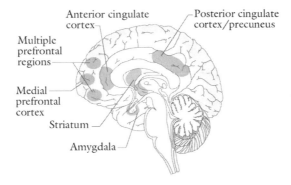

Brain regions in which neural growth occurs as a result of meditation.

WHAT EMOTIONAL REGULATION CAN DO FOR YOU

Like the brain of Graham Phillips, your brain is rewiring itself constantly. The brain adds neural capacity to regions you exercise. Choose a different experience, like meditation, and your brain begins working differently. Change your mind, and information starts to flow along new neural pathways in the brain. The brain's neurons reconfigure themselves accordingly, firing and wiring to fit the new pattern. As the mind directs, the brain responds.

Let's unpack the key elements of Graham's story for a moment. There are five:

- A 22.8 percent increase in the volume of the part of the brain responsible for emotional regulation

- Enhanced brain response time, better memory, increased cognitive powers, improved behavioral abilities

- A more relaxed and energy-efficient brain

- Changes in the brain in just 8 weeks

- No drugs, surgery, supplements, or major life changes—just mindfulness

Imagine having 22.8 percent more nerve cells in your brain to handle the task of emotional regulation. *Emotional regulation* may be jargon from neuroscience, but those two words have a big impact on your daily life. Better emotional regulation means that you're not derailed by common challenges such as:

- Getting triggered by co-workers at your job

- Annoying things your spouse or partner says or does

- Being startled by sudden noises or sights

- The problematic behavior of your children

- What politicians say and do

- Being stuck in traffic

- Stories in the news

- The way your body looks and functions

- Winning or losing at games or conflicts with others

- Religious conflicts or views held by others

- The stock market, your investments, and the economy

- Staying calm when people around you are stressed out

- Being short of time or feeling overwhelmed

- The amount of money you have or expect to have
- The way other people drive their cars
- Your age and how your body is changing
- Crowds, shopping, and close physical proximity to other people
- Other people's opinions that clash with yours
- Your expectations about the way your life ought to be
- The way your parents think and what they say
- Having to wait in line or wait for something you want
- The enviable lifestyles of movie stars and celebrities
- People who make unwanted demands on your time and attention
- The possessions you have or don't have
- Annoying relatives you interact with at family gatherings
- Random mishaps of daily life
- Getting or not getting promotions, rewards, and other things you want
- . . . and anything else that routinely annoys you

Imagine having a brain with vastly increased ability to master those challenges, preventing them from compromising your happiness. Meditation doesn't just change your state—the way you feel at the moment. It changes your traits—the enduring aspects of personality engraved in your brain that govern your outlook on life. Among the positive traits fostered by meditation are greater resilience in the face of adversity, more sympathy for others, and increased compassion for oneself (Goleman & Davidson, 2017). It also leads to a greater degree of self-regulation, making you the master of your emotions rather than a slave to them.

A classic 1972 study called the Stanford marshmallow experiment tested emotional regulation in preschool children. A marshmallow was put in front of them, after which they were left alone in a room. They were promised that they would get a second marshmallow if they could refrain from eating the first one for 15 minutes. Thirty years later, the lives of those who could regulate their emotions were better in many ways. They achieved higher scores on college entry exams. They earned more money and created happier marriages. They had a lower body mass index (BMI) and fewer addictive behaviors (Schlam, Wilson, Shoda, Mischel, & Ayduk, 2013).

The parts of the brain tasked with emotional regulation are also the ones that handle working memory, as revealed by MRI scans (Schweizer, Grahn, Hampshire, Mobbs, & Dalgleish, 2013). Working memory involves awareness, enabling you to remain focused on an activity and to sort relevant from irrelevant information. When your emotions are disturbed, those parts of the brain go offline for use by working memory. You then make poor decisions. When you learn effective emotional regulation, as Graham Phillips did, you are able to control your emotions, freeing up the brain's memory circuits to run your life wisely.

YOUR EVERYDAY SUPERPOWER

This is the everyday superpower that you possess: second by second, you are changing your brain by the way you use your mind. The consciousness of your mind is becoming the cells of the matter of your brain.

We're impressed when we see on-screen superheroes who can change their bodies at will. They may develop mental brilliance, like the hero in the movie and TV series *Limitless,* who takes an experimental drug called NZT that unlocks the full potential of his brain. Or the X-Men, each one of whom has a unique superpower gift.

Yet you, at this very moment, possess the superpower to change your brain. With each thought you think, as you direct your attention, you're signaling your brain to create new neural connections. Use this power deliberately, rather than allowing random thoughts to flow through your mind, and you start to consciously direct the formation of neural tissue. After a few weeks, your brain changes substantially. Keep it up for years, and you can build a brain that's habituated to process the signals of love, peace, and happiness.

This isn't a comic book or sci-fi movie; this is your life! Changing your brain is something you're doing every day. Now it's time to direct the process deliberately in a way that improves your life. Just as you upgrade the operating system of your computer or smartphone, you can upgrade your brain by changing your mind. Mind to matter.

ELECTRICAL CONDUCTORS
GENERATE ENERGY FIELDS

Tiny electrical currents run through the neurons in your brain, just like the electricity that runs through the copper wire in the electrical cords powering your appliances. As a whole, the brain seethes with electrical activity. This produces an energy field around the brain. When you get an MRI or EEG, medical professionals can read the energy field of your brain. It's a magnetic field in the case of an MRI, and it's an electrical field in the case of an EEG. Electricity and magnetism are two sides of the same coin: electromagnetism.

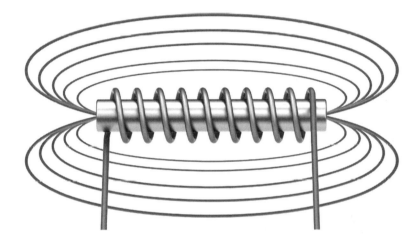

When an electric current is passed through a conductor, it produces a magnetic field. This is true whether the conductor is a power cord or a neuron.

There are many other forms of energy as well, and your brain and mind are constantly interacting with them. One of these is light. All living tissues emit photons, or light particles, and the type and intensity of the photons they emit vary. Even individual cells emit photons. A healthy cell emits a steady stream, while a dying cell sprays out its photons all at once like the burst of radiation from a collapsing supernova.

Light, electricity, and magnetism create the energy fields used in biological signaling. Biologist James Oschman states, "Energy is the currency in which all transactions in nature are conducted" (Oschman, 2015).

THE ANTENNAE IN YOUR CELLS

Imagine two magnets. Sprinkle iron filings around them and you'll see the lines of energy their fields produce. The copper cords powering your appliances and the neurons firing in your brain work the same way. They generate fields.

Now place a bigger magnet nearby. It will exert an influence on the iron filings, and the pattern of the whole energy field will change. Add an even bigger magnet and the field shifts again. Fields within fields produce complex patterns of energy.

The neurons in your brain act like those magnets. They generate fields. Those fields shape the matter around them, just the way the magnets cause the iron filings to form symmetrical patterns.

Bigger fields outside the body, such as the gravitational field of the Earth, act like the bigger magnets. They shift the pattern of your body's fields. They act on your brain and your cells, while your body also exerts a tiny influence on those bigger fields. Our bodies are influencing these big fields while also being influenced by them.

Your body's electromagnetic field extends about five yards or meters from your body. When you're five meters away from another person, your field begins interacting with their field. The two of you might be saying nothing, yet your energy fields are shaping each other in an invisible dance of communication (Frey, 1993).

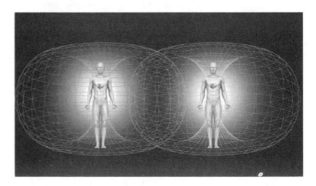

When two people are in close proximity, their fields interact.

For decades, microtubules, with their rigid form, were assumed to be no more than structural elements of the cell. Just as your body has a skeleton that provides a rigid structure to which other structures of the body attach, microtubules are the girders and scaffolding of the cell.

However, like antennae, microtubules are hollow. They are long cylinders. This property allows them to resonate, like a drum. And like antennae, their structure makes them capable of receiving signals from energy fields (Hameroff & Penrose, 1996). Microtubule signaling has been proposed as a method by which the body's complex systems are coordinated among trillions of cells (Oschman, 2015).

The Shaman and the Cardiac Surgeon

The fields of your body can interact with the fields of other people at great distances. A former cardiac patient named Richard Geggie told me this story during my research for a book called *The Heart of Healing* (Smith, 2004):

"In the early 1990s I was in Toronto, Canada. I went to see my doctor because I felt tired and listless. He sent me to have an electrocardiogram. Later that day, when he got the results back, he told me that my heart was at serious risk. He told me to stay calm, not exert myself, keep nitroglycerine pills with me at all times, and to not go outside alone.

"The doctors administered several tests over the course of the following three days, and I failed them all because my arteries were severely clogged. They included an angiogram, another electrocardiogram, and a treadmill stress test. When I started the bicycle test, the clinic staff didn't even let me finish. They stopped me partway. They were afraid I was going to die on the spot, my arteries were so clogged. As a high-risk patient, I was given an immediate appointment for heart bypass surgery.

"The day before the surgery, I woke up feeling much better. I went to the hospital and I was given an angiogram. This involved shooting dye into my arteries through an injection in my thigh. The surgeons wanted to discover the exact location of the blockages prior to the operation. I was prepared for surgery. My chest was shaved, and the doctors were about to mark my skin where they planned to make the incision.

"When the new angiograms came back from the lab, the doctor in charge looked at them. He became very upset. He said he had wasted his time. There were no blockages visible at all. He said he wished his own arteries looked as clear. He could not explain why all the other tests had shown such severe problems.

"I later discovered that my friend Lorin Smith [a Pomo Indian medicine man] in California, upon hearing of my heart trouble, had assembled a group of his students for a healing ceremony the day before the second angiogram. He covered one man with bay leaves and told him that his name was Richard Geggie. For the next hour, Lorin led the group in songs, prayers, and movement. The next day, I was healed."

When I last followed up, 13 years later, Geggie was still in excellent health. The phenomenon of distant healing is well documented, with scores of studies showing its effects (Radin, Schlitz, & Baur, 2015).

DIRECTING THE FLOW OF CONSCIOUSNESS

You can direct your consciousness, the way Lorin Smith did toward Richard Geggie's healing. Consciousness isn't something that simply is; it's something that can be controlled and pointed in a desired direction. When you direct your consciousness, you harness the power of your mind, activate the splendid machinery of your brain, and influence the environment around you (Chiesa, Calati, & Serretti, 2011).

You do that in visibly obvious ways, like deciding to plant a vegetable garden. After your mind makes the decision, you use your consciousness to direct the project. Your brain signals your body to drive your car to the local gardening store, where you buy fertilizer, tools, and seeds. You plant, water, and tend your garden, and a few months later, you have a crop. Your crop began in consciousness and ended in the material reality of a homegrown meal. A thought eventually produced a thing.

Take a look around you right now. The colors in the carpet began as a thought in someone's mind. That person chose the particular shades and textures that wound up in the finished product. Someone else decided the dimensions of your cell phone and laptop computer. Every proportion in your home began as a thought in the consciousness of the builder. We use invisible fields such as cell signals, Bluetooth, and wireless networks every day. A wireless network uses a router to send a signal into the surrounding environment. In the presence of a receiver, such as your smartphone or laptop, information is exchanged. The field of energy created by the router makes communication possible between your laptop and every device accessible to the router.

Though the fields are invisible, they are efficient conductors of information. Even electricity can now be transmitted wirelessly from one device to another.

You also interact with your environment in invisible ways, through the energy fields in which you're immersed. Through your brain, mind, and cells, your consciousness projects signals into the fields around you (Oschman, 2015).

Genius inventor Nikola Tesla is often quoted as saying, "If you wish to find the secrets of the universe, think in terms of energy, frequency, and vibration."

We use invisible energy fields, such as cellular networks, to transmit information every day.

When we originate an idea in consciousness, we send signals into the universal field. Transmission requires hardware, in the form of the brain, as well as software, in the form of the mind. Signals traveling through neural pathways create energy fields, and those fields change depending on the content of consciousness. Healing involves field effects, whether local or distant.

CURING MICE OF CANCER

My friend and colleague Bill Bengston, Ph.D., is a professor of sociology at St. Joseph's College. With various teams of researchers, he has conducted provocative experiments that demonstrate the healing potential of energy fields (Bengston, 2010).

Bill started out as a skeptic. When he finished his degree in sociology in 1971, he had no time for people who claimed paranormal powers. But he was an open-minded skeptic, and when he met healer Bennett Mayrick, he put him to the test. Ben said there was something wrong with Bill's car, and Bill was disappointed. He happened to have had the car inspected the day before, and he knew there was absolutely nothing wrong with it.

Bill's skepticism remained intact for half the drive home—when the car's entire exhaust system crashed to the ground.

Bill got to know Ben well over the next few years and eventually had an opportunity to apply real science to test Ben's skills. Bill had joined the faculty at City University of New York, and one of his fellow faculty members, Dave Krinsley, designed an objective experiment to measure whether human energy could produce healing (Bengston & Krinsley, 2000).

The design was simple. Mice would be injected with mammary cancer, or adenocarcinoma, a procedure that had been used in scores of other studies. In cancer studies, tumors are induced in the mice, after which researchers try various chemicals to see if they will alter the course of the disease. The longest an injected mouse had ever survived was 27 days. After injection, the cancer tumors grow rapidly in the mice, and they die in 14 to 27 days (Lerner & Dzelzkalns, 1966).

The mice in Krinsley's study would be randomized into two groups in order to provide a control. The control mice would be kept in a different building to eliminate the possibility of healing effects due to proximity to the treated mice.

Unfortunately, the shipment of mice did not arrive at the lab on schedule. There were repeated delays, and Ben lost interest in the experiment, as he had other priorities. Dave encouraged Bill to do the healing in Ben's stead.

Eventually, the mice arrived and were injected. Bill began to hold the cage of experimental mice in his hands for an hour each day. His hypothesis was that if healing energy were real, the mice would not develop tumors in the way they normally did.

A week into the treatment, two of the mice developed visible tumors. Bill was bitterly disappointed. When all five developed tumors, Bill asked Dave to put the mice out of their misery, as the experiment had clearly failed.

When Dave arrived, he commented on how healthy Bill's mice appeared to be despite the tumors. They were running around their cages, full of energy, behaving as though they were healthy. The control mice in the other lab, he told Bill, weren't doing well. Two had already died.

He argued, "Perhaps the treatments are slowing down the cancer even if they can't prevent it. There's no record of a single mouse living past day 27. Get one to live 28 days and we'll have a world record. Experiments rarely turn out the way they're supposed to. That's why they're called experiments!"

Around day 17, much to everyone's surprise, the tumors on Bill's mice began to change. They became ulcerated, with scabs replacing the hair on their skin. By day 28, Bill confided to the mice that they were making history. The ulcerations began to disappear and the fur grew back.

Mouse with tumor.

A week later, Bill's mice were examined by a biologist, who relayed the news to Dave: "The mice are cancer-free."

SKEPTICISM IS NO BARRIER TO BEING A HEALER

The experiment was replicated at different times by different researchers who extended the design in interesting ways. The research teams found that when more mice were treated, the effect was stronger. When the effect was very strong, even mice in the control group in a different building began to improve, and some did not die (Bengston, 2007).

In some studies, Bill trained graduate students to perform the healing. He chose people who, like himself, were skeptics. He eliminated true believers from the pool of healers.

The cages in which the mice were kept were held by Bill or the students.

This made no difference. The mice recovered whether treated by Bill or by skeptical students. Not only did the mice recover, but they also developed immunity to adenocarcinoma. If they were injected later, they no longer developed cancer. Bill also tried treating water that was then given to the mice. This was as effective as using the healing practice on the mice themselves.

Bill required the students to keep notebooks describing their personal experiences. Examination of their notes revealed that at first many of them did not believe they were taking part in an experiment in healing. They thought that they, not the mice, were the subjects being studied. They believed they were unconscious stooges being secretly tested to determine just how gullible they were.

This is called the nocebo effect. It's the opposite of the placebo effect. With placebo, people's belief that they will get better can produce a cure. Patients with nocebo can make themselves sick through their beliefs. People who don't believe in the possibility of healing, like the skeptical grad students, introduce the nocebo effect into their work.

The mice had no opinions, which is what makes animals useful for studies in which researchers wish to eliminate the placebo effect. Bill's skeptical students also didn't believe in healing. So it wasn't belief that was producing the healing.

The most likely explanation for the healing is energy fields. Many of the students, as well as Bill himself, described feeling their hands getting hot as they felt the healing energy begin to flow. They also described a cessation of that feeling when the healing session was complete. They learned to discern exactly what the flow of healing energy through their hands felt like.

Variants of the experiment found that distance was not an obstacle. Whether the mice were in close proximity to or far from the healer did not matter. Energy healing does not appear to be confined by the usual barriers of time and space (Oschman, 2015). Distant intentionality can be as effective as the presence of a healer in the room (Schmidt, Schneider, Utts, & Walach, 2004).

In her book *The Intention Experiment,* medical journalist Lynne McTaggart summarizes six studies using EEG or MRI machines to show that healers are able to affect the brain waves of people at a distance. She concludes that "the receiver's brain reacts as though he or she is seeing the same image at the same time" (McTaggart, 2007).

Bill Bengston also found that he personally was able to change the EEG of a distant human subject. After the experiments with mice, Bill began to offer energy healing to human beings and found that tumors, whether cancerous or benign, often disappeared.

Her Doctor Said: "This Doesn't Make Sense"

Bill Bengston has recorded many case histories from his work with patients with tumors. Here's one in which a patient's doctors were baffled by the changes they saw after energy healing.

"Janis, who was in her 20s, had been diagnosed with ovarian torsion, which means twisted fallopian tubes, along with cysts, causing the ovarian tissue to die. An operation was scheduled, carrying with it the chance that she would become infertile. After I treated her a few times . . . when Janis went for her pre-op exam, her doctor was astonished: 'There are no growths!'

"He referred her to a specialist, who was just as puzzled. He mused aloud while looking at her slides, 'You've got growths in this photo, but they're gone in the next one. You've got twisted tubes in this photo, but now they're gone. This doesn't make sense.' . . . Janis's doctors cancelled her operation" (Bengston, 2010).

CAN HEALING BE LEARNED?

As Bill's skeptical graduate students discovered, healing can be learned. My friends Donna Eden and David Feinstein manage the largest energy medicine program in the world, Eden Energy Medicine. Their program has over 1,000 graduates. Hundreds of stories confirm that energy healing works for humans as well as mice (Eden & Feinstein, 2008).

In the 1980s, I argued that healing was a special ability that only certain gifted individuals possessed. Throughout history, there have been remarkable people who demonstrated verifiable healing powers.

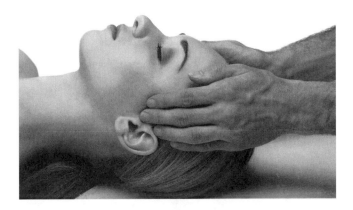

Hands-on healing session.

In *Soul Medicine,* a book I co-authored with Norm Shealy, M.D., founder of the American Holistic Medical Association, we talk about several of these people (Shealy & Church, 2008). Our standard of a verifiable cure was a doctor's diagnosis showing that the patient had a disease, followed by a second diagnosis after healing showing that the patient did not have that disease. Studying these practitioners suggested to me that healing was an unusual gift. Bill, David, Donna, and many others have proved me wrong.

Energy medicine programs such as those offered by Bill and Donna now show that healing is a skill that can be taught. Case studies written by their students include patients who have recovered from serious conditions such as cancer, heart disease, and autoimmune diseases.

I founded a nonprofit called the National Institute for Integrative Healthcare (niih.org). On our website, we maintain a list of studies of energy healing published in peer-reviewed scientific journals. To be included on this list, studies need to meet the following criteria:

- They assess the use of hands-on healing or interventions in the body's energy field.

- They use energetic exercises or techniques to balance the body's energy systems.

- The explanation they use for the effects of treatment is based on changes to the body's energy field.

The list excludes methods such as acupuncture and EFT (emotional freedom techniques) because these have their own online databases. Nonetheless, there are over 600 studies on the list. If you include EFT, acupuncture, and other energy healing methods, there are over 1,000 studies showing that energy healing is effective for a wide range of conditions, including those listed in Table 1.

Alzheimer's	HIV/AIDS
Anxiety	Insomnia
Arthritis	Irritable bowel syndrome
Asthma	Low back pain
Autism	Memory
Burnout	Menstrual distress
Burns	Migraines
Cancer	Mood disorders
Cardiovascular disease	Motion sickness
Carpal tunnel syndrome	Obesity
Children's behavioral issues	Pain
Cognitive impairment	Post-traumatic stress disorder (PTSD)
Cortisol	Prostate cancer
Dementia	Pulmonary disease
Depression	Skin wounds
Diabetes	Smoking
Drug addiction	Stroke
Fibromyalgia	Substance abuse
Headache	Thyroid dysfunction
High blood pressure	

Table 1. Conditions for which energy healing has been shown to be effective.

This compelling body of evidence shows that consciousness—directed by intention, working through energy fields—can produce radical changes in matter. "Skull and skin are not limiting boundaries of energy and information," says UCLA psychiatrist Dan Siegel in his book *Mind* (Siegel, 2017).

Though healing can occur at the level of small animals, such as mice, as well as at the level of larger animals, such as *Homo sapiens*, and can happen at a distance, just how large can the effect get?

The answer is: very large. Whole societies have been changed by a change of mind in a single person. In every age, there are people who have asked "Why?" and "Does it have to be this way?" and "How can we do things differently?" Even when facing a social condition that has been unchanged for centuries, the mind of a single person is sometimes able to change the matter of an entire society.

Mind is able to change matter at the level of the very small—atoms and molecules. Scaling up, it can change matter at the level of cells, organs, and bodies. Getting bigger still, it can change social groups and even whole countries. There are many historical examples of people who've changed first at the level of their own minds and then gone on to have an impact that shapes the world. We'll look at several examples of how individual mind change can scale up to produce enormous social shifts.

HOW A MIND CHANGE ELIMINATED INFECTIOUS DISEASE

Josephine Baker was the first woman to graduate with a doctorate in public health from New York University. In 1908, she was appointed head of the city's new Bureau of Child Hygiene.

She understood the link between poverty and illness and was possessed by a single-minded desire to eliminate human suffering. She introduced many reforms in New York City (Baker, 1925).

Baker instituted a program called the Little Mothers' League to train girls 12 and up in basic infant care. At a time when both parents were usually working outside the home, this improved the health of small children.

Josephine Baker.

Baker standardized the dosage of silver nitrate being placed in the eyes of newborns to prevent syphilis. Before her innovation, there was no standard dose, and some babies were given so much silver nitrate that they went blind.

She established standards for the quality of milk. At that time, the milk fed to most youngsters was watered down and then adulterated with other substances such as flour, starch, or chalk to make it look like the real thing.

Nineteenth-century cartoon depicting the health hazards of tainted milk.

In the middle of World War I, Baker published an editorial in the *New York Times* in which she calculated that the mortality rate of children in New York City was higher than that of soldiers on the Western front. This caused a sensation and highlighted the need for public health reforms (King, 1993).

Baker was determined to control the spread of typhoid fever, one of the major killers of both adults and children. The disease had taken the life of her father, a factor that motivated her choice of career. With a colleague named George Soper, she began to map areas of the city marked by outbreaks of typhoid. At a time when the germ theory of disease was not yet widely accepted, her team identified individuals at the epicenter of each outbreak.

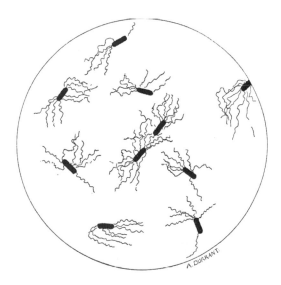

Typhoid bacillus.

TYPHOID MARY

One of these individuals was Mary Mallon, an immigrant from County Tyrone in Ireland. Mary served as a cook to various wealthy families. Josephine Baker and George Soper discovered that wherever Mary worked, outbreaks of typhoid followed shortly thereafter. When she prepared food, she transmitted the typhoid bacillus to those who ate it.

Mary was taken for evaluation and testing, and enormous quantities of the typhoid bacillus were found in her blood. She had no symptoms herself, however, and did not believe she was sick.

Though she was released on a promise to pursue a profession other than cooking, she soon went back to her old ways. Josephine Baker tracked her down again and knocked on the family's front door with a police escort.

Mary ran out the back door and eluded the police. But Josephine, more determined than the boys in blue, tracked her down in a neighbor's potting shed. Mary was huddled in a corner. Josephine sat down on top of Mary and yelled for help until the police arrived. Typhoid Mary was out of circulation for good.

Typhoid Mary.

Josephine Baker's reforms were bitterly contested by the medical establishment. When her campaign against typhoid fever became successful, a group of Brooklyn pediatricians petitioned the mayor to abolish her office. They complained that the supply of sick children to their practices was drying up.

Hearings were held in Congress to stop her. She was mocked as a woman, and critics declared that her efforts would eliminate medicine as a profession for promising young men. Nevertheless, she persisted—and eventually prevailed. By the time she retired, New York had the lowest rate of infant mortality in the United States.

Baker's reforms spread quickly. Her standards were adopted by 35 other states and in 1912 became the basis for the national Children's Bureau. Within a few years, terrifying diseases such as smallpox, typhoid, and cholera were virtually wiped out. That's the power of mind change as it plays out on a large social scale. Anthropologist Margaret Mead is famously supposed to have said, "Never think that a small group of thoughtful, committed citizens cannot change the world. Indeed, it's the only thing that ever has."

AN IDEA WHOSE TIME HAS COME

When you change your mind, sending new signals through the neural pathways of your brain, altering the energy fields all around you, interacting with the fields of others, you have no idea how far the effect might travel.

We see this in great social movements such as the abolition of slavery. In about 50 years, slavery went from an institution that had been with us since the dawn of humankind to being abolished worldwide. Women's suffrage and civil rights followed the same trajectory.

Women's suffrage poster.

Great social movements begin in the consciousness of just a few people. They spread slowly at first, then propagate with accelerating speed. As French novelist Victor Hugo said, "One withstands the invasion of armies; one does not withstand the invasion of ideas" (Hugo, 1877)—or, as it is more popularly paraphrased, "There is nothing more powerful than an idea whose time has come."

An idea that begins in just one mind can take over the world. What are the ideas with which you fill your consciousness every day?

CREATING FROM THE INSIDE OUT

In my first career, in book publishing, I came into contact with many best-selling authors. One day, I asked myself, *What do they have in common?* Reflecting on that question changed the direction of my life.

One of the characteristics common to best-selling authors is a focus on creation. They are much more interested in producing information than consuming it. The flow of words and images tends to be from the inside out, not the outside in. They certainly read and watch videos like the rest of us. But they tend to spend much more time pouring information out of their consciousness than sucking information into their consciousness. Given a choice of reading (inflow) or writing (outflow), they write.

Most people are passive. They take information in. They listen to the radio, watch shows and movies, and read the occasional book. They are consumers of information rather than producers of information. They are constantly influenced by the information they are consuming.

When it comes to best-selling authors, the flow of information tends to run in the opposite direction. They are much more interested in the information they can produce than what they can consume. They are active producers of information rather than passive consumers of information.

DELILAH AND THE INFORMATION FIELD

I remember a picnic with a group of friends a few years back. One member of the group was a woman in her 50s named Delilah who I hadn't seen for a couple of years but with whom I'd previously shared many warm conversations. She had always been pretty, bright, and healthy. Financially secure, she had no need to work, but she enjoyed a moderately successful career as a classical pianist.

We were sitting on the grass in the park on a beautiful spring day after a morning of group free-form dance. As we talked, Delilah shared her distress about what was happening in the world.

There were a lot of problems for her to be distressed about. Wars in several regions. Refugees. Natural disasters. Pollution. The loss of ground water. Mass extinction. Rising sea levels. The poor quality of governance. Deforestation.

News will rarely make you happy.

As we talked, I got a clear picture of the flow of information in Delilah's life. Whenever she was driving, she had her car radio tuned to an all-news station; she read the newspaper daily and watched television news. Note the use of the word *news* three times in that sentence. She was absorbing all this information from the outside world and spent much of her time engaged in the process.

This did not make her happy. I noticed how much Delilah seemed to have aged since our last conversation, and how heavy her energy felt as she described the flood of problems that filled her worried mind. Even though she was healthy, smart, and financially set for life, her mind was consumed by worry. She attuned her consciousness to the bad stuff, like a vacuum cleaner sucking in garbage. Filling her mind with problems led to a mind filled with garbage.

The places to which she turned her attention led to Delilah's immersion in the energy field of bad news. Conditioned by her consciousness, her brain was busy growing the neural circuits of stress. Her mind was guiding her brain to enhance those neural pathways, making them larger and more efficient at carrying their habitual signals. With every increase in capacity, her mind became more attuned to bad news.

Delilah believed that the bad things she heard on the news were happening "out there." She could claim with complete justification that the news items with which she was filling her thoughts were objectively true.

Yet the truth was that she was creating her own stress-filled reality by the direction in which she chose to turn her attention. Focusing on the news sparked the creation of new neurons in those circuits, which created stronger electromagnetic fields, which in turn sensitized her further to similar signals. Her stress had as much to do with her subjective creation of mind as it did with the objective state of the world.

SELF-DIRECTED NEURAL PLASTICITY

That's the risk you take when you're a consumer of information rather than a producer. When the flow of information is from the outside in, you hold your consciousness hostage to the consciousness of the people producing the information. When the container of your mind is being filled with unhappy input, it's hard to maintain a happy state.

When you allow others to fill your consciousness, you are at the mercy of their consciousness.

My wife, Christine, also consumes information constantly. However, she chooses inspirational material. She listens to her favorite transformational speakers during the long drives she takes to work. She reads inspirational books and watches nature shows on television. Her family and friends share inspirational quotes in their e-mail exchanges. She is bathing her mind in information from the outside, and her choice of uplifting material makes her a happy and wise presence.

That's the place from which she then creates. She'll tell you about an exciting new art project she's designed or a powerful new idea she's learned. Those are the things that fill her mind.

The thoughts, beliefs, and ideas that fill your consciousness exert a powerful influence on the world outside your brain. You are constantly creating. You can use that power to create intangibles such as a nurturing emotional environment. You can also use that power to create tangible material conditions. There are many examples of changes that have begun inside the mind of a single person like Josephine Baker and expanded to change the world.

Launching Mind into Space

In the sphere of technology, one person whose personal vision has reshaped entire industries is Elon Musk.

Elon Musk is famous as the founder of several successful businesses, including Tesla and Solar City. He sold his first product at the age of 12. It was a game called Blastar for which he'd written the code.

After applying unsuccessfully for a job at Netscape and dropping out of Stanford University, he founded a company called Zip2, which Compaq later purchased for $307 million. He then cofounded PayPal and cashed out when eBay purchased it.

While Musk's businesses thrived, his personal life hit some rough patches. On a vacation in his native South Africa, he contracted cerebral malaria, which is fatal in about 20 percent of cases. He lost 45 pounds and had a near-death experience. Two years later, his first son died at the age of 10 weeks.

Musk founded his third company, SpaceX, in 2002, with the audacious goal of making commercial spaceflight possible.

The launch of the first SpaceX rocket in 2006 ended in a fireball. Along with the incinerated rocket went the millions of dollars Musk had put into the venture. He was undeterred, however, and afterward wrote: "SpaceX is in this for the long haul and, come hell or high water, we are going to make this work" (Malik, 2006).

The following year, the company launched its second rocket. It failed to reach orbit when the engines shut down prematurely, leaving SpaceX with two strikes against it, and a founder who was desperately short of cash.

In the third launch, in 2008, the two stages of the rocket collided after separating. Its payload—which included Musk's first cargo for NASA, as well as the ashes of Star Trek's James "Scotty" Doohan—wound up in the ocean.

SpaceX launch.

Musk was now completely out of money and on the verge of bankruptcy. He was saved only by an eleventh-hour investment from eccentric billionaire Peter Thiel.

Today, Musk's companies—Tesla, SpaceX, and Solar City—are enormously successful. Yet it took perseverance through setback after setback to get to that point. Musk's mind-set is relentlessly positive, whatever the challenge. His mind has been the source of multiple game-changing material realities.

WHAT WORLD WILL YOU SHAPE WITH YOUR BRAIN?

What's in your mind, and what kind of material world might you create with it?

You have this magnificent brain and mind, capable of creating wealth, happiness, health, and well-being in your own life and the lives of those around you. Your consciousness is powerful—much more powerful than you realize.

Most of us are using just a tiny fraction of our ability, not even realizing that our minds create matter. This book is about harnessing your superpower consciously to make a wonderful life for yourself and those around you. You're already turning thoughts into things. You're doing it every day unconsciously. Now it's time to do it systematically and deliberately.

In the coming pages, you will meet many people like Josephine Baker, Elon Musk, Lorin Smith, and Bill Bengston, who have turned thoughts into things. Information flows out from them into the universal field, and their consciousness conditions the space around them to produce manifestations in material reality.

The concept that mind creates matter is not a metaphysical proposition. It's a biological one. In the chapters ahead, you'll begin to experience for yourself how your brain creates matter in the form of neurons and synapses in response to your consciousness. Consciousness and matter interact with the fields around you, and the result is material reality.

You'll begin to use your consciousness deliberately, building matter through intention flowing from the inside rather than by accident based on what's coming at you from the outside. You'll discover the community of conscious people who are building reality for the highest and best for the whole planet, and discover that you're part of an enormous creative community working for good. Welcome to the future of mind and matter!

PUTTING THESE IDEAS INTO PRACTICE

Activities to practice this week:

- As soon as you wake up in the morning, place your hand over your heart and feel love.

- Buy a journal. Write down a list of your intentions. What are 10 things that would transform your life?

- Breathe and send healing intentions to someone who is sick.

- Make a donation of 10 percent of your next paycheck to a charity dedicated to social change.

The Extended Play version of this chapter includes:

- An audio interview with Bill Bengston, Ph.D.

- Stanford marshmallow experiment video and full story

- A full list of conditions improved by energy therapies

- Women whose inventions changed the world

To access the Extended Play version, visit:
MindToMatter.club/Chapter1

CHAPTER 2

How Energy
Builds Matter

"Land ho!" the lookout sang. The day was September 6, 1522, and the port ahead was Sanlúcar de Barrameda, Spain. The ship was the *Victory,* commanded by Captain Juan Sebastián de Elcano.

The *Victory* was the last survivor of five ships commanded by Portuguese mariner Ferdinand Magellan. With a well-equipped fleet, he set out from Spain on September 20, 1519, with the goal of circumnavigating the globe via the Spice Islands.

Magellan first sailed south to Africa. From there, he crossed the Atlantic to Brazil. He followed the Brazilian coast, searching for a strait that would lead to the Pacific Ocean. Traversing the entire length of South America, he spent the winter in the sheltered bay at Puerto San Julián, Argentina, near the southern end of the continent.

On Easter day, his captains mutinied, but Magellan was able to subdue the rebellion. He executed one mutineer and beached one of the others.

On October 21, he finally found the passage he'd been looking for, now called the Strait of Magellan. By that time, one ship had been wrecked and a second one had deserted the convoy.

It took the remaining three ships 38 days to round the treacherous promontory of Tierra del Fuego. When Magellan saw the Pacific at the other end of the strait, he wept for joy. Ninety-nine days later, after sailing across the tranquil ocean, he landed at the island of Guam on March 6, 1521. His men were starving. They had chewed the leather straps of their tunics to stay alive.

The survivors resupplied in the Philippine islands. In two ships, laden with spices, they began the journey home. One ship was lost at sea, and only the *Victory* straggled back to Spain. Only 22 of the original 270 men survived.

Ferdinand Magellan.

Magellan was not one of the survivors. He had died en route. On April 27, while fighting as an ally of the chief of the Philippine island of Cebu against a tribe on the neighboring island of Mactan, Magellan was struck by a poisoned arrow. His retreating comrades left him to die.

Magellan's voyage was made possible by a remarkable electromagnetic invention, the compass. Invented in China, the first reference to it appeared in a manuscript written in 1040 (Vardalas, 2013). It describes an "iron fish" that when suspended in water, always pointed south.

A Song dynasty scholar named Shen Kuo wrote another account in 1088. He said that when "magicians rub the point of a needle with lodestone, then it is able to point to the south. . . . It may be made to float on the surface of water, but it is then rather unsteady. . . . It is best to suspend it by a single cocoon fiber of new silk attached to the center of the needle by a piece of wax. Then, hanging in a windless place, it will always point to the south." Indeed, this must have looked like magic in the 11th century, when electromagnetic fields were unknown.

Nineteenth-century Chinese compass.

About 200 years before Magellan's voyage, the first European compass was used in Amalfi, Italy. Mariners of seafaring nations such as England, France, Holland, Spain, and Portugal recognized the importance of this technological marvel and developed and refined the design.

Without the compass, Magellan's remarkable feat of navigation would have been impossible. A thin sliver of magnetized metal suspended in the center, it points to Earth's magnetic north pole regardless of where on the globe it is located. Lines of magnetic force surround Earth's mantle and are detected by the compass's needle.

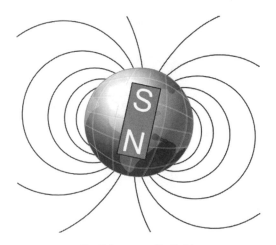

Earth's magnetic field.

Celestial bodies such as stars and planets have electromagnetic fields. Small objects such as crystals and rocks have them too. So do living beings. You have a field around your body, and it extends about five yards or meters out.

FIELDS ARE BEAUTIFUL—AND EVERYWHERE

Electromagnetic fields are now being measured around increasing numbers of plants and animals. In a study published in the prestigious journal *Science,* a research team investigated the electromagnetic relationship between flowers and the bees that pollinate them.

They found that bees can detect the fields around flowers and use the information to determine which flowers have the most nectar (Clarke, Whitney, Sutton, & Robert, 2013). Study co-author Daniel Robert, a biologist at the University of Bristol, says, "We think bumblebees are using this ability to perceive electrical fields to determine if flowers were recently visited by other bumblebees and are therefore worth visiting."

The electromagnetic properties of the fields around living beings came as a surprise to scientists immersed in matter-bound explanations. Thomas Seeley, a behavioral biologist at Cornell University, commented after reading the study, "We had no idea that this sense even existed."

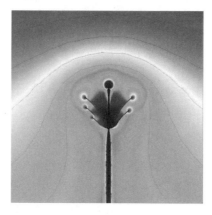

A flower's electromagnetic field.

The ability to perceive electromagnetic fields has now been measured in algae, worms, ants, insects, anteaters, platypuses, and hummingbirds.

Research has recently shown that dolphins are also able to detect electromagnetic fields. The Guiana dolphin is a species that lives close to estuaries in protected waters off the coast of South America. German researchers tested these river dolphins and found that they were sensitive to even very weak electrical currents (Czech-Damal et al., 2011).

The researchers then investigated how the dolphins were able to detect these fields, and they found small hair follicles around the dolphins' mouths. The indentations are surrounded by nerve endings, well supplied with blood vessels, and are filled with gel. Scientists believe these are the sensory organs by means of which the dolphins detect fields.

FIELDS CREATE THE SHAPES OF MOLECULES

I vividly remember my first experience with electromagnetism. In my first-grade science class, we sprinkled iron filings onto a piece of paper. As we moved magnets around under the paper, they rearranged the iron filings. Without touching, even at a distance, fields were able to rearrange matter. Because this simple experiment is repeated millions of times each year around the world, it's easy to forget how amazing it is. We take it for granted that fields exist and are able to shape matter, yet we somehow forget to apply this concept when we're struggling with the challenges of everyday material life. Whether we scale up large—to the size of a planet or a galaxy—or scale down small—to the size of a single atom—we find fields. Each cell of your body has its own unique electromagnetic field. The molecules of which your cells are built also have fields. Electromagnetism is central to the processes of biology.

Aside from water, most of the molecules in our bodies are proteins. Our bodies manufacture more than 100,000 different types of proteins. They're large and complicated molecules, with strings of atoms folded around each other to make intricate designs. When a cell is synthesizing a protein, it creates these folds the same way my first-grade science class moved iron filings.

Protein molecules are intricately folded.

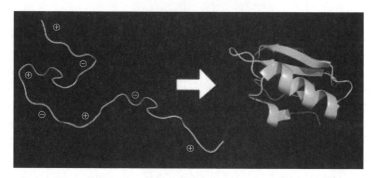

Protein before and after folding. Electrical charges at different points on the molecule determine how it shapes itself.

Each part of the string of molecules making up a protein has its own positive or negative charge. If two parts of the string are both negatively charged, they repel each other. The same is true of positively charged parts. On the other hand, negatives and positives are attracted to each other. These forces of attraction and repulsion mold the big and complicated protein string into its designated shape.

STALKING THE WILD FIELD

Willem Einthoven was an eccentric Dutch physician born in 1860. In the late 1890s, he set out to measure the electromagnetic field of the human heart. He began building a device called a galvanometer. Einthoven faced a great deal of skepticism and opposition, and to many of his medical colleagues, who were used to looking only at matter, the notion of invisible energy fields seemed suspect.

His first attempts were unpromising. His machine weighed 600 pounds (270 kg) and needed five people to operate it. A water-filled radiator system was required to cool the powerful electromagnets on which it relied.

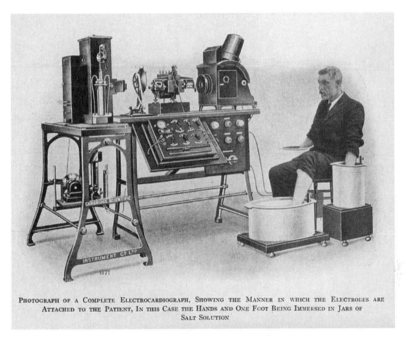

PHOTOGRAPH OF A COMPLETE ELECTROCARDIOGRAPH, SHOWING THE MANNER IN WHICH THE ELECTRODES ARE ATTACHED TO THE PATIENT, IN THIS CASE THE HANDS AND ONE FOOT BEING IMMERSED IN JARS OF SALT SOLUTION

An early electrocardiogram device.

After years of painstaking work, Einthoven developed a galvanometer much more sensitive than any available at the time. He was able to hook up subjects and measure their heart rates. He eventually built up a substantial theory of how the heart functioned and what the readings of electrocardiograms (EKGs) meant for diagnosis and treatment.

As for his critics? Einthoven had the last laugh, winning the Nobel Prize for medicine in 1924. He inspired the search for the field of the brain, which was discovered in 1926. Later researchers were able to map the field of even a single cell.

An early EEG recording, showing the electromagnetic activity of the brain.

WHAT ARE FIELDS DOING?

Harold Saxton Burr was a visionary researcher who became a professor at Yale School of Medicine in 1929. He began to study the energy fields around animals and plants, measuring ways in which matter (atoms, molecules, and cells) is organized by those fields as organisms develop and grow. In a key paper in 1949, he mapped the electromagnetic field around a single nerve. His careful measurements showed a field much like the iron filings around the magnet in my first-grade science class. The field was strongest closest to the nerve and became weaker moving outward from the nerve (Burr & Mauro, 1949).

Burr's huge insight was that fields weren't just *produced by* living organisms, but that fields *created* matter, providing lines of force around which matter could arrange itself into atoms, molecules, and cells.

Harold Saxton Burr.

In his book *The Fields of Life* (1973), Burr used the analogy of the iron filings with which I played as a child. If you shake the iron filings off the paper and add new ones, they arrange themselves into the same patterns as the discarded ones. It is the field that is organizing the filings; the field is not being produced by the filings.

Burr wrote: "Something like this . . . happens in the human body. Its molecules and cells are constantly being torn apart and rebuilt with fresh material from the food we eat. But, thanks to the controlling [life]-field, the new molecules and cells are rebuilt as before and arrange themselves in the same pattern as the old ones" (Burr, 1973, pp. 12–13).

For instance, when you cut your finger and your skin regrows, the field provides the blueprint around which the new cells organize themselves. Energy is not an epiphenomenon of matter; energy is *organizing* matter.

For many of his experiments, Burr used salamanders. He measured the voltages on the outer membranes of salamander eggs, and found that one spot had maximum voltage, while a spot 180 degrees opposite had minimal voltage. He marked both spots.

When the salamanders grew to maturity, he found that what had been the point with the strongest field in the egg had become the head. The point with lowest electrical activity was always the tail. The field appeared to be organizing the matter of the egg during gestation and development.

Burr used mice to determine if the energy field played a role in cancer. He measured their fields and noted which mice later developed cancer. After taking more than 10,000 measurements, he found that the electromagnetic signature of cancer appeared in the mouse's energy field before any detectable cellular malignancy was evident.

Thermography scan of a couple doing yoga.

ENERGY CREATES MATTER

In a landmark study published in 1947, Burr turned his attention to human disease to determine if his observations might have therapeutic value. He and his colleagues examined women with uterine cancer. They found that these women's uteruses had an electromagnetic charge that was different from the charge of healthy uteruses (Langman & Burr, 1947).

Burr then looked at a group of healthy women who did not have a diagnosis of uterine cancer. Those women who had the electromagnetic signature of uterine cancer—even though they were apparently healthy—were the ones who went on to develop cancer later. Cancer was showing up *in the field of energy* before it showed up *in the cells of matter*. Burr's work demonstrated that it is not the case that material organs and organisms like hearts and uteruses and salamanders and mice create energy fields. Energy fields form the templates around which matter condenses. Change the field and you change matter.

Though this understanding may be relatively recent in modern science, it is actually not an entirely new concept. An ancient saying in traditional Chinese medicine is "The mind controls the qi, and the blood follows the qi." By *qi* (also spelled *chi*) the ancient sages were referring to life energy, and by *blood* they meant the matter of the body. Energy directs matter.

WHAT IS H_2O?

Water is so familiar to us that many of us take it for granted. It makes up 70 percent of the volume of our bodies and comprises a similar percentage of the surface of the planet. We drink it and bathe in it every day without giving it a second thought. While people other than chemists can't recite the formula for any other molecule, everyone knows that the formula for water is H_2O. Yet it turns out that this most common of substances holds profound lessons about the relationship of energy to matter.

If I ask you, "What is H_2O?" you're likely to answer, "Water, of course." Certainly, if I hand you a glass of H_2O at room temperature, it's water. But if I add energy to the water by placing it on the stove, it becomes steam. It's still H_2O, but the increase in energy has completely changed the material form it takes.

If I take the same H_2O and place it in the freezer, subtracting energy, the matter changes form again. It becomes ice. The decrease in energy has again completely altered the form of the matter. This is one analogy that my colleague Eric Leskowitz, M.D., of Harvard Medical School, an expert on energy in acupuncture, uses to explain the effect of energy on matter. In similar ways, energy underlies the form matter takes in a huge number of ways that we don't usually notice.

H$_2$O can exist in several different states yet still be water.

WATER AND HEALING

In a remarkable series of experiments at McGill University, pioneering researcher Bernard Grad examined the effect of healing energy on animals and plants.

The healing was provided by a former Hungarian cavalry officer named Oskar Estebany, who could heal people by projecting energy from his hands. He was not trained in any way, and he had discovered his gift by accident when massaging horses. He believed that this energy was electromagnetic in nature and that it was a natural human ability. Grad first tested Estebany's abilities on mice. Four rows of small puncture wounds were made on their backs, and Estebany was instructed to "heal" only the two center rows. Sure enough, these rows healed faster than the outer rows. Estebany's mice also healed significantly faster than those held by students.

Grad then tested the effect of treated water on the growth rate of barley seeds. When provided with water held by Estebany for 30 minutes, more of the seeds germinated and the resulting plants grew taller. Their chlorophyll content increased, and the quality of leaf growth was significantly enhanced (Grad, 1963). Other researchers also found highly significant improvements in plant growth or seed germination after healers treated the plants (Scofield & Hodges, 1991; Kronn, 2006).

One rigorous study examined water treated by therapeutic touch practitioners (Schwartz, De Mattei, Brame, & Spottiswoode, 2015). The molecule H_2O has two hydrogen atoms bonded to a single oxygen atom. The angle of the bond between them can be measured, just as you can open a hinge partially and measure the angle it forms. The angle of the molecular bond of normal water is 104.5 degrees.

After 45-minute therapeutic touch sessions, the water showed highly statistically significant changes in its absorption of infrared light, which demonstrated that the bonding angle between the oxygen and two hydrogen atoms was altered by contact with the healing field. This particular experiment was very carefully blinded and controlled. Other researchers have also found alterations in the molecular structure of water after contact with a healer (Lu, 1997; Kronn, 2006).

Penn State University materials science professor Rustum Roy conducted many studies of the structure of water. He found that water molecules have a variety of potential configurations in which they can bond together. These can be altered by passing specific frequencies through the water. Water resonates with these frequencies, and the resulting water can have healing properties (Rao, Sedlmayr, Roy, & Kanzius, 2010).

Chinese qigong master Xin Yan has demonstrated the ability to alter the molecular structure of water dramatically, even at a distance. Researchers from the Chinese Academy of Sciences conducted 10 experiments with Dr. Yan. In the first, he stood near the water. In the other nine, he was at a distance of between 7 km and 1,900 km. In all cases, he was able to affect the water while allowing a control sample to remain unchanged.

When performing studies showing that energy healing cured cancer in mice, Bill Bengston noted similar changes in the infrared properties of water held by the healer (Bengston, 2010). He also reviewed research showing that the energy fields of a healer's hands can change how fast cellular enzymes catalyze and, in red blood corpuscles, increase the content of hemoglobin, the compound that carries oxygen to our cells.

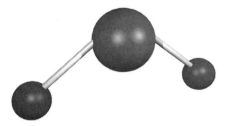

H_2O is an oxygen atom bonded to two hydrogen atoms at an angle of 104.5 degrees.

aᴅᴇʟɪɴᴇ ᴀɴᴅ ᴛʜᴇ Hᴇᴀʟɪɴɢ Sᴛᴀʀs

In the early 1980s, I interviewed a cancer survivor named Adeline. I was working on a project recording spontaneous remissions. Among the many stories I heard, hers stands out to me.

By the time Adeline was diagnosed with uterine cancer in her early 30s, it had spread throughout her body. Adeline's doctors recommended surgery followed by chemotherapy and radiation. Her chances of survival were small.

Unwilling to surrender her body to the ravages of treatment, she decided that instead, she would make her last months as serene as possible.

Adeline began to take long walks in the redwoods of Northern California where she lived. She also took long baths each day, letting water out as it cooled and topping the bath off with hot water. As she lay in the tub and walked through the forest, she imagined tiny glittering healing stars raining from heaven. They passed through her body, and whenever the point of a star touched a cancer cell, she imagined the cancer cell popping like a burst balloon.

Adeline ate the healthiest diet possible, meditated every day, read inspirational books, and terminated her relationships with people whose company was upsetting to her. Aside from a couple of close friends, most of her time was spent in solitude.

Her walks became longer, and she found herself feeling better physically than she'd felt her entire life.

When she went back to the hospital for a checkup nine months later, Adeline's doctors could find no trace of cancer in her body.

Adeline changed her energy in every possible way. She changed the energy of her physical environment by immersing herself in nature. She filled her mind with positive and specific images like the healing stars and with the uplifting energy of inspirational books. She ate food with an elevated energetic signature. She eliminated the negative energy of unhappy friends. She bathed daily, a practice that fills the body with electrons, countering the free radicals that are a major source of oxidative stress and cell degeneration.

In this pervasive environment of positive healing energy, directed by consciousness, the matter of Adeline's body began to change. Her cells responded, and her body began to eliminate the malfunctioning cancerous tissue. She used energy to heal her material body, and she never went back to her old habits.

Adeline became so accustomed to feeling good that it became her new normal. When I interviewed her seven years later, she was still meditating, eating clean, and living a low-stress lifestyle—and she was still cancer-free.

Adeline's story shows that it's not just gifted healers like Oskar Estebany who heal with energy. We can heal ourselves as well when we adjust our consciousness to the frequency of healing. The matter of our cells responds to the energy of our consciousness.

We're all familiar with the parlor trick of an opera singer breaking a wine glass. When the frequency of the singer's voice raises the energy of the molecules in the glass to the critical limit, they shatter. This is a well-known illustration of a little-known field of study called cymatics, the science of how sound affects matter. Dive deeper into cymatics, and we find that sound is as full of astonishing properties as water.

The resonant frequency of sound vibration can shatter a wine glass.

CYMATICS: HOW FREQUENCY
CHANGES MATTER

Ernst Chladni was a 19th-century German physicist and musician. He is called the father of acoustics for his pioneering experiments with sound. His father was a strict disciplinarian who did not allow young Ernst outside to play each day until he had finished his rigorous studies.

Chladni had an extremely sensitive musical ear, able to discern very small differences between frequencies. After obtaining two degrees, one in law and one in philosophy, Chladni became interested in the study of sound. Inspired by other scientists who had made energy fields visible, he developed a new device.

Fine sand was placed on top of a thin metal plate and a violin bow was drawn along the side of the plate. This caused the plate to vibrate. Different vibrational frequencies produced different patterns in the sand.

Chladni plate.

Chladni became famous for his public demonstrations, and he traveled throughout Europe year after year. This brought him into contact with many other scientists, and he progressively developed his ideas. He published his seminal work, *Acoustics,* in 1802, founding a new scientific field.

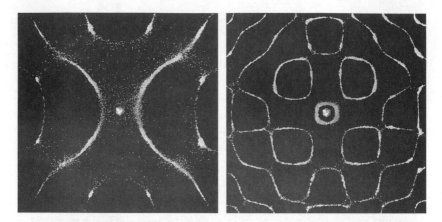

The frequency of sound passed through a Chladni plate produces different patterns. Above, 1305 Hz and 5065 Hz. Below, 2076 Hz and 2277 Hz.

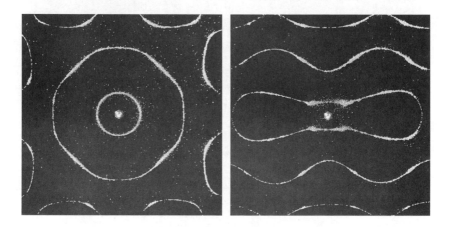

The study of how sound affects matter is called cymatics. Following Chladni's pioneering work, scientists have been examining the effects of vibrational tones on various substances. Vibrations can change the configuration of material objects dramatically and immediately.

A modern Chladni plate is attached to a scientific instrument called a vibration generator. When the frequency is adjusted, the metal vibrates at different rates. When a substance with a contrasting color, such as white sand, is sprinkled on the plate, patterns are visible. That's because when certain frequencies are passed through molecules, they produce distinct shapes. Generally, the higher the frequency, the more complex the pattern it produces in matter.

Various types of matter can be used to illustrate the effect of energy passing through Chladni plates. Salt and sand are popular media. Living organisms such as seeds also respond.

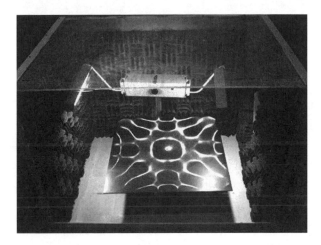

A large Chladni plate at the Harvard University natural sciences laboratory.

Chladni plates and vibration generators are popular items in high-school science classes. They can be purchased online or easily made at home using simple materials. Yet as a demonstration of how energy organizes matter, they are a powerful reminder that every frequency that passes through our bodies and minds is organizing the molecules of our bodies.

SOUND VIBRATIONS CREATE SQUARE WATER

Water can also be made to change shape in response to vibration. When water comes out of a tube, the shape of the stream is round. If certain frequencies are played nearby, however, it changes its regular form into a series of right angles or a spiral.

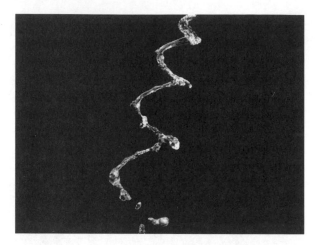

**A stream of water changes shape in response
to sound vibration from a speaker.**

Another way to visualize the impact of energy frequencies on matter is to pass sound waves through a dish of water. As the frequency is changed, the patterns in the water change too. Certain types of classical music produce complex and beautiful patterns in the water, while other frequencies, such as those found in harsh music, produce chaotic and disorganized wave forms.

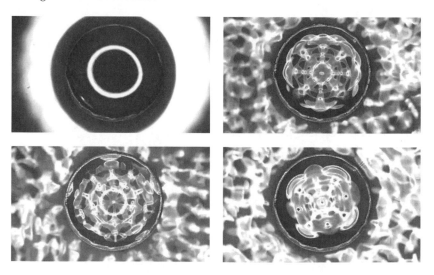

**Water in a backlit glass dish changing shape as various
energy frequencies are passed through it.**

YOUR PERSONALITY IN A DROP OF WATER

A fascinating series of experiments at the Aerospace Institute (officially, the Institute for Static and Dynamics for Aerospace Constructions) in Stuttgart, Germany, used water as a medium. The studies, performed by Professor Dr. Bernd Helmut Kröplin, measured the effect of different people on water.

A large group of students participated in one experiment. Each one filled a hypodermic syringe with water and squeezed a series of droplets onto a microscope slide. Kröplin's team then took photographs of the droplets.

They found that each person's group of droplets looked quite different from the droplets produced by the others. The droplets produced by the same person, however, were virtually the same. Even if the person squeezed out 20 droplets, a similar pattern was discernable in all 20. But that group of droplets looked different from the droplets produced by the next person, and the next. It seemed that passage through the energy field of a person produced an indelible and consistent impact on the matter, in the form of water, that they handled.

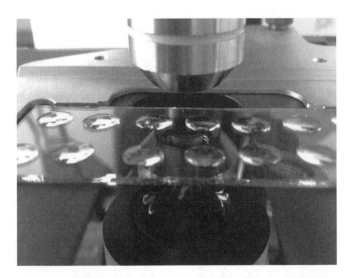

A subject produces a series of droplets on a microscope slide.

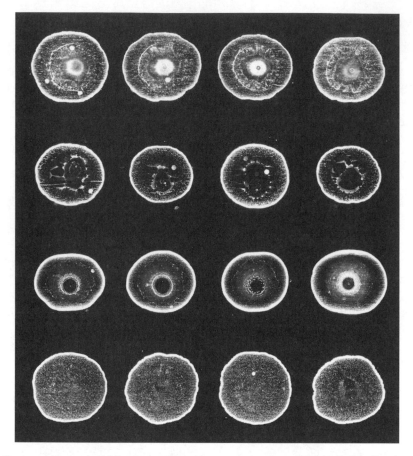

However many droplets are produced by a person, they all look similar. Yet they are completely different from a series of droplets produced by another person.

Just as the fingerprints of every one of the eight billion people on the planet are unique, the energy field of each person is unique. When water passes through a person's energy field, the shapes it assumes are always the same, while different from the shapes produced by any other person. Kröplin and his associate Regine Henschel describe their latest research in their book *Water and Its Memory*, saying, "To our surprise, we could demonstrate that the drop image is changed in the vicinity of the experimenter by the individual energy field around him or her. Each experimenter creates an individual, reproducible set of drop images without any special mind or thought activity" (Kröplin & Henschel, 2017).

Another study, this time on the effects of distant intention on water, was performed by a research group at the Institute of Noetic Sciences (IONS) in Petaluma, California.

A group of 2,000 people in Tokyo focused positive intentions on water samples inside an electromagnetically shielded room in Petaluma. Such rooms, also known as Faraday cages, are lead-lined chambers designed to screen out all known forms of radiation. Fiber-optic cables connect the instrumentation inside the room to the lab outside, so that even conventional electromagnetic fields are screened out.

Unknown to the group of earnest intenders in Tokyo, however, similar water samples were being held in a different location as controls.

Photographs of ice crystals formed from both sets of water were then viewed by 100 independent judges. They found the shapes in the treated water more beautiful than those in the untreated water (Radin, Hayssen, Emoto, & Kizu, 2006).

  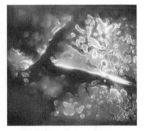

| Water exposed to the music of Mozart. | Water exposed to the music of Vivaldi. | Water exposed to heavy metal music. |

Your body is 70 percent water. That water is responding to the vibrations around it as certainly as the particles on the Chladni plates or the droplets on Dr. Kröplin's microscope slides. When you are flooding the water molecules of your body with the vibrations of healing energy, you are entraining them in sympathy with wellness, while discordant vibrations have the opposite effect. Immerse your mind in positive energy and at least 70 percent of the matter in your body comes into sync with that elevated state.

How Sound Cured Jim's Alcoholism and Cardiac Disease

By Frances Dachelet, R.N., licensed acupuncturist, acutonics practitioner

Jim, a 40-year-old married man, sought treatment for intermittent heart palpitations that had been active over the previous month. He reported that when his heart started to race, he felt anxiety, shortness of breath, and chest pain.

He was admitted to the hospital the first time it happened and had a complete heart workup that was negative for myocardial infarction or any specific heart problem. Jim had been married for one year and was the father of a six-month-old baby boy. He worked full-time as a physician's assistant in an emergency care setting and found his work busy and rewarding.

Jim had a long family history of alcoholism. His father had been physically abusive to him, his siblings, and his mother. Jim had received some therapy in the past to deal with particular childhood problems.

Jim admitted that he hides and covers many of his feelings with humor and sarcasm. He worries about being a good enough father, husband, and physician's assistant. When he doubts himself, he uses alcohol to calm his worries. He admitted to having a problem with drinking, although he had reduced the number of times he drank to excess.

Jim eats a vegetarian diet and has hot meals with his family that his wife prepares. He reported consuming too much dairy and cheese and had gained weight since getting married. He acknowledged the need to drink more water, that he will go for long periods of time not drinking liquids at all during a day, then having a beer or cocktails at night.

He was assessed energetically with:

- Shen disturbance (agitation of the spirit)
- Imbalances of the liver, spleen, and kidney meridian energies
- Intergenerational alcoholism
- Heart chakra issues
- Fear

At the first treatment, Jim came in with heart palpitations and was visibly uncomfortable and frightened. Treatment strategies for this visit were to calm the spirit, slow the heart rate and breathing, and strengthen the kidney energy to anchor the energy of the heart and lung acupuncture meridians.

The treatment was started with tuning forks for grounding, centering, and stabilizing kidney meridian energy. Tuning fork intervals were applied to points for calming the spirit and nourishing and balancing the heart energy.

Grounding on kidney points was repeated, and Jim reported feeling calm and a sensation he described as his heart slowing down. He was less anxious and visibly relaxed on the treatment table.

Extraordinary vessels were used to address the intergenerational issues, drawing on their primordial connection to Source to open to those deep-seated childhood issues. Tuning fork combinations were used to break through the familial issues.

The session ended with additional grounding, using kidney points located on the feet. Jim reported feeling calm and rested.

Dietary, hydration, and exercise recommendations were made to Jim. He reported no palpitations or panic symptoms following his first treatment.

Subsequent treatments focused on nourishing kidney energy and balancing the nervous system while continuing to address familial patterns and to provide nurturance.

High-octave tuning forks were added and sounded above the body to clear and heal the body's subtle energy field.

The treatment series ended by grounding the energy shifts, using kidney points on the feet.

Jim reported that after his first treatment, the palpitations did not return. Though he still experienced occasional stress and anxiety, he felt much better. He continued to work on his diet and stopped drinking alcohol. He was investigating an outpatient rehabilitation program and considering treatment.

ENERGY FLOWS ALONG
ACUPUNCTURE MERIDIANS

Acupuncture meridians such as the kidney, liver, and spleen meridians used in Jim's treatment sequence have been used for healing for thousands of years. The meridians and the acupoints along them were identified in a Chinese book called *The Yellow Emperor's Classic of Internal Medicine* that is more than 2,000 years old.

Meridians were also known in Europe. A mummified body found in the Alps in 1991 exhibits 61 tattoos. Some are shaped like crosses or targets. Scientists have studied the mummy, called Otzi, extensively and can identify the diseases from which he suffered. Some of the tattoos are directly on the acupoints for those particular conditions. Otzi's corpse is some 5,400 years old, making it apparent that human beings have known for millennia about the link between these points and healing.

Some of the tattoos on Otzi's body are on acupoints.

FINDING ACUPOINTS ON YOUR BODY

Nowadays it is easy to find acupoints on a body using a handheld skin galvanometer. Acupoints are excellent conductors of electricity, since they have only 1/2000th of the resistance of the surrounding skin. Low resistance equals high conductance, as with wires that run through a power cord. When these low-resistance points are stimulated, energy flows through them easily.

When I teach live workshops, I often use a galvanometer to find acupoints on a volunteer's body. This makes it apparent to participants that acupoints aren't just some ancient Chinese fiction. They're real and they're measurable, and when energy therapies use them for healing effect, the flow of energy in the body is altered.

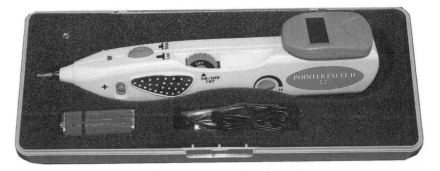

Acupoints can easily be identified using a handheld galvanometer.

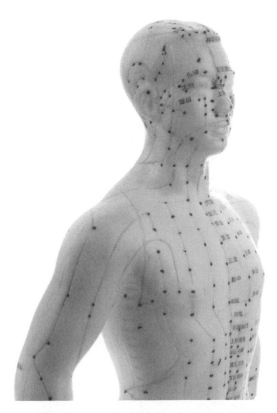

Acupoints and meridians of the upper body.

An energy psychology method that uses acupoints is called Emotional Freedom Techniques (EFT). This is the most popular of the more than 30 different energy psychology methods that exist today. EFT is used by over 20 million people worldwide. It stimulates acupoints on the body's meridians by tapping on them with the fingertips. For this reason, EFT is often simply called tapping. Its popularity has grown rapidly over the last two decades because it's easily learned, quickly applied, and effective. I wrote the most recent edition of the handbook describing the method, *The EFT Manual,* to make the version of EFT used in studies more widely available (Church, 2013).

That evidence-based form is called clinical EFT, and there are now over 100 clinical trials published in peer-reviewed psychology and medical journals attesting to its efficacy. Meta-analyses of EFT for depression, anxiety, and PTSD show that its treatment effects are much greater than those of drugs or talk therapy.

EFT uses some simple elements drawn from talk therapy but adds the ingredient of tapping on acupoints. It takes less than a minute to tap through them all, and psychological distress usually diminishes immediately.

I've presented EFT workshops at many medical and psychology conferences and noticed that doctors usually take readily to EFT. They are very aware of the contribution that stress makes to physical disease. I've had several doctors tell me that after tapping, patient issues resolved without further need for conventional allopathic treatment. As Chuck Gebhardt, M.D., observed in the following account after seeing swelling subside immediately after acupoint tapping, "Nothing in my traditional medical training in anatomy, physiology, or pathology even hinted at what I am now witnessing."

a Flu Shot Gone Wrong

By Chuck Gebhardt, M.D.

I am a traditionally trained American physician who has been using a somewhat modified version of EFT for about six months. As readers would expect, I have been seeing great success and tremendous value to my patients. I specialize in internal medicine and I am one of six physicians in a private practice in southwest Georgia.

I typically treat my patients as I always have, but if they are experiencing acute discomfort during our visit, I will try to treat the discomfort with tapping or pressure on acupoints (if circumstances allow). Before I introduce this technique, though, I examine, diagnose, and treat all important problems as I usually do, including their acute problems that I am about to target with a new and unusual intervention after the traditional work is done. Now for the story.

Bill received a flu shot from my very able assistant with no initial problem. He is a 60-year-old gentleman whom I treat for hypertension and hypercholesterolemia. He is otherwise completely healthy, well balanced, and down to earth, with no psychological problems of any kind.

Early the next morning, he called and reported that within hours of the shot his left arm began to throb with pain and swell. . . . In my office, the area of swelling was the size of about a half of a hardboiled egg (very dramatic indeed). It throbbed and hurt him so much, he couldn't stand for his shirt sleeve to touch it. It was intensely red and very warm to touch. His temperature was 100.5°F, and he had beads of cold sweat on his forehead (called diaphoresis).

I prescribed an antihistamine, pain medicine, and a steroid dose pack to be started immediately and instructed him to call us right away if he had any trouble breathing or felt like he might pass out.

As he was about to leave with his prescriptions in hand, I decided to tap on some of the meridians on his head, left shoulder, and left arm to see if I could relieve his discomfort somewhat until the medications would take effect.

Tapping on several spots seemed to help a little, but when I tapped on the inside of his left elbow at a spot that acupuncturists call L5, he said: "Wow! That is helping a lot." Over the next 30 seconds, while I continuously tapped on L5, the inflamed, swollen lump shrunk to about one-tenth its initial size, the redness faded, and it stopped hurting.

His low-grade temperature and diaphoresis resolved, and his feeling of malaise was also gone. This response was jaw-dropping amazing for both me and him. He even pounded on the previously exquisitely tender spot with his fist to show how well it now felt. His grin was ear to ear. When I saw him again about a month later, he said the pain and swelling never came back, so he didn't see any need to fill the prescriptions I had written for him.

> This was one of the most dramatic responses to acupoint stimulation I have witnessed, but it is only one of many I see on a daily basis in my practice.
>
> Nothing in my traditional medical training in anatomy, physiology, or pathology even hinted at what I am now witnessing. As you know, anyone who watches these dramatic improvements knows immediately that our previous understanding of how our bodies and our minds work is in need of important revisions and redirected research. This is very exciting.

Dr. Gebhardt is one of many physicians using EFT for physical ailments. At one conference, a doctor came up to me, grasped my hands, and expressed his gratitude for the training in EFT I had given at that same conference two years earlier. He told me that at his clinic they now use EFT with every new patient during the intake process. This typically clears the emotional aspects of the presenting problem, and after that the doctors can address what's left—the parts of the problem that are truly medical.

Energy Healing for Champion Swimmer Tim Garton after Stage 2 Non-Hodgkin's Lymphoma

Tim Garton, a world-champion swimmer, was diagnosed in 1989 with stage 2 non-Hodgkin's lymphoma. He was 49 years old and had a tumor the size of a football in his abdomen. It was treated with surgery followed by four chemotherapy treatments over 12 weeks, with subsequent abdominal radiation for 8 weeks. Despite initial concern that the cancer appeared to be terminal, the treatment was successful, and by 1990 Tim was told that he was in remission. He was also told that he would never again compete at a national or international level. In 1992, however, Tim Garton returned to competitive swimming and won the 100-meter freestyle world championship.

In early July of 1999, he was diagnosed with prostate cancer. A prostatectomy in late July revealed that the cancer had expanded beyond the borders of his prostate and could not all be surgically removed.

Once again, he received weekly radiation treatment in the area of his abdomen. After eight weeks of treatment, the cancer had cleared.

In 2001, the lymphoma returned, this time in his neck. It was removed surgically. Tim again received radiation, which left severe burns on his neck. The following year, a growth on the other side of his neck, moving over his trachea, was diagnosed as a fast-growing lymphoma that required emergency surgery.

He was told that the lymphoma was widespread. An autologous bone marrow and stem cell transplant was done at this time, but it was not successful. There was concern that the tumors would metastasize to his stomach. His doctors determined at this point that they could do nothing more for him. He was told that highly experimental medical treatments, for which there was little optimism, were the only alternative. He was given an injection of monoclonal antibodies (Rituxan), which had been minimally approved for recurrent low-grade lymphoma. Rituxan is designed to flag the cancer sites and potentially help stimulate the immune system to know where to focus.

At this point, Tim enlisted the services of Kim Wedman, an energy medicine practitioner trained by Donna Eden. Tim and his wife went to the Bahamas for three weeks and took Kim with them for the first week. Kim provided daily sessions lasting an hour and a half. These sessions included a basic energy balancing routine, meridian tracing, a chakra clearing, and work with the electrical, neurolymphatic, and neurovascular points.

Kim also taught Tim and his wife a 20-minute twice-daily energy medicine protocol, which they followed diligently, both during the week Kim was there and for the subsequent two weeks. The protocol included a basic energy balancing routine and specific interventions for the energy pathways that govern the immune system and that feed energy to the stomach, kidneys, and bladder.

Upon returning to his home in Denver, in order to determine how quickly the cancers might be spreading, Tim scheduled a follow-up assessment with the oncologist who had told him, "There is nothing more that we can do for you." To everyone's thrill and surprise, Tim was cancer-free. He has remained so during the four years between that assessment and the time of this writing. He has been checked with a PET scan each year, with no cancer detected.

CREATING MATTER FROM INFINITE MIND

The big picture in all this research is that energy builds matter. We know that we are immersed in energy fields, from Earth's magnetic field to the fields produced by the hearts of the people closest to us. We know that our organs have fields and our cells have fields. These fields change in response to intention and the activity of a healer—and that healer can be us.

We know that disease shows up in a person's energy field before it becomes evident at the level of matter and that the water that makes up our bodies is sensitive to the energy fields around it. We know that sound frequencies change matter and that even the act of observing subatomic particles can change their behavior.

Finally, we see that when energy is applied with the intention of healing, matter often follows. Ancient healing systems such as acupuncture, as well as modern variants such as EFT, all show the effect of energy on our cells. Over a thousand studies of energy healing show that it is effective for both psychological conditions (e.g., anxiety and depression) and physical symptoms, including pain and autoimmune diseases.

Although science used to regard energy fields as epiphenomena of matter, the evidence now suggests that matter is an epiphenomenon of energy. The implication for healing is that when we change our energy fields, the cells of our material bodies respond.

Albert Einstein understood the relationship of energy to matter. His famous equation is $E = mc^2$. The E stands for "energy" and the m stands for "matter." They are in balance on opposite sides of the equation. He wrote, "What we have called *matter* is *energy,* whose vibration has been so lowered as to be perceptible to the senses. There is no matter."

We can choose to remain materialists. Faced with imbalances in our lives, disturbances in our emotions, and diseases in our bodies, we can look for material solutions like pills or surgery or recreational drugs to make us feel better.

We can also choose the path of energy. When people change energetically, matter follows right along. Faced with the inevitable challenges of being human, we can take Einstein's advice and shift the E side of the equation. Simple, broadly effective, and elegant, working at the level of energy frees us from the tyranny of matter. We address our problems at the level of cause rather than effect.

As we free our attention from fascination with matter, we perceive the intelligence innate in energy. Shifting to the level of detached consciousness opens us to the infinite possibilities contained in the nonlocal field of infinite intelligence.

When we create in alignment with this universal nonlocal field, we are in touch with the field of infinite possibilities. We are no longer bound by the limited subset of possibilities offered by matter. This interaction patterns the cells of our bodies, from water molecules to neurons, and aligns our material form with the endless possibilities in the field of infinite intelligence. Habituating ourselves to living there, we create entirely different lives than are possible when we remain bound by the limitations of material thinking.

PUTTING THESE IDEAS INTO PRACTICE

Activities to practice this week:

- Sing for at least a few minutes each day when you're alone.

- Experience water deeply. Take a walk by a body of water, enjoy a bath, splash in a fountain. Notice the ripples and reflections.

- Before you drink a glass of water, hold it to your heart and radiate blessing toward it.

- Use sound consciously. For the entire week, fast from all music other than meditation music channels.

- Write your observations of your experiences of sound and water in your journal.

The Extended Play version of this chapter includes:

- Studies of life-forms able to detect electromagnetic fields

- Best cymatics videos

- The sound patterns of Ernst Chladni

- Sound healing case histories

- Dawson's galvanometer video

- Water memory videos

- Professor Rustum Roy's presentation on the changes in the properties of water

To access the Extended Play version, visit: MindToMatter.club/Chapter2

CHAPTER 3

How Our Emotions Organize Our Environment

On a bright spring morning in 1892, a young German soldier named Hans Berger was riding high. He was taking part in military exercises in the town of Würzburg, and his unit was pulling artillery pieces into position with their horses.

Suddenly, Berger's horse reared up on its hind legs, throwing him to the ground right in front of one of the wagon wheels. At the last second, Berger's desperate companions halted the momentum of the gun just before it crushed him. Berger escaped death with nothing more than a dirty uniform.

That evening, he received a telegram from his father in Coburg, asking about his well-being. His father had never sent him a telegram before. That morning, Berger's older sister had been "overwhelmed by an ominous feeling . . . convinced that something terrible had happened to him" and urged her father to send the telegram.

Berger struggled to understand how his feelings of terror might have been communicated to his sister over 100 kilometers away. He had been planning to become an astronomer but now changed his mind, and after his discharge from the army, he became a psychiatrist instead, studying the workings of the brain (Millett, 2001).

In June of 1924, he had the opportunity to study the brain of a 17-year-old boy who had a gap in his skull as a result of an earlier surgery to remove a brain tumor. He wanted to see if he could measure brain activity. After weeks of modifications to his equipment in the wake of unsuccessful readings, to Berger's excitement, he finally observed "continuous oscillations of the galvanometer."

He wrote in his journal: "Is it possible that I might fulfill the plan I have cherished for over 20 years and even still, to create a kind of brain mirror: the electroencephalogram!" (Millett, 2001).

Hans Berger.

In 1929, after refining his equipment and skills, Berger described the first two brain waves ever discovered: alpha and beta. Unfortunately, Berger's work ran counter to the brain theories then prevalent in contemporary medicine, and his work was rejected by most of his colleagues. British and American scientists believed that what he was measuring was the result of an electrical artifact, and one wrote that he was "highly skeptical of the possibility of recording anything of significance from the surface of the brain."

Berger was forced into retirement from his university professorship and his health worsened. He sank into depression and took his own life in 1941. It was not until consciousness researchers began to investigate the link between mind and brain in the 1960s that EEGs came into widespread use. They're now used to map states of consciousness as well as brain function, and new waves such as gamma continue to be discovered (Hughes, 1964).

THE COMMUNICATING BRAIN: CLAPPING "THE WAVE"

I travel to New York often, and I love going to see Broadway musicals. When *The Book of Mormon* opened, I was one of the first to buy tickets.

Members of the audience were laughing all the way through. At the end, the cast got a standing ovation.

Suddenly, the applause changed. Rather than a thousand people clapping separately, everyone began to clap in rhythm. *Clap, clap, clap, clap.* The rhythmic clapping become so insistent that the actors came back onstage for an encore. The clapping communicated approval to the actors, and they responded with another song.

The neurons in your brain do something similar. They fire together in rhythmic patterns, communicating with each other across the brain. These patterns are measured in cycles per second, or Hertz (Hz). Imagine an audience clapping together slowly. That's a slow brain wave, with millions of neurons firing together slowly. Imagine an audience clapping quickly. That's a fast brain wave, with millions of neurons firing together quickly.

Today's EEGs calculate wave patterns from each of the brain's many different parts. They typically use 19 electrodes attached to the surface of the scalp.

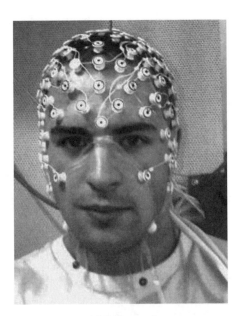

A typical 19-electrode array.

One research team observed, "Scientists are now so accustomed to these EEG correlations with brain state that they may forget just how remarkable they are. . . . A single electrode provides estimates of synaptic action averaged over tissue masses containing between roughly 100 million and 1 billion neurons" (Nunez & Srinivasan, 2006). When we see brain wave changes on an EEG, it indicates that the firing patterns of billions of neurons in our brains are also changing.

WHAT BRAIN WAVES ARE AND WHAT THEY DO

There are five basic brain waves that are picked up by a modern EEG. Gamma is the highest brain wave frequency (40 to 100 Hz). It's most prevalent at times when the brain is learning, making associations between phenomena and integrating information from many different parts of the brain.

A brain producing lots of gamma waves reflects complex neural organization and heightened awareness. When monks were asked to meditate on compassion, large flares of gamma were found in their brains (Davidson & Lutz, 2008).

They were compared to novice meditators who had meditated for an hour a day the week before. The novices had brain activity similar to that of the monks. But when the monks were instructed to evoke a feeling of compassion, their brains began to fire in rhythmic coherence, like the audience clapping at *The Book of Mormon* musical.

The flares of gamma waves measured in the brains of the monks were the largest ever recorded. The monks reported entering a state of bliss. Gamma is associated with very high levels of intellectual function, creativity, integration, peak states, and of feeling "in the zone." Gamma waves flow from the front to the back of the brain about 40 times per second (Llinás, 2014). Researchers look to this oscillating wave as a neural correlate of consciousness (NCC), a state linking the brain's activity with the subjective experience of consciousness (Tononi & Koch, 2015).

Brain researchers talk about the amplitude of a brain wave and that simply means how big it is. A high amplitude of gamma means a big gamma wave, while a low amplitude means a small one. Measurements of brain waves show peaks and valleys. The distance from the peak to the trough is the amplitude. Amplitude is measured in microvolts, and brain waves typically measure between 10 and 100 microvolts, with the faster waves like gamma having the lowest amplitude.

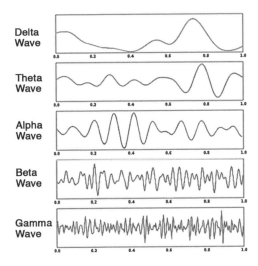

EEG brain waves from slowest to fastest.

The next fastest wave is beta (12 to 40 Hz). Beta is typically divided into two parts: high beta and low beta. High beta is your monkey mind. High beta (15 to 40 Hz) is the signature brain wave of people with anxiety, people experiencing frustration, and people under stress.

The more stressed people become, the higher the amplitude of the beta their brains produce. Negative emotions such as anger, fear, blame, guilt, and shame produce large flares of beta in the EEG readout.

This shuts down the brain regions that handle rational thinking, decision making, memory, and objective evaluation (LeDoux, 2002). Blood flow to the prefrontal cortex, the "thinking brain," is reduced by up to 80 percent. Starved of oxygen and nutrients, our brains' ability to think clearly plummets.

Low beta is the band that synchronizes our bodies' automatic functions, so it's also called the sensorimotor rhythm frequency, or SMR (12 to 15 Hz).

Beta is required for processing information and for linear thinking, so normal levels of beta are fine. When you focus on solving a problem, composing a poem, calculating the best route to your destination, or balancing your checkbook, beta is your friend. SMR represents a calm, focused mental state. It's stress that produces high beta, especially above 25 Hz.

Alpha (8 to 12 Hz) is an optimal state of relaxed alertness. Alpha connects the higher frequencies—the thinking mind of beta and the associative mind of gamma—with the two lowest frequency brain waves, which are theta (4 to 8 Hz) and delta (0 to 4 Hz).

Theta is characteristic of light sleep. When we dream vividly, our eyes move rapidly and our brains are primarily in theta. Theta is the frequency of rapid eye movement (REM) sleep. Theta is also the dominant frequency of people under hypnosis, healers, people in trances, and people in highly creative states (Kershaw & Wade, 2012). The recollection of emotional experiences, both good and bad, can trigger theta.

The slowest frequency is delta. Delta is characteristic of deep sleep. Very high amplitudes of delta are also found in people who are in touch with nonlocal mind, even when they're wide awake. The brains of meditators, intuitives, and healers have much more delta than normal.

The eyes of people who are in deep dreamless sleep don't move. Delta waves also predominate in such non–rapid eye movement (NREM) sleep.

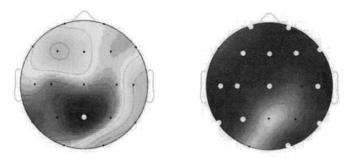

On this type of chart (a "z-score" chart), the middle shade indicates normal activity, and the two lighter shades progressively reduced activity. The two darker shades indicate increased activity. The brain on the left shows a variety of activity. The brain on the right is highly active at the middle frequencies of theta, a common pattern in experienced healers.

AWAKENING FROM EVERYDAY REALITY

EEG pioneer Maxwell Cade noticed that alpha, in the middle of the range of frequencies, forms a bridge between the two high frequencies of beta and gamma and the two low frequencies of theta and delta (Cade & Coxhead, 1979). Biofeedback and neurofeedback skills focus on teaching people how to get into an alpha state. The ideal state is enough alpha to link all of the other brain rhythms together. High beta is minimized, so that there is very little monkey mind and anxiety. There is a balanced amount of gamma and theta, and a wide base of delta.

Maxwell Cade.

A biophysicist, Cade had worked on radar for the British government before turning his attention to measuring states of consciousness. He developed his own machine, the "mind mirror," in 1976. It is unique among EEG devices in that it provides a clear visual snapshot of brain waves.

His student Anna Wise described the machine as follows: "What sets the Mind Mirror apart from other forms of electroencephalography was the interest, on the part of its developer, not in pathological states (as in the case of medical devices), but in an optimum state called the Awakened Mind. Instead of measuring subjects with problems, the inventor of the Mind Mirror sought the most highly developed and spiritually conscious people he could find. In the flicker of their brainwaves, he and his colleagues found a common pattern, whether the subject was a yogi, a Zen master or a healer."

THE AWAKENED MIND

Using the mind mirror, over 20 years, Cade recorded the brain wave patterns of more than four thousand people with strong spiritual practices. He found the Awakened Mind state was common in this group. Cade also noticed another similarity: they all had high amounts of alpha.

As noted, alpha waves are right in the middle of the spectrum, with beta and gamma above, and theta and delta below. When someone in the Awakened Mind state has lots of alpha, it creates a link between the high frequencies above and the low frequencies below. Cade called this the alpha bridge, because it bridges the conscious mind frequencies of beta with the subconscious and unconscious mind frequencies of theta and delta. This allows a flow of consciousness, integrating all the levels of mind.

Cade wrote: "The awakening of awareness is like gradually awakening from sleep and becoming more and more vividly aware of everyday reality—only it's everyday reality from which we are awakening!" (Cade & Coxhead, 1979).

Max Cade with first 1970s version of the mind mirror.

I developed a meditation method called EcoMeditation that's very simple, yet it's consistently and automatically able to bring people into the Awakened Mind EEG pattern. EcoMeditation uses EFT tapping to clear obstacles to relaxation. It then takes you through a series of simple physical relaxation exercises that send signals of safety to the brain and body. It does not rely on belief or philosophy; instead, it's based on sending the body physiological cues that produce a deeply relaxed state automatically. The instructions are free at EcoMeditation.com.

During EcoMeditation, we see lots of delta brain waves as well. Delta is where we connect with many resources above and beyond the local self. As noted, people in trance states, as well as healers, artists, musicians, and intuitives, tend to have plenty of delta.

Those in a creative trance, such as a composer making music or a child at play, usually have lots of delta. They lose all awareness of the outer world as they become absorbed in their creativity. They're mostly in delta, with some theta and alpha, and just enough beta to function (Gruzelier, 2009).

It's been fascinating to me to speak to people whose brains show a high amplitude of delta during meditation. They report transcendent experiences. They describe feeling one with the universe, an exquisite sense of harmony and well-being (Johnson, 2011). Albert Einstein referred to this as an expansive state of consciousness in which we "embrace all living creatures and the whole of nature." Scientists can be mystics too!

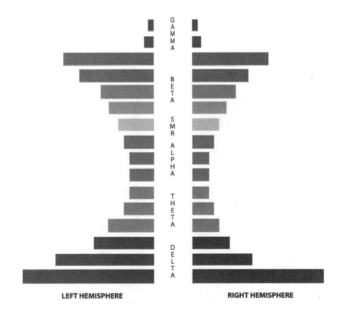

LEFT HEMISPHERE   RIGHT HEMISPHERE

Display from the mind mirror. Normal brain function: note that all six frequencies are present, with balance between left and right hemispheres.

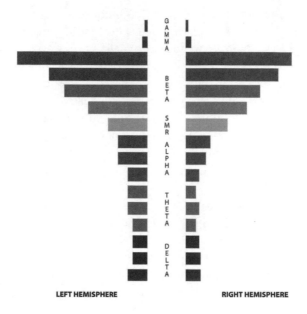

Anxiety: A person with anxiety has a lot of high
beta and little alpha, theta, or delta.

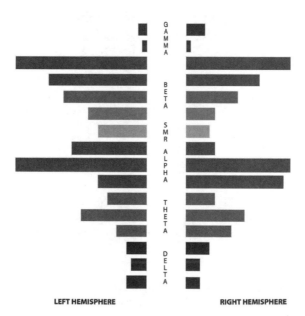

Increase in alpha activity: A subject breaking through to integration
has flares of alpha, even though they still have a pronounced anxiety,
which shows up as beta. They're also amplifying theta, though the waves
are not balanced equally between left and right hemispheres.

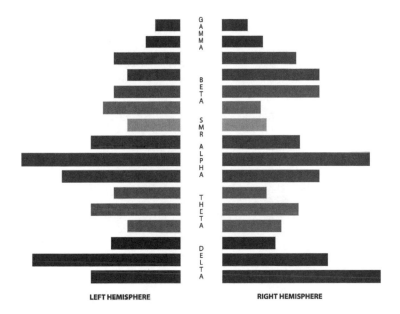

Balance between brain activities: The "Awakened Mind" pattern, with large amounts of delta and theta, and lowered beta. Plentiful alpha provides an "alpha bridge" between conscious mind (beta) and unconscious and subconscious levels (theta and delta).

The Musician Trapped inside the Programmer

At a live workshop, I taught EcoMeditation to Prem, a 42-year-old man with moderate anxiety. He was a computer programmer who wanted to bring more creativity into his life. Prem played the guitar but rarely made time for it, even though it was his favorite hobby. "I just don't have time for myself," he said. One of his core beliefs was "Life is tough. You have to apply yourself. There's no time for play."

When we began the session, Prem's EEG showed a high degree of beta waves in both the left and the right hemispheres of his brain. Beta is the wave typical of stress. His alpha waves were minimal.

Alpha is the ideal wave, one of relaxed alertness, linking the high and low frequencies.

Prem's EEG readout showed plenty of theta and delta, but his minimal alpha amplitude was like a bottleneck; he didn't have access to his creative side. His high amplitude of beta is also characteristic of people with chronic anxiety, stress, and burnout (Fehmi & Robbins, 2007).

Once Prem settled into the EcoMeditation routine, he had big flares of alpha in both the right and the left hemispheres of his brain, though larger on the right. His anxious, stressed-out beta waves disappeared. His brain began to produce gamma waves, which it had not been doing before.

Prem was not a meditator and said that he had taken meditation classes but never succeeded in establishing a routine meditation practice. However, EcoMeditation quickly settled him into a deep state. His brain waves stabilized in the Awakened Mind pattern.

In the absence of stress, the blood rushed back into his prefrontal cortex, and his thinking became clear as he gained access to the biological and intellectual assets in the executive centers of his brain.

At that workshop, we tested the biological responses of participants as well as their psychological states before and after the workshop. Prem's set point for cortisol, the primary stress hormone, dropped significantly. When our stress levels drop, biological resources are freed up for cell repair, immunity, and other beneficial functions.

This was evident in Prem's levels of salivary immunoglobulin A (SIgA), a key immune marker. They rose significantly between the beginning and the end of the workshop. His resting heart rate dropped from 79 to 64 beats per minute (bpm), while his blood pressure dropped from 118/80 to 108/70. All these indicators reflected the newly balanced function of his brain.

Similar positive effects were noted for other workshop participants. For the whole group, average cortisol levels declined and SIgA levels rose. Resting heart rate dropped from 70 to 66 (Groesbeck et al., 2016).

Once we reversed the stress response with EcoMeditation, Prem began to see the light side of life. The blood began to flow back into his forebrain and his whole hard drive came back online. He felt empowered. He knew he had resources. He knew he had the capacity for play. He regained a sense of control in his life. He had a sense of agency, of self-efficacy, and his whole story changed.

When I tested Prem afterward by having him repeat his opening statement that "Life is tough . . . there's no time for play," he burst into laughter. "That sounds like my dad speaking," he observed, and he scowled and wagged his finger as he mimicked a stern father rebuking his playful child.

Prem practiced EcoMeditation throughout the workshop and, by the end, could quickly induce that relaxed state. He began planning time to play guitar and honor his creative side.

Session at a workshop with a participant hooked up to an EEG.

WHEN CONSCIOUSNESS CHANGES, BRAIN WAVES CHANGE

The energy fields of brain waves and the matter of neural pathways are in a constantly evolving dance. When consciousness changes, brain waves change and different neural pathways are engaged.

The extremes are love and fear. When we're in a state of fear, our alpha bridge disappears. We may still have theta and delta, but we're cut off from the resources of our subconscious mind and its connection with the universal whole.

Beta waves flood the fearful brain. It's in survival mode.

When we're in a state of bliss, our brains show the Awakened Mind pattern. A step beyond, they can also move to a symmetrical pattern Cade called the Evolved Mind. As our consciousness is filled with love, our brains function very differently, with large amounts of theta and delta, plus an alpha bridge to connect our conscious with our subconscious mind.

Emotions create brain states. Brain waves measure the fields generated by consciousness. Passing signals through the neural bundles engaged by love, joy, and harmony creates a characteristic energy field (Wright, 2017). When monitoring the brains of people doing EcoMeditation, EEG expert Judith Pennington observed that "theta and delta progressed their patterns from the Awakened Mind to the Evolved Mind state."

Emotions also create neurotransmitters. Among these are serotonin, dopamine, endorphins, oxytocin, and anandamide (Kotler & Wheal, 2017). Serotonin is associated with satisfaction, and dopamine with a sensation of reward. Endorphins block pain and increase pleasure. Oxytocin is the "bonding hormone," and it stimulates feelings of closeness and intimacy with others. Anandamide is called the "bliss molecule," and it's named after the Sanskrit word for happiness. It binds to the same receptors in the brain as THC, the primary psychoactive molecule in marijuana. When mind changes, it creates molecular facts in the form of these neurotransmitters. As they flood our brains, we feel satisfied, secure, bonded, blissful, and serene. When our minds enter elevated emotional states, we're literally getting high—on drugs produced by our bodies.

BRAIN WAVES EXPRESS THE FIELDS GENERATED BY EMOTION

An influential study examined the brain wave patterns of meditators from five different contemplative traditions ranging from qigong to Zen (Lehmann et al., 2012). It compared their brain function in a normal state of consciousness and in meditation.

One of the challenges of such research is that a single hour of EEG recordings of a single subject yields millions of pieces of data. It tells you the predominant frequencies of each part of the brain millisecond by millisecond, and these frequencies are changing constantly. Interpreting this huge mass of data requires experience and a model to describe what you're looking for.

After building a complete picture of how the entire brain functions, the investigators in this study concluded that the most informative model was to compare beta with delta. They measured the ratio of beta to delta before meditation, during meditation, and after meditation. While the meditation traditions offered very different teachings, from chanting to movement to sitting still, what they all had in common was a reduction in beta and an increase in delta.

The researchers identified "globally reduced functional interdependence between brain regions," a change in brain function suggesting a dissolution of the sense of an isolated local self. This brain pattern of low beta and high delta typified what they termed "the subjective experience of non-involvement, detachment and letting go, as well as of all-oneness and dissolution of ego borders" as the consciousness of meditators shifted into oneness with the nonlocal universal field.

That is the same brain wave pattern I've seen in the EEG readouts of hundreds of meditators who are describing states of flow, altered consciousness, and connection with the universal nonlocal field in which the borders of the local self dissolve.

THE EXPERIENCE OF THE MYSTICS

At one workshop, we videotaped statements from people whose brains showed enormous amounts of delta. We asked them what they had experienced during the meditations. One woman named "Julie," who suffered from depression, described it like this:

"At first, having my eyes closed was annoying. I could feel every little scratchy itchy feeling in my skin. My throat tickled, and I wanted to cough. I could hear the guy next to me breathing, and that was annoying too. But then I began to forget about all that stuff, and a feeling of peace came over me.

"I could feel the breath going inside my body. And going out again. It felt like a river flowing. I started to float, like I was a helium balloon or something.

"I seemed to go to another place, and it was beautiful. I could feel the rocks and trees and ocean, and I seemed to be part of it all, like I was absorbed into this perfection of everything there is in the cosmos.

"These four huge blue beings drifted near me, and I felt incredible love and connection flowing out of them. They were like outlines of people but transparent and about 15 feet high. Made out of a beautiful royal blue mist.

"I've been so worried about all the stuff going on in my life lately, but one of the beings drifted close to me and I felt reassured. Like she was telling me everything is going to be okay. My heart filled up with love, and I realized that love is everything.

"She gave me a shiny diamond crystal to remind me that she's always there for me. I put it in my heart. It melted all the miserable, depressed pain that's been living there for too long, and the pain became drops of water that fell into the ground.

"When you told us to come back into the room, I felt like I was a million miles away. I brought that feeling of peace back into my body. It was hard to come back, and I realize part of me is there all the time."

COMMONALITIES IN MYSTICAL EXPERIENCE

What Julie described is a typical mystical experience. Human beings have been having transcendent experiences since the dawn of consciousness, and hers had characteristics similar to many others:

- A pervasive feeling of peace
- The falling away of worry and doubt
- A felt sense of detachment from local self and the limitations of the body
- An experience of oneness with nonlocal mind, including nature, the universe, and all of life
- A meeting with a symbolic guide
- Receiving a symbolic gift that carries healing power
- The integration of the gift with her body and her local self
- A sense of being changed by the experience

The neuroscientists I've worked with have instructed experienced meditators to provide prearranged signals during meditation, such as tapping their forefinger three times when they feel the experience of oneness. We can time-stamp this spot on the EEG readout. This has allowed us to correlate their internal experience with brain states.

When their local self abandons its preoccupation with the body to merge with nonlocal mind, we see large flares of delta. The high-amplitude delta wave becomes stable when the meditators integrate the two states, such as when Julie communed with the blue being who gave her the gift (Pennington, 2017).

Once people start to make meditation part of their daily lives, they develop higher amplitudes of alpha, theta, and delta than they had before.

Mystical experiences throughout history show similarities. Tukaram, an Indian saint of the 17th century, wrote the following poem, "When I Lose Myself in Thee" (Hoyland, 1932):

> When thus I lose myself in Thee, my God,
> Then do I see, and know,
> That all Thy universe reveals Thy beauty,
> All living beings, and all lifeless things,
> Exist through thee.
>
> This whole vast world is but the form
> In which Thou showest us Thyself,
> Is but the voice,
> In which Thyself Thou speakest unto us.
>
> What need of words?
> Come, Master, come,
> And fill me wholly with Thyself.

In Tukaram's poem, we can see characteristics similar to Julie's experience. He loses his sense of local self, disappearing into nonlocal consciousness. He has an experience of oneness with the universe. He feels the universe communicating with him, a state of unity in which no words are necessary.

Though there were no EEGs around in the 17th century to map the brain waves of mystics such as Tukaram, we can infer the types of neural signaling occurring in their brains by examining similar experiences in people like Julie.

**Indian saint Ramakrishna often spontaneously
entered states of mystical experience.**

Indian saint Ramakrishna (1836–1886) would go into states of bliss that lasted for hours at a time. His body became stiff, and he became so absorbed in his transcendent experience that he was unaware of his surroundings. When he emerged from meditation, he was often unable to speak for a while. Once, after regaining the power of speech, he described seeing a light like a million suns. A luminous form emerged from the light, took human shape, then reintegrated with the light.

Theologian Huston Smith is the author of the textbook *The World's Religions* and an expert on mystical experience. He states that experiences of oneness are common to mystics throughout history. The experience is not dependent on time or culture. Mystics aren't talking secondhand about oneness; they're talking firsthand about experiences of oneness (Smith, 2009).

When they descend from the mountaintop, they share their experience with those around them. Inspired, their listeners often venerate them and may even build religions around them. What all the mystics are pointing to, however, is the direct experience of oneness. This is an order removed from the secondhand experience mediated by intercessors such as priests and religious rites.

Mystics don't disagree with one another or believe their own path is superior to another, because they've all had the same experience. Only second-tier religious authorities come into conflict. While religions are different, the mystical experience is one. Smith holds that the mystical experience is the pinnacle of human consciousness (Smith, 2009).

The breakthrough of modern science is that we can now chart the information flow in the brains of mystics, just as the ancient mariners charted the unknown seas. Science is now showing us objectively what mystics like Smith have known subjectively, that mystical experience produces common and predictable patterns in the brain.

The brain's right parietal lobe is responsible for positioning the body in relationship to its surroundings and distinguishing the boundary between self and other. Neuroimaging studies show that in ecstatic states, this region goes offline (Kotler & Wheal, 2017). When Ramakrishna and other mystics describe their sense of local self fading into a merger with a universal nonlocal mind, the experience is echoed in the objective function of their brains. As their oxytocin spikes, they bond with the universe, and as their brains flood with anandamide, they enter bliss.

DELTA WAVES AND CONNECTION WITH NONLOCAL CONSCIOUSNESS

My friend and colleague Dr. Joe Dispenza has been collecting brain scans at meditation workshops for many years and now has a compendium of over 10,000 scans. Studying the patterns that are common to this group of mind maps gives us fascinating insights into the experience of workshop participants.

What we see in Joe's collection is people with much more theta and delta than usual. The baseline amount of delta in the brains of meditators is much greater than those in "normal" brains (Thatcher, 1998). Meditators have practiced releasing their attachment to local mind and immersing themselves in experiences of oneness with nonlocal mind.

Repeated meditation moves the brain into a new zone of functioning that includes much more delta than the old normal. When Joe tested first hundreds and then thousands of such brains, what he noticed was that they were processing information in a way that was very different from the average brain (Dispenza, 2017).

Activity in many of these people is in the red zone, which means that the amount of delta is two deviations from the mean greater than that found in a database of normalized mind maps (Thatcher, 1998). The practical meaning of this statistic is that only 2.5 percent of the general population has the delta function we're seeing in experienced meditators. Neuroscientists measuring the changes in brain waves during Joe's advanced workshops found that over the four days of a workshop, the brain's baseline delta activity increases by an average of 149 percent (Dispenza, 2017).

Delta brain waves range in amplitude from 100 to 200 microvolts from peak to trough (ADInstruments, 2010). When testing people in Eco-Meditation workshops, we often see amplitudes of over 1,000 microvolts. Sometimes we see surges of over a million microvolts. Most EEG equipment is not even able to measure so much delta.

This correlates with powerful spiritual experiences such as the ones reported by today's Julie and yesterday's Tukaram. They have been reported by mystics from all traditions for thousands of years. We can't objectively measure an experience like the sense of local self and local mind dissolving into nonlocal self and universal mind. We can, however, measure how the brain having such an experience processes information. The common denominator is enormous amplitudes of delta waves. This energy is matched by molecules like serotonin and dopamine, as well as the ecstasy neurotransmitter anandamide and the bonding hormone oxytocin. These types of experience are not isolated exceptions. Research shows that 40 percent of Americans and 37 percent of Britons have had at least one transcendent experience that took them beyond local mind. Often they describe it as the most important experience of their lives, shaping everything that came later (Greeley, 1975; Castro, Burrows, & Wooffitt, 2014).

Few talked about their experiences with others, however. Children didn't tell parents. Patients didn't tell doctors. Wives didn't tell husbands. Because this type of conversation is outside our normal social conventions, we don't have the language or context to conduct it.

That doesn't mean these experiences aren't happening. When we start to look for them, encounters with nonlocal mind are all around us.

THETA WAVES AND HEALING

Sometimes such altered brain states are accompanied by rapid healing. In a meditation workshop taught by Joe Dispenza, a Mexican man we'll call "José" described similar mystical experiences (Dispenza, 2017).

José had come to the workshop shortly after being diagnosed with a cancerous brain tumor. He was due for a life-threatening operation soon. During one of the meditations, José—like Julie—saw otherworldly beings. One of them reached his hand into José's skull and rooted around inside for a while. José felt vivid physical sensations as though his scalp were being cut open and his brain tissue rearranged.

The day after the workshop, José rearranged his schedule so that he could get a new X-ray. He flew to Houston to consult with doctors at MD Anderson, a famous cancer clinic, before returning home. The new scan, taken just a day after the workshop, showed that all traces of the tumor had disappeared.

During intense healing experiences, we often see high amplitudes of theta waves on the EEG. Theta has been mapped as the signature brain wave during energy healing sessions (Benor, 2004). If one person is offering healing to another, we see big theta waves in first the healer, then the healee. The switch often happens at the moment the healer feels his or her hands becoming warm—the subjective experience of energy flow (Bengston, 2010).

In one study, a healer and client were both hooked up to EEGs. The healer's EEG readout showed 14 periods of sustained theta at the frequency of exactly 7.81 Hz. The client's EEG shifted to the same frequency, demonstrating entrainment between healer and healee (Hendricks, Bengston, & Gunkelman, 2010).

THE DOCTOR WHO COULDN'T HEAL

In one of my trainings, "Anise," a brilliant doctor, volunteered to work on her issues in front of the whole group while hooked up to an EEG monitor. Anise had earned not only an M.D. but also a doctorate in pharmacology. In addition, she was certified in healing touch and several other modalities.

Anise had been diagnosed with fibromyalgia 13 years earlier. The symptoms, such as joint pain, fatigue, and "brain fog," were sometimes severe, other times less so. She had eventually become so debilitated, however, that she was no longer able to work.

On the day of the training, her pain level was 7 out of 10, and her brain fog was so extreme that she was barely able to comprehend the lectures. She walked with difficulty and needed to prop herself up with three pillows in order to feel comfortable enough to function.

Anise had a high degree of frustration and anger at herself because her husband, "Dal," who was also attending the workshop, now had the whole financial burden of providing for the family, including their two teenage daughters. Another source of anger was the experience that "despite all my training, I can't heal myself."

Although we sometimes see "one-minute wonders" during workshops, this was not the case for Anise. Hers was a long and complicated session. She had difficulty creating a vision for her future because she could not imagine herself getting better.

Gestalt therapist Byron Katie has clients ask themselves provocative questions that challenge their assumptions about self and the world. One of these questions is "Who would I be without this story?" Another way of asking it is "What contribution is this disability making to my life?"

I asked this of Anise. The question triggered a memory of a time when she was eight years old and being emotionally abused by a family member. She got sick, and her illness became her shield. When Anise was bedridden, she could retreat into her bedroom and didn't have to deal with her tormentor.

Once we identified the core issue that sickness might be a solution masquerading as a problem, we used energy psychology techniques to release all her anger at her childhood persecutor, who was still very much present in her life.

Her pain went down to a 1 out of 10, and she began to smile and then laugh at the predicament she'd created for herself. "My nemesis has never become successful," she realized, and she felt empowered in that relationship for the first time in her adult life.

She began to talk about the possibilities for her future. She'd been offered a great job in Brazil but hadn't considered it because she didn't think she could function physically without the resources she enjoyed in the United States. Now that possibility opened up for her. "How about it?" she asked her husband. "I would love to," Dal responded, his eyes shining.

At the end of our session, Anise stood up and walked around the room. As her pain subsided completely, she swung her arms and legs freely, with a full range of motion. She left the workshop that day to have dinner with Dal and discuss their positive future. Not only had her consciousness shifted, but her body had been freed up dramatically as well.

CONSCIOUSNESS SHIFTS THE WAY THE BRAIN PROCESSES INFORMATION

During sessions with clients hooked up to an EEG, what we typically see at the start of a session is a lot of high beta, indicating worry and stress. There's little alpha, gamma, or theta. The absence of alpha means clients are unable to bridge their conscious minds (beta) and their creativity, intuition, and connection to the universal field (theta and delta).

As clients experience flashes of insight, we see large flares of alpha in both the left and the right hemispheres of the brain. During Anise's aha moment of realizing that her tormentor had never become anything like as successful as she was, her alpha flared out so wide that it exceeded the measuring capability of our device.

By the end of the session, we saw the typical Awakened Mind pattern in Anise's brain. She had a small amount of high beta, indicating that her critical thinking capacities were online. But she had more SMR (low beta), showing that she was in touch with her body. She had large amounts of theta and an even greater amplitude of delta, showing a connection with her creativity, intuition, and the universal information field. Her gamma had increased, demonstrating a greater ability to make connections between disparate parts of the brain and process information in an integrated way.

While her psychological breakthroughs were profound, her physiological functioning as diagrammed on her EEG readouts showed real-time brain changes. She wasn't simply experiencing a psychological change; the way her brain organized information was shifting too.

This is more than simply a change in the mind. This is a change in the brain itself, as new neural bundles wire themselves together. New neural bundles are constantly being formed and old ones pruned throughout our lives (Restak, 2001).

When we meditate, tap, use another form of energy psychology, or otherwise shift our consciousness, the brain changes quickly. The brain can be intentionally changed by the mind, especially by what is known as attention training (Schwartz & Begley, 2002). True transformation repatterns neural pathways. Eventually, the entire state of the brain shifts and establishes a new and healthy level of homeostasis.

One research team notes that "an accelerating number of studies in the neuroimaging literature significantly support the thesis that . . . with appropriate training and effort, people can systematically alter neural circuitry associated with a variety of mental and physical states that are frankly pathological" (Schwartz, Stapp, & Beauregard, 2005). We can take our dysfunctional brain networks and alter them with our minds.

It's not just mystics and healers who produce large alpha bridges and theta flares when they're in ecstatic states. Groups for whom high performance is critical are finding that tuning the brain in this way produces big leaps in achievement. U.S. Navy SEALs need to operate effectively in rapidly changing combat conditions. Using millions of dollars of advanced EEG equipment in a "Mind Gym" specially constructed in Norfolk, Virginia, they learn to enter a state they call ecstasis (Cohen, 2017). Once they "flip the switch" into ecstasis, their brains are in a state of flow, an altered reality in which super-performance becomes possible. Other peak performers, such as elite courtroom lawyers, Olympic athletes, and Google executives, also train themselves to enter ecstasis.

The characteristics of these flow states are described in the book *Stealing Fire* (Kotler & Wheal, 2017). Among them are selflessness and timelessness. People in ecstasis transcend the boundaries of local mind. EEG readings show that the prefrontal cortex of their brains, the seat of a sense of self, shuts down. Beta-wave mental chatter ceases. They gain distance from the anxious obsessions of local mind. Their internal chemistry changes as "feel-good" neurotransmitters like serotonin, dopamine, anandamide, and oxytocin flood their brains.

In this state they gain a nonlocal perspective. They are open to an infinite range of possible options and outcomes. The self, rather than being trapped in a limited fixed local reality, is able to try on different possibilities. This "knocks out filters we normally apply to incoming information," leading to associative leaps that facilitate problem solving and super-creativity. Kotler and Wheal (2017) review the research on the performance gains produced by these brain wave states. These include a 490 percent improvement in mental focus, a doubling of creativity, and a 500 percent increase in productivity.

During ecstasis, whether found in the ancient accounts of Tukaram or the modern experiences of Julie and the Navy SEALs, people have common experiences. These are linked to neurotransmitters: entering a state of bliss (anandamide), a sense of detachment from the body that encapsulates the local self (endorphins), local self bonding with the nonlocal universe (oxytocin), serenity (serotonin), and the reward of being changed by the experience (dopamine).

These are the characteristics of upgraded minds, and we now have EEGs and neurotransmitter assays to measure the changes they produce in matter. In the past, ecstatic states were attainable only by mystics, and it took decades of study, rigorous practice, ascetic discipline, and spiritual initiation. Today, "we now know the precise adjustments to body and brain that let us recreate them for ourselves" at will; technology is providing us with "a Cliff Notes version of . . . how to encounter the divine" (Kotler & Wheal, 2017). Today, the highest-performing humans in the fields of sports, business, combat, science, meditation, and art are inducing them routinely. Tomorrow, as we map the physiology of these states and turn ecstasis into a learnable skill, they will be available to everyone.

My Brief Career as an Artist, or Dodging the Bullets of Belief

My career as an artist began at age five and started off badly.

My family had just transplanted themselves to America, and I found myself involuntarily incarcerated in Howard Elementary School in Colorado Springs, Colorado. My British accent attracted unfavorable attention from the teachers. To fix the problem, they consigned me to remedial speech classes, where I developed a stutter and a speech impediment.

One day, I brought an art project home to show my parents. Along with all the other kindergartners, I'd been instructed to draw a cowboy. I did my best, and my teacher noticed how good the drawing looked. Flushed with this rare show of approval, I took my drawing home and showed my mother.

She burst out laughing and ridiculed the drawing. She danced around the dining room, shrieking and pantomiming the anatomically inaccurate angles of the cowboy's arms and legs. Crushed, I retreated to the bunk bed on the enclosed porch that I shared with my sister. I never drew another human form again, confining my doodles to ships and aircraft.

Until I turned 45 years old.

I began to meditate daily as well as tap regularly. I examined my core beliefs. One of these was *I'm no good at art.*

Is that really true? I asked myself. Along with a woman I was close to at the time, who happened to own an art gallery, I signed up for a one-day watercolor class at the local college.

The moment I picked up the brush, it felt alive in my hand. I entered an effortless state of flow. I felt as though I'd been painting for a century. I was a sponge for knowledge, learning every technique the teacher knew in just that one day. My artsy girlfriend couldn't believe I was a novice and suspected I'd obtained a clandestine degree in art somewhere along the line.

Next, I took a two-day class in painting the human face in watercolor. I again sucked the teacher dry, insisting on knowing her advanced techniques before the end of the first day.

I then began to paint regularly. Being a methodical sort, I numbered each painting in the order I completed it—1, 2, 3, and so on—instead of giving them names. They were mostly faces. I painted my love. I painted my confusion. I painted my pain.

Watercolor #13: Angel of destiny.

Once I had eight paintings, I took the best four to a local coffee-shop-cum-art-gallery. The owner was impressed and booked me for a one-man show. The opening was in six weeks. "Come the day before and hang 36 pieces," he said.

I tried to look nonchalant as I walked out the door, but inside I was quaking. Thirty-six pieces! He didn't know I'd only done eight in my whole life, if you exclude the cowboy. Now I had to come up with around 30 more in six weeks, on top of my 60-hour workweek and being a single dad to my two young children!

During breaks at work, I began to paint methodically. I realized I could meet the deadline, but only if I took a cue from Henry Ford and set up my paintings on a production line. Very un-artsy, but necessary.

I arranged three easels side by side in a row. Each watercolor wash takes about 10 minutes to dry before you can apply the next one. So I would apply a layer to one easel and then work on the following one. Then on to the third. By the time I circled back to the first painting, the wash had dried, and I could repeat the process.

Watercolor is a demanding medium. The paint is transparent, so you can't cover up a mistake the way you can using opaque media like oil or acrylic. If you mess up a wash or allow a drop of the wrong color to fall on the paper, the painting is ruined. The pressure was on to finish and frame those 30 paintings. As I entered the flow state, I found that I could hold the plan of each of the three paintings in my mind while simultaneously applying the paint effortlessly.

I met the deadline and opened my first art show. People loved the images, and I sold several pieces. Emboldened, I approached the most prestigious local venue, City Hall. They rotated local artists every few weeks. Again, the manager immediately booked me for a one-man show. Again, I painted and enjoyed the process of exhibiting.

Then the opportunity arose to co-author a book, called *Soul Medicine*, with my mentor, Dr. Norm Shealy. I decided to switch my energies and very limited free time into writing instead of painting. Halfway through the largest and most ambitious piece I'd ever painted, I laid down my brushes forever and began to write instead.

Art show invitation.

The experience was full of lessons for me. One is that our heads are full of beliefs that aren't true—in my case, things like the core belief *I'm no good at art*. Another lesson is that these core beliefs arise from early childhood experiences. They shape our entire lives, and unless we challenge them, we can spend our lives demonstrating the lies we were told as children. Most of my subsequent career has been spent helping other people identify and challenge their limiting core beliefs.

One of the friends who came to the grand opening of my City Hall exhibit was a woman named Alice. She was a fused-glass artist who had been struggling to make a living at her craft for years. Alice said to me, "I'm awed. One-person shows are impossible to get. I've never been able to land one." I didn't reply to Alice. Inside my head, I wiped my metaphorical brow and thought, *Whew, I'm glad I didn't know that. I've only had two shows. I had no idea they were hard to land.*

Another watercolor artist at the reception painted landscapes. She exclaimed, "But you paint portraits. Faces are the most difficult thing to paint in watercolor!" My mental self-talk was: *Who knew? Not me . . . Dodged another belief bullet.*

Once I disintegrated one belief, I began to disintegrate others. I began to question all the beliefs that had kept me small and limited. I began to reclaim parts of myself that I'd disowned because of the disapproval of parents, teachers, partners, and friends. I began to find out who I was and become that person, instead of confining myself to the limitations set up by the people around me.

That's what the human potential movement is all about. We have vast abilities, powers, and insights within. They may be constrained by the blindness of the people around us, but they're still there. We're much bigger than we've believed. Once we begin to take off the blinders and step into our full magnificence, we become shapers of the world around us rather than reflections of the limitations of the past.

Watercolor #21: Heart's Too Big.

Every moment is the moment you decide: Will I be that magnificence, or will I continue to pretend I'm less than what I know I am?

Imagine if I had played it safe and stuck with my trusty tried-and-true core belief I'm no good at art. Imagine if I'd consulted my experienced friends in advance and discovered that one-man shows are impossible to obtain and that faces are the most difficult thing to paint. The result would have been no art classes, no one-man shows, no explosion of creativity, perhaps no book and no life-changing career in writing and research. That's the consequence of living in the box of your old beliefs: no new mind, no new matter—instead of living in an open world of new mind, new matter.

As a thought experiment, imagine that you continue, for the rest of your life, to hold the beliefs about yourself that you hold today. That's one option at the fork in the road ahead. If you take the other direction at the fork, you challenge every limiting belief in your head and reach out far ahead for your potential. You succeed sometimes, you fail at other times, but either way you grow. You start to discover the boundaries of who you really are instead of the boundaries your teachers and parents held about you. Your new mind becomes your new matter.

You truly are at the crossroads at this very minute. Which direction will you choose? My mission in this book is to encourage you to say, "I know I have greatness in me, and I'm determined to express it fully!"

Social scientists used to believe that our personality is formed very early in life and does not change much over time. A 1989 headline in the *New York Times* proclaimed "Personality: Major Traits Found Stable through Life" (Goleman, 1987). It reported on a study showing that our core traits, such as anxiety, friendliness, and appetite for new experiences, are fixed.

The longest personality study ever conducted, however, shows that our personalities can change beyond recognition over the course of our lives (Harris, Brett, Johnson, & Deary, 2016). It began with data from a 1950 survey of 1,208 14-year-olds. Six questionnaires were used by their teachers to evaluate six personality traits.

Sixty years later, researchers tracked down the original respondents, now aged on average 77. They found that there was little overlap with their teenage selves. Where they expected to find a good deal of stability of personality traits, they were surprised to find little, with one exclaiming that "there is hardly any relationship at all" (Goldhill, 2017).

Our childhood beliefs and traits don't have to dog us through life. As we take responsibility for change and practice desirable habits of mind consistently, we can shift dramatically. The changes might not show up in a week or a month, but consistent practice over time can turn you into a completely different person.

EMOTIONS SHAPE THE WORLD AROUND US

We think of ourselves as autonomous individuals, making our own decisions and leading our own lives. In reality, we are part of a matrix of connection. We are connected to each other through our neural networks and by means of invisible energy fields.

Our thoughts and emotions are not contained within our minds and bodies. They affect people around us, often without their knowledge. Their thoughts and emotions are affecting us too—at the subconscious and unconscious levels.

Prior research has shown that brains synchronize when sharing information. When one person speaks while another listens, the brain regions active in the speaker light up in the listener too.

Biomedical engineers at Drexel University, in collaboration with psychologists at Princeton, developed a wearable brain-imaging headband to measure this phenomenon (Liu et al., 2017). It builds on work using functional magnetic resonance imaging (fMRI) to examine the activity of the language areas of the brain. Especially when the speaker is describing a vivid and emotional experience, the listener's brain activity mirrors that of the speaker.

The researchers recorded one English-speaking subject and two Turkish-speaking subjects telling a real-life story. Their brains were scanned while they were speaking. The recording was then played back to 15 English-only speakers while the investigators measured activity in the parietal and prefrontal areas of the listeners' brains. These regions are involved in our ability to discern the goals, desires, and beliefs of other people. Those areas lit up when the listeners heard the English story but not the Turkish ones. The researchers also found that the greater the degree of "coupling" between brain areas in listener and speaker, the better the degree of comprehension. This shows that the better our brains are at mirroring the experience of others, the more we understand them.

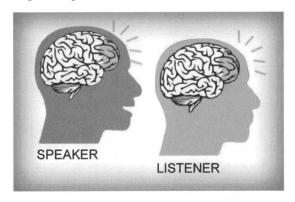

Brain coupling during communication.

ENERGY FIELDS AT A DISTANCE

Energy fields can affect others at a distance as well. Eric Leskowitz, M.D., a psychiatrist from Harvard Medical School's Spaulding Rehabilitation Hospital, visited the Institute of HeartMath in Boulder Creek, California, in 2007. While blindfolded and meditating, his heart rate and heart coherence were continuously monitored by the lab technicians.

Heart coherence is associated with increased alpha brain wave activity. It is a state in which the interval between heartbeats is regular and constant. It's produced by positive emotions such as love and compassion. Negative emotions disrupt heart coherence.

At random intervals unknown to Leskowitz, expert meditators standing behind him were given a signal to enter heart coherence themselves. As they did so, Leskowitz's heart coherence also increased (Leskowitz, 2007). Without touching him, they were able to shift his heart-brain function.

A follow-up study measured the same effect in 25 volunteers in a series of 148 ten-minute trials, and it found the same phenomenon of heart entrainment at a distance (Morris, 2010). The author stated that "a coherent energy field can be generated and/or enhanced by the intentions of small groups of participants. . . . The evidence of heart rhythm synchronization across participants supports the possibility of heart-to-heart bio-communications."

Our bodies and brains are synchronizing with people around us all the time. When we observe others being touched, our brains light up in the same way as if we were being touched (Schaefer, Heinze, & Rotte, 2012). That's because our brains contain mirror neurons that echo the sensations we're observing. These mirror neurons even fire in sympathy with facial expressions and tones of voice, indicating that we are very sensitive to both verbal and nonverbal emotional cues provided by those around us.

It is not only positive emotions that can be transmitted from person to person. Our brains are also attuned to the pain of another. Researchers in Birmingham, England, showed college students images of people suffering from localized sports injuries or from receiving injections. Almost a third of the students felt pain at the same site portrayed in the photographs they were looking at.

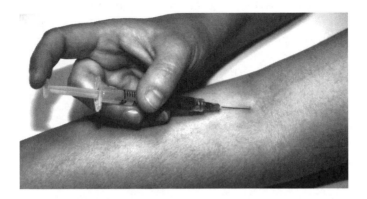

Receiving an injection.

The researchers then used an fMRI machine to compare the brains of 10 students who had felt only an emotional reaction to the images against another 10 students who had actually felt physical pain. All 20 students showed increased activity in the areas of the brain that process emotions. But only those who had actually felt the pain physically had activity in the brain regions that process pain (Osborn & Derbyshire, 2010).

As another example, babies cry not just when family members are in distress, but even when strangers are upset (Zahn-Waxler, Radke-Yarrow, Wagner, & Chapman, 1992). Their nervous systems have a high degree of entrainment with those around them, and the structures in the emotion-processing parts of their brains light up in response to the emotions of others.

EMOTIONAL CONTAGION

Emotions are contagious (Hatfield, Cacioppo, & Rapson, 1994). When your best friend laughs, you're likely to laugh along with her. When she's depressed, you're equally likely to feel blue too. Just as you can get the flu by walking into a classroom full of sick second-graders, you can pick up emotions from the people around you—for instance, walking into that classroom and feeling happy when you hear all the second-graders laughing at a joke. Emotions are contagious in the same way infectious diseases are contagious. This isn't only true of negative emotions such as fear, stress, and sadness. It is also the case for joy and contentment (Chapman & Sisodia, 2015).

Framingham is a charming New England town in Massachusetts, 19 miles from Boston. Now home to 17,000 families, it was first settled in the mid-1600s. Late in that century, Framingham received an influx of families from nearby Salem, people who were seeking to escape the infamous Salem witch trials. That part of town is still called Salem's End.

In medical literature, the town is famous for the Framingham Heart Study. In 1948, a farsighted group of researchers from the National Heart Institute set up an ambitious research project to find the cause of heart disease and stroke, both of which had been rising steadily in the first half of the century.

Framingham Common.

They recruited 5,209 Framingham residents between the ages of 30 and 62 and performed a comprehensive battery of psychological and physical tests. Subjects returned every two years for follow-up. In 1971, the study enrolled a second generation, consisting of 5,124 of the original participants' children and the children's spouses, and today many of the grandchildren and great-grandchildren of the original participants still participate.

The gold mine of data obtained by the study has enabled researchers to look at much more than heart disease. A sub-study of 4,739 people over 20 years looked at their happiness levels and how these levels affected those around them (Fowler & Christakis, 2008).

This study found that one person's happiness can boost that of another for time periods as long as a year. When a person in the Framingham social network became happy, the chances that a neighbor, spouse, sibling, or friend would become happy increased up to 34 percent. Living within a mile of a friend who became happy increased a participant's chance of happiness by 25 percent.

"You would think that your emotional state would depend on your own choices and actions and experience," observed study co-author Nicholas Christakis, a medical sociologist at Harvard University. "But it also depends on the choices and actions and experiences of other people, including people to whom you are not directly connected. Happiness is contagious." Barbara Fredrickson, the author of *Love 2.0*, calls this positivity resonance (Fredrickson, 2013). When the frequency of our consciousness is love, we naturally connect with others who resonate with that shared energy field.

THE RIPPLE EFFECT OF HAPPINESS

Not only did happy people affect those around them, but happiness also showed a ripple effect. Three degrees of separation out, people became happier. Having a friend know someone who was happy increased the chances of happiness by as much as 15 percent, and even in the next layer out, the likelihood was still 6 percent.

Negative emotions were also contagious, but not as much. Having an unhappy connection increased the chances of unhappiness by an average of 7 percent, as opposed to 9 percent for happiness.

Emotional contagion is present in groups too (Barsade, 2002). It can influence group dynamics and can lead to improved cooperation, enhanced task performance, and decreased conflict. "Emotional contagion, through its direct influence on employees' and work teams' emotions, judgments, and behaviors, can lead to subtle but important ripple effects in groups and organizations," says Sigal Barsade, author of several influential studies of emotional contagion. Positive emotion and mood in a team member, especially the leader, enhances the performance of the whole team. But stressed leaders will degrade the performance of everyone around them.

An Organizational Culture Corroded by Emotional Contagion

By Stacene Courvallis

Our company manufactures specialized construction equipment, and is admired by others in our industry as an example of tightly-focused growth.

As the recent construction boom expanded, so did we. We hired a lot of new people quickly, and one of those was Wilma, a senior executive who reported to me. Her resume looked perfect, and she'd passed the interviewing process with flying colors.

Three months into her job, her performance was good, but Wilma had begun sharing concerns with me about various projects and people. A couple of other executives who usually left work early. A budget overrun in another department. An engineer with sensitive proprietary information who was friends with a peer at a competing company.

She framed her observations in terms of concern for the health of our organization, and I was grateful to her for pointing them out.

Emotional energy, whether positive or negative, spreads throughout a team.

Soon Wilma's gripe sessions became a regular part of my workload, and she continued to discover problems. She felt that the corporate culture was too lax and that the other executives didn't give me enough respect. She believed we needed to sharpen our mission statement and our goals. She believed we could downsize our workforce and increase our profit margins.

I started to wonder if there was much more wrong with the company than I had perceived, and I became suspicious of other members of the executive team. The exuberant, fun tone of our office began to erode, despite our accelerating financial success.

Then our CFO, Jason, asked for a confidential meeting with me. He told me that Wilma had been talking to him about the failings of others in the office, and Jason did not believe her concerns were warranted. As I dug deeper, I discovered a pattern. She took other executives into her confidence, smearing all the managers except the person she was talking to.

I also realized that the real problem was me. I had been sucked into Wilma's stories, and lost my own sense of trust in our people, and security in the company's direction. I had been unconsciously transmitting this to the rest of the team, leading to the loss of our emotionally uplifting organizational culture.

Some quick web searches soon revealed that this malaise had a name: emotional contagion. Unhealthy emotions can spread among people in close proximity just the way diseases spread. Our whole company had become infected.

Once I identified emotional contagion, I could see it in every organization I encountered. I went into a courtroom and felt the thick fog of discontent and unhappiness that filled the building. I went into the local music store and noticed that the smiles of employees seemed genuine, and they were truly having fun as they interacted together.

I let Wilma go late on a Friday afternoon. On Monday morning, the mood in the entire office had changed. People were relaxed once again. Our company felt like a fun and creative place to work once more. The flow of conversation was no longer guarded. Trust had returned. With the carrier of the bad feelings removed, the previous positive emotional tone quickly reasserted itself. Best of all, I felt good about myself and the company again.

EMOTIONAL CONTAGION SHAPES THE WORLD

Emotions aren't contagious just at the level of a team, family, or community. They're contagious on the much larger scale of social networks.

A massive experiment with 689,003 Facebook users found that emotional contagion doesn't even require contact between people (Kramer, Guillory, & Hancock, 2014). Entire groups of people can come into emotional coherence, and their brain waves change, potentially generating a huge combined field.

The study used an automated system to change the amount of emotional content in the news feeds of Facebook users. When user timelines were manipulated to reduce positive emotions, according to the study authors, "People produced fewer positive posts and more negative posts; when negative expressions were reduced, the opposite pattern occurred."

This demonstrates that "Emotions expressed by others on Facebook influence our own emotions, constituting experimental evidence for massive-scale contagion via social networks." It showed that nonverbal cues and personal interaction weren't necessary for emotional contagion to occur.

Though it's happening below the level of our conscious awareness, we're sharing our emotions with others all the time, including through online social networks. A study conducted by the University of Vermont found that photographs posted on Instagram reflect the mood of the person posting them. The researchers compared photos posted by depressed people with those posted by people who were not depressed. They compared 43,950 photos posted by 166 individuals. Half of these had been diagnosed with clinical depression during the previous three years (Reece & Danforth, 2017).

The investigators discovered that depressed people manipulated their photos to have darker tones. Their most popular choice of filter was one called Inkwell, which removes color and makes photos black and white. Happy people were more likely to use a filter called Valencia, which gives photos a warmer and brighter tone. Depressed people literally drained the color out of what they shared with others.

Using these color choices as a tool for diagnosing depression was successful 70 percent of the time. That's substantially higher than the 42 percent success rate of general practice doctors.

THE NUREMBERG RALLIES

The unconscious spread of negative emotions has been directing human societies for millennia, long before social media came along. It's nothing new. Examples of mass hysteria can be found throughout the pages of history. In the 1930s, Adolf Hitler staged huge rallies in Nuremberg, Germany, to whip up enthusiasm and showcase the power of Germany and the National Socialist Party to the nation and the world.

Huge banners, goose-stepping marchers, martial songs, torchlit processions, fireworks, and bonfires enthralled the hundreds of thousands of spectators. Long speeches by Adolf Hitler and other Nazi Party luminaries laid out party ideology. The emotional contagion of the spectacular events helped unite the country behind Hitler's vision.

The 1934 rally drew over a million people. The American journalist William Shirer had recently arrived to cover Germany for the Hearst newspaper group and decided to attend. In his diary, he records his impressions of his first evening in the grand medieval city. He found himself carried along in a wave of humanity. In front of the hotel where Hitler was staying, 10,000 people chanted, "We want our Führer!"

Adolf Hitler addressing the 1934 Nuremberg rally.

Shirer wrote, "I was a little shocked at the faces, especially those of the women, when Hitler finally appeared on the balcony for a moment. They reminded me of the crazed expressions I once saw in the back country of Louisiana on the faces of some Holy Rollers. . . . They looked up at him as if he were a Messiah, their faces transformed into something positively inhuman."

The following morning, Shirer attended the opening ceremony of the rally. He wrote, "I'm beginning to comprehend, I think, some of the reasons for Hitler's astounding success. . . . This morning's opening meeting . . . was more than a gorgeous show; it also had something of the mysticism and religious fervor of an Easter or Christmas Mass in a great Gothic cathedral. The hall was a sea of brightly colored flags. Even Hitler's arrival was made dramatic. The band stopped playing. There was a hush over the thirty thousand people packed in the hall. Then the band struck up the *Badenweiler March*. . . . Hitler appeared in the back of the auditorium and followed by his aides, Göring, Goebbels, Hess, Himmler, and the others, he strode slowly down the long centre aisle while thirty thousand hands were raised in salute."

To those attending, the event was intoxicating. Shirer records that "Every word dropped by Hitler seemed like an inspired Word from on high. Man's—or at least the German's—critical faculty is swept away at such moments, and every lie pronounced is accepted as high truth itself" (Shirer, 1941).

That's the power of emotional contagion. Like the reign of Hitler, the Salem witch trials, the Red Scare of the 1960s, the 1994 Rwandan genocide, the 2003 Iraq war, the Great Recession of 2007, and the North Korean nuclear standoff, such times of mass hysteria usually end badly for all concerned.

MARKET AND COMMODITY BUBBLES

Stock market bubbles are another example of emotional contagion. Investors forget the ups and downs of the business cycle in a wave of speculative buying. In 1996, Federal Reserve Board chairman Alan Greenspan called it "irrational exuberance." In his book *The Ascent of Money*, historian Niall Ferguson states, "Booms and busts are products, at root, of our emotional volatility" (Ferguson, 2008).

Ratios of the stock prices of companies relative to their income as of February 20, 2018 (Shiller, 2017). The historic median is 16, meaning that company stocks are typically valued at 16 times their historic earnings. Ratios above 16 indicate a bubble. In early 2018, the ratio stood at 33.

On October 16, 1929, Irving Fisher, an economics professor at Yale University, announced that American stock prices had "reached what looks like a permanently high plateau."

He was very wrong. The market slipped a few days later, then crashed and crashed again. Over the next three years, the market declined by 89 percent. It did not regain its 1929 level until 1954.

In seeking to explain the crash, legendary economist John Maynard Keynes was well aware of the emotional contagion that had gripped the national psyche, calling it a "failure of the immaterial devices of the mind" (Ferguson, 2008).

Bubbles have been seen throughout history. In 1634, the prices of Dutch tulip bulbs began to rise, and speculators entered the market. The Dutch tulip mania began. Some bulbs changed hands 10 times a day, at ever higher prices. By January 1637, rare tulip bulbs sold for more than the price of a house. On February 5, the bubble abruptly collapsed.

Wagon of Fools **by Hendrik Gerritsz Pot.**

The emotional contagion of tulip mania was captured in a 1637 painting by Hendrik Gerritsz Pot called *Wagon of Fools*. It depicts a group of Dutch weavers who have dropped their looms to follow a wagon topped by Flora, goddess of flowers. She carries bouquets of tulips in her arms and is accompanied by alcoholics, moneylenders, and the double-faced goddess Fortuna. The assembly is being led to their deaths in the sea.

The feelings we feel when our brain wave patterns are hijacked by emotional contagion are real. We have a spike in stress-related beta waves and a drop in alpha. It takes a strong mind to remain unaffected by the mass hysteria around us. We can't easily discern an emotion being given to us secondhand from one arising within our own neural network.

MAPPING THE ENLIGHTENED BRAIN

Historical observers have been able to describe the extremes of consciousness. The continuum ranges from the emotional contagion that drives whole civilizations to war to the enlightened states of the mystics.

Modern neuroscience, however, gives us the ability to map the neural signaling involved in consciousness and describe the signaling pathways active in the emotional brain.

When we record the brain waves of people having mystical experiences, we translate subjective states of consciousness into objective pictures of brain function. As consciousness shifts away from fear, distress, and the worries of the local mind, brain waves change. This indicates that different neural pathways are being engaged, which in turn alters the brain's electromagnetic field. Subjective feelings of inner peace can now be mapped objectively using EEGs to provide an objective picture of information flow in the brain.

During mystical experiences, mind leaves matter. Consciousness ceases to identify exclusively with the local self, and EEG readings show large flares of alpha waves as the alpha bridge is created between conscious and unconscious reality.

Consciousness then transcends attachment to the local self to merge with nonlocal mind. The EEG shows first flares and then large, steady amplitudes of delta waves, the signature wave of nonlocal mind and connection with the universal field.

When altered states are experienced, the EEG records large amplitudes of alpha, theta, and delta simultaneously. When physical healing takes place, such as the dissolution of José's tumor, flares of theta are usually evident.

In this union of local brain and nonlocal mind, a transformation occurs. Symbols such as the beings Julie saw and the crystal she received become emblems of a new personal reality that integrates local and nonlocal mind. At the conclusion of the mystical experience, the person returns to local reality. However, they are changed. They may have brought back a gift representing emotional or physical healing, such as the crystal Julie placed in her heart. The process produces a release of old stuck energy—in Julie's case, the depression that melted like raindrops and fell to the ground. They may experience physical healing, such as the disappearance of José's brain tumor.

Matter is changed by mind. Many studies show that meditators have higher volumes of brain tissue, better sleep, fewer diseases, increased immunity, enhanced emotional health, reduced inflammation, slower aging, increased intercellular communication, balanced neurotransmitters, greater longevity, and less stress.

Our transformed mental, emotional, and physical states then radiate around us. As we become happier, we affect the people we associate with. They in turn affect people around them, and the effects of mind change ripple through the community. Positive emotional contagion occurs.

Jesuit philosopher Pierre Teilhard de Chardin coined the term *noosphere*, sometimes translated as *orb of awareness*, to describe the field of consciousness produced by humankind. Include all the rest of life on Earth and you have the *psychosphere*, or orb of consciousness of everything in the field. I also use the term *emosphere* to describe the collective emotional tone of the planet.

We are part of the field of healing in the psychosphere of humankind. Our energy is out of phase with the negative emotions infecting society; we don't participate in those fields. Our change of mind has produced a new material reality, one that supports our health and spiritual transformation.

PUTTING THESE IDEAS INTO PRACTICE

Activities to practice this week:

- Practice EcoMeditation for at least 10 minutes each morning and evening.
- Foster positive emotional contagion by deliberately connecting with other people.
- Spend at least 10 minutes with your spouse at the beginning and end of each work day.
- Talk about the things your spouse wants to discuss and practice summarizing what they tell you.
- When you're in a store, look the people helping you in the eye.
- Practice smiling at other people to foster positive emotional connections.
- In your journal, note any petty annoyances that trigger you.

The Extended Play version of this chapter includes:

- Audio interview with psychiatrist Eric Leskowitz, M.D.
- The seven steps of EcoMeditation
- Emotional contagion videos
- Additional case histories and references

To access the Extended Play version, visit:
MindToMatter.club/Chapter3

CHAPTER 4

How Energy Regulates Dna and the Cells of Our Bodies

You are not the same person you were a second ago, let alone yesterday. Your body is replacing cells and rejuvenating its systems at a frantic pace.

Your body contains some 37 trillion cells (Bianconi et al., 2013). That's a much bigger number than the count of galaxies in the known universe. Old cells are dying and new ones replacing them all the time. Each second, over 810,000 cells are being replaced.

Your body produces one trillion new red blood cells per day (Wahlestedt et al., 2017). That's a big number; with all its zeros it can be expressed as 1,000,000,000,000.

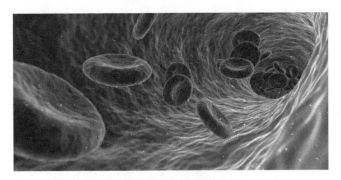

Red blood cells circulating.

As they circulate through your veins and arteries, red blood cells carry oxygen and nutrients to every other cell in your body. Each blood cell has a lifetime of about four months, after which the liver extracts its vital ingredients and sends the rest to the spleen for recycling. You don't have a single red blood cell in your body that you had six months ago. Every one has been replaced.

YOUR BODY IS CONSTANTLY REGENERATING ITSELF

The lining of your digestive tract also undergoes rapid turnover. It's replaced every four days. Your lung tissue? Every eight days. Even the densest of tissues, your bones, are constantly regenerating, with 10 percent of your skeleton being replaced each year.

There are about 84 billion neurons in the brain, along with a similar number of non-neural cells (Azevedo et al., 2009). Our brains are growing new neural cells continuously, and each cell can connect with thousands of others, weaving an interconnected web of an estimated 150 trillion synapses (Sukel, 2011). Our brains are replacing at least one neuron per second (Walløe, Pakkenberg, & Fabricius, 2014).

The hippocampus is the part of the brain responsible for memory and learning. It's constantly adding new neurons and synapses while pruning others. Some neural pathways are shrinking, and the volume of those parts of the hippocampus diminishes. Other neural pathways are growing, with their volume expanding.

When a patient has a liver transplant, half the liver of the donor is typically removed and transplanted into the body of the new host. Yet so fast do liver cells regenerate that within eight weeks the donor's liver has grown back to its original size (Nadalin et al., 2004). The oldest cell now in your liver is about five months old

Cell Type	Turnover Time	BNID
blood neutrophils	1-5 days	101940
bone osteoblasts	3 months	109907
bone osteoclasts	2 weeks	109906
cardiomytes	0.5-10% per year	107076, 107077, 107078
cervix	6 days	11032
colon lining cells	3-4 days	107812
fat cells	8 years	103455
Intestine Paneth cells	20 days	107812
lens cells	lifetime	109840
liver hepatocyte cells	0.5-1 year	109233
lungs alveoli	8 days	101940
oocytes (female gametes)	lifetime	111451
pancreas beta cells (rat)	20-50 days	109228
platelets	10 days	111407, 111408
red blood cells	4 months	101706, 107875
skeleton	10% per year	107076, 107077, 107078
skin epidermis cells	10-30 days	109214, 109215
small intestine epithelium	2-4 days	107812, 109231
sperm (male gametes)	2 months	110319, 110320
stem cells	2 months	109232
stomach	2-9 days	101940
tongue taste buds (rat)	10 days	111427
trachea	1-2 months	101940
white blood cells Eosinophils	2-5 days	109901, 109902

**The regeneration of cells occurs at different rates in different tissues.
This table shows the renewal rates of some of these. The acronym BNID
refers to the Harvard University Database of Useful Biological Numbers.**

Even the heart regenerates. Until very recently, scientists believed
that the heart does not regenerate and that once heart cells have died,
they are not replaced. But recent research shows that heart tissue contains
regions of stem cells that are available to replace damaged or dead cells
and that the entire heart regenerates at least three times in the course of
a person's life (Laflamme & Murry, 2011).

The corneal cells on the surface of your eye can regenerate within
24 hours. Your skin is being entirely replaced every month. The lining of
your stomach is renewing itself every week and your colon even faster.
The self you were yesterday is not the self you are today.

Cell division.

Welcome to the new you!

This continual turnover of the fundamental building blocks of our bodies has profound implications for how quickly and completely we can heal.

Our bodies are programmed to heal. Healing is not something we get from a prescription, a doctor, an herb, or an alternative therapist. Healing is what our bodies do naturally and normally every second of every day. The deeper our understanding of the healing process, the better equipped we are to turn mind to matter.

YOUR BODY USES THE MATERIAL YOU MAKE AVAILABLE TO IT

When you look in the mirror each morning, you might believe you're seeing yesterday's face staring back at you. But during the previous day, your body replaced some 60 billion cells. You're a different physical being than you were the day before.

This extensive daily remodeling of the body isn't happening in a vacuum. You are shaping the quality of cells your body produces with material inputs such as the food you eat and the water you drink. When you eat high-quality food, your body has the raw materials with which to create high-quality proteins, the molecular building blocks of cells.

When you eat low-quality food, the body only has substandard materials out of which to fashion new proteins. When your food lacks vital nutrients, your body is forced to make compromises, and those trade-offs can eventually damage your health.

Most of us know to choose healthy food and not eat junk, yet we're often much less discriminating about the energy we absorb.

Think of your body as a factory and the cells it produces as cars. If the finest steel is being delivered to its loading docks by freight companies, and it has excellent glass, flexible rubber, and advanced composites at its disposal, the factory can build high-quality cars.

But if the rubber is brittle or the glass opaque or the steel weak, the final product is compromised. The factory can't build excellent cars out of shoddy ingredients. If the matter going in is inadequate, the matter emerging from your body's manufacturing cycle will be of poor quality. Garbage in, garbage out.

That's the matter end of the equation. What about energy?

CELLS REGENERATE IN A FIELD

Cells also replicate in an energy environment. Just as poor-quality matter is going to produce poor-quality cells, inferior energy is going to result in inferior molecules. Energy fields bathe our bodies, and the type of energy in which cell regeneration takes place determines the biological outcome.

Right now, I'm enjoying a delicious cup of Earl Grey tea. I went to the kitchen, popped a tea bag into a cup, filled the cup with the tangy water from my well, and put the cup inside the microwave. I set the timer for two minutes, sufficient to bring the water to a boil.

Though they're invisible, the waves inside the microwave oven caused the water in my teacup to change state. In two minutes, the water went from a room temperature of 70°F to boiling, 212°F. Matter was changed by energy.

In the same way, our cells are bathed in the surrounding energy fields. These fields change the matter of our cells, even though they're invisible. Strong radiation, such as that released in nuclear reactor disasters, can cause cells to mutate.

What happens when your cells are bathed in the energy of love, appreciation, and kindness created by a vibrant and coherent brain? Just the opposite. They're nurtured in the radiant fields of positive emotion.

Here is one of my favorite healing stories. Glenda Payne faced a truly desperate situation as her body began to degenerate. How she used her mind to save herself has inspired thousands of people.

From Terminal Muscular Degeneration to Dancing around the Room

By Glenda Payne

I had a job I loved. I was the wholesale program manager for a greenhouse manufacturing company. I was just expanding our market into France when I began to notice strange symptoms. Climbing the stairs was becoming more and more of a struggle. I would feel as though I had just run a mile up a steep hill. My thigh muscles would hardly lift my legs. By the time I reached the top stair, I would be gasping for breath.

Despite taking time off to rest, I found that the muscle pain and weakness escalated, with a frightening new symptom: terrible shortness of breath leading to blackouts. Simple activities such as hand-washing dishes, standing in line at a public counter, or pushing a grocery cart would leave me in an embarrassed heap on the floor, desperately gasping for breath and fighting blackout. One afternoon, I was standing in the office talking with a co-worker and

I helplessly slid to the floor, lost in a black tunnel. After that, I could no longer drive. I never went back to work again.

My doctors could find no explanation. After five years of expensive tests, going to specialist after specialist, I finally got a diagnosis: a rare condition called mitochondrial inclusion body myositis. I was told there was nothing they could do for me.

My life spiraled down into one of hopeless despair. I was ready to give up. My world was reduced to my living room couch or my bed.

One spring, my sister shared a five-minute video demonstration of EFT tapping. We became hooked on tapping. That summer, we heard Dawson Church interview Dr. Joe Dispenza in a webinar.

In the interview, Dr. Dispenza related his own medical miracle story. He had been a professional bicycle racer. During an event, he was directly hit by a large truck as he was navigating a turn. His injuries were serious, with little hope that he would recover enough to walk again. He shared how he used his mind to communicate to the nerves and cells of his body while he was strapped to a bed, utterly motionless. He projected an image of his healthy body into what he called the unified field of consciousness. It worked.

As I lay there in my constant state of painful, exhausted fatigue, I latched onto the hope that if he could find full recovery, I could too!

Dawson worked with me on a live call during that same webinar. Hearing Dr. Dispenza's story and tapping with Dawson for a few minutes on that call changed my life. My sister and I both knew that tapping was helping us clear major issues we'd been plagued with our whole lives. We chose to pursue certification.

In October, we enrolled in our first certification class with Dawson. He worked with me again in a demonstration. At the end of the four-day workshop, I approached Dawson with the words, "Notice what's missing?" I dropped my cane and proceeded to dance in front of the whole room. I had arrived at the hotel for that workshop in a wheelchair. I left dancing. I haven't used my scooter since that day.

In the three years since I first listened to that interview with Joe and Dawson, I've completed my EFT practitioner certification program, simultaneously completed energy psychology certification, written and published a book, and completed an initiation as a shaman. I'm currently working on material for a second book and a blog.

I still have good days and bad days. I still need lots of rest. My cane is still my companion on most outings, though I find I am using it less and less. I am able to go on hikes again, though they are brief, of short distance, and must be on level ground. Inclines can still do me in. And I have to plan at least one full day of rest after. I've learned to listen to my body.

Glenda four years later.

The happier I get using all of the tools now available to me, the happier my body is too, and the more activity I can handle. I have turned what was once a hopeless existence full of lonely despair into a life of joyful inspiration. I enjoy whatever life chooses to offer me in each moment.

I have a limited, part-time practice, but the people I work with provide the impetus to continue being kind to my body. A well-rested me can be more available to my clients and my readers. *I love this work!* I hope that one day my story will prove to be as life-changing and inspirational to them as hearing Dr. Joe's story was to me.

WHEN SERIOUS DISEASES SIMPLY DISAPPEAR

I believe that many cases of remission from serious diseases are influenced by mental fields. The bodies of these people are being bathed in positivity while the cells are replicating and growing. When every one of those 810,000 new cells that your body creates each second is born in an energetic environment of kindness and love, it shapes their development.

When we create mental, emotional, and spiritual fields of love and kindness, we provide a healthy energetic ecosystem in which our bodies regenerate.

The spontaneous remission of cancer without treatment has historically been viewed by the medical profession as a rare phenomenon. One of the first authors to make an estimate stated that it probably happened in 1 out of every 80,000 cases (Boyd, 1966). A contemporary estimate was 1 in 100,000 cases (Boyers, 1953).

Modern studies, however, are discovering that remission is common. One found that about a fifth of breast cancers are healed by mind and body without the need for medical intervention (Zahl, Mæhlen, & Welch, 2008). Others report a similar percentage of patients healing spontaneously from a type of cancer that affects white blood cells (Krikorian, Portlock, Cooney, & Rosenberg, 1980). A bibliography of medical reports of spontaneous remission found over 3,000 cases reported in the medical literature (O'Regan & Hirshberg, 1993).

The spread of cancer requires signaling and cooperation between groups of cancer cells. This signaling is triggered by stress (Wu, Pastor-Pareja, & Xu, 2010). Adrenaline, also called epinephrine, is one of our two main stress hormones, the other being cortisol. High levels of adrenaline trigger the spread of ovarian cancer cells far away from the primary tumor. They also activate an enzyme called FAK that inhibits the destruction of cancer cells and hastens death (Sood et al., 2010). A different enzyme, one that destroys prostate and breast cancer cells, is immobilized by adrenaline (Sastry et al., 2007).

When we lower our stress levels, we reverse these effects, sometimes quickly. Researchers report tumors shrinking to less than half their original size within a few hours of an emotional healing session (Ventegodt, Morad, Hyam, & Merrick, 2004). Among those who experience spontaneous remission or survive much longer than usual after a diagnosis, a change in worldview is common. They become more altruistic in their relationships with others and actively involve themselves in their treatment (Frenkel et al., 2011). Anandamide, the "bliss molecule" generated by meditation, also inhibits the formation of cancer cells. As mind changes, so does matter.

Altruism and connection with others are hallmarks of those who heal.

THE SHRINKING TUMORS

Energy healing researcher Bill Bengston, whom you read about in a previous chapter, was the subject of several randomized controlled trials in which he and his graduate students were consistently able to heal cancerous tumors in mice. He then began to apply his method to people. The following story is an example of the healing that can occur when cells are bathed in positive energy fields (Bengston, 2010).

One of Bill's students, Laurie, was diagnosed with terminal breast cancer. It had spread first to her lymph nodes and then metastasized throughout her body. She was given four months to live. Bill recounts:

"Against all advice, she opted to be treated by me. . . . For two months I treated Laurie six days a week, sometimes many hours a day. So intense was the process that I developed alarming lumps in my own armpits and groin, which disappeared when I physically disconnected from her.

"The usual medical tests administered by her doctors, including X-rays, blood work, and CAT scans, showed her tumors to be shrinking. Eventually, they disappeared. . . . Laurie and I celebrated the fifth and tenth anniversary of her remaining cancer-free."

The invisible microwaves of kindness might be bathing the regenerating cells of the bodies of people like Laurie to produce healing. When those 810,000 cells that are being created by our bodies every second are marinating in the energy of positive emotion, they're being shaped by the field.

When our consciousness shifts, and we begin to make deliberate changes, as Glenda and Laurie did, we change the character of the energy in which our new cells are being formed. Maintain those positive mental states for a few weeks and trillions of new cells have now been shaped by them.

Let's now look at the direct evidence for the influence of human-generated energy on cell formation.

ENERGY GUIDES CELL FORMATION

As researchers have exposed cell cultures to ranges of frequencies, they have shown that some are particularly beneficial to the growth of certain types of cells. Some of the frequencies that stimulate the growth of healthy cells are the very frequencies generated by our brains. The electromagnetic fields of our brains, generated by our consciousness, may produce direct effects on cellular regeneration.

Most of the signals to which our cells are most sensitive are at the very lower end of the frequency spectrum. These microcurrents aren't involved in carrying energy. Instead, they carry information (Foletti, Ledda, D'Emilia, Grimaldi, & Lisi, 2011).

Cells are typically sensitive to very narrow frequency bands. These are called frequency windows because cells will respond to frequencies in these narrow ranges but not to those above or below that range.

Frequency windows are the narrow bands of energy to which particular cells respond.

A review of 175 papers published in the scientific literature from 1950 to 2015 found that certain frequencies triggered cell regeneration and repair. In the words of the authors, "Waves affect cells . . . only at specific frequencies, being separated by wide ranges of non-effective frequencies" (Geesink & Meijer, 2016, p. 110). These frequencies are similar to a musical scale, with harmonic resonance between frequencies on the scale, just as there are in a pleasing chord played on the piano. The authors listed the physical effects that various frequencies exert:

- Stimulate the formation of nerve cells and synapses

- Repair spinal cord tissue

- Reduce the symptoms of Parkinson's disease

- Inhibit the growth of cancer cells

- Improve memory

- Synchronize the firing of neurons in different parts of the brain

- Increase attention

- Speed wound healing

- Decrease the activity of inflammatory cells

- Increase bone regeneration

- Reduce the degeneration of nerves in diabetics

- Trigger the expression of beneficial genes

- Promote the growth of connective tissue like ligaments and tendons

- Increase the amount of stem cells circulating in the body

- Stimulate stem cells to differentiate into muscle, bone, and skin

- Enhance the activity of white blood cells in the immune system

- Catalyze the synthesis of growth hormone

- Regulate free radicals (oxygen atoms regarded as the primary cause of aging)

- Repair heart muscle by inducing cells to assemble and graft onto damaged tissue

BIOMARKERS AS INDICATORS OF HEALTH

As we look at the fascinating research showing the effect of energy fields on cells, you'll be captivated by the healing potential of this work. You'll see the possibility of radically improving your health and that of the people around you.

You'll also notice that there are several common biological markers that scientists examine. These include gene expression, growth hormone (GH) levels, aging markers called telomeres, and numbers of circulating stem cells. The reason researchers use these biomarkers is that they correlate with the activation of our immune and inflammation systems.

Healthy activities reduce inflammation and boost immunity. The goal for health is to have a highly functional immune system and as little systemic inflammation in the body as possible.

Stem cells are "blank" cells that can turn into any other type of cell. They circulate through the body, and when we need to repair skin cells from a cut on our finger or lung tissue damaged by smoke, stem cells turn themselves into whatever specific type of cell is required. They can change into bone cells, muscle cells, lung cells, or skin cells, depending on the body's needs. Their versatility makes stem cells extremely important to healing, and researchers use a count of their numbers as a proxy for how effectively an immune system is functioning.

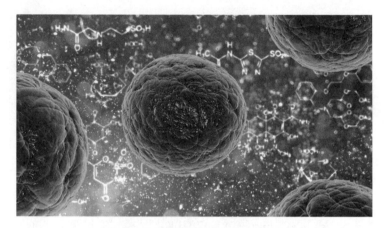

Stem cells are "blank" cells that can turn into any other type of cell as required by the body.

Another common substance of interest is growth hormone, or GH. Though the word *growth* is in its name, that doesn't mean it makes us grow larger. GH repairs and regenerates our cells. When we sleep, we typically produce more GH as our bodies repair the tissues damaged by the day's activities. To keep our bodies young, healthy, and strong, we need high levels of GH. Patients whose vitality is depleted often have low levels of GH. So if a treatment produces a higher concentration of GH, it's beneficial to our system.

Oxidative stress is another common focus of research. Though the type of oxygen we breathe in the air is stable, that's because it is composed of two oxygen atoms bonded together (O_2). However, single oxygen atoms, unpaired with a second atom, damage our cells. They're called free radicals. Oxidative stress, the product of free radicals, is regarded as the most universal cause of aging.

Another much-studied molecule is telomerase. Telomeres are the endcaps of the chromosomes in our cells, and they shorten slightly every time a cell divides. Telomerase is an enzyme that adds DNA molecules to the ends of telomeres. As we grow older, the chains of DNA in the telomeres on the ends of our chromosomes decline at a rate of about one percent a year. This makes telomere length an extremely stable marker of biological aging.

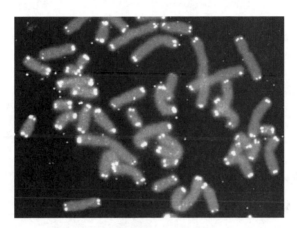

The bright spots at the ends of the chromosomes are telomeres.

When people are stressed, their cells die more quickly because of the wear and tear on their molecules. To replace the cells killed by stress, the body's cells have to divide more often to make replacements. As cells divide more frequently, their telomeres shorten more quickly. Stressed people lose telomere length fast, while healthy people have long telomeres. This is one reason why stressed people die at younger ages than those who know how to relax. Scientists can tell our biological age from the length of our telomeres, making this a popular genetic test.

BRAIN WAVES AS WINDOWS TO THE MIND

There are thousands of studies showing the energy field frequency windows that affect cells and molecules. What I'm particularly interested in is the frequencies generated by our own brain waves, especially delta, theta, alpha, and gamma. That's because these are naturally occurring frequencies in our bodies. As our brain frequencies change, they affect our cells. I'm fascinated by how we can change our cellular environment using our own naturally generated brain waves.

When in my trainings I teach people to meditate and tap, their levels of these four brain waves increase. They are frequencies you can induce yourself—no medications, herbs, beliefs, or mind-altering substances required!

A century of study has demonstrated that our brains produce the energy fields we measure as brain waves. It's also shown that mental states such as the ones we generate during meditation and tapping produce unique energy fields. Very slow waves like delta, theta, and alpha, as well as very fast waves like gamma, change dramatically when we induce these states of mind. As we examine the research associated with each of the five brain wave frequencies, from slowest to fastest, you'll notice an exciting range of healing events associated with each.

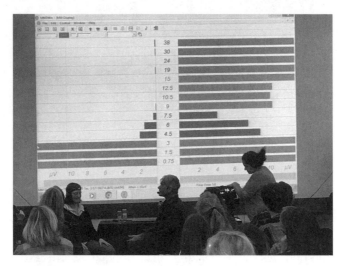

A conference participant hooked up to an EEG during a live therapy session. The entire audience can see her brain waves.

Delta

The slowest brain wave, delta, from 0 to 4 Hz, is associated with many beneficial changes in living tissues. Key studies of normal brains have pointed to some of the links between healing and frequencies in the 0–4 Hz range.

A group of sleep investigators hooked men up to EEG monitors before they went to bed in order to study sleep patterns (Gronfier et al., 1996). In addition to the EEG readings, growth hormone levels were measured every 10 minutes. The researchers found that when delta waves were at their peak in the brain, the secretion levels of GH were highest.

In a different group of men of a wide range of ages, from teenagers to octogenarians, an association was found between delta and GH production (Van Cauter, Leproult, & Plat, 2000). Production of both of these declined progressively, the older the men were. GH is synthesized during periods of delta wave sleep.

Ahmed and Wieraszko (2008) took slices of live tissue from the hippocampus, the part of the brain that governs memory and learning. They found that a very low frequency in the delta band, 0.16 Hz, increases activity in the synaptic connections between neurons in the hippocampus. This suggests that memory and learning may be enhanced by delta activity.

Researchers from Washington University School of Medicine in St. Louis, Missouri, looked at beta-amyloids, sticky plaques between neurons in the brain characteristic of Alzheimer's disease (Kang et al., 2009). They found that during sleep, when brains are primarily in theta and delta brain wave states, beta-amyloid production in the brain ceases, and toxic material is cleared away. The effect was greater in deep sleep, the phase of sleep in which our brains are in delta.

When analyzing RNA and five proteins that are involved in the production of telomerase, a group of researchers found peak resonance in these molecules in the frequency bands of 0.19 and 0.37 Hz (Cosic, Cosic, & Lazar, 2015). What is striking about this study is that other frequencies did not affect telomerase. The molecule was exquisitely sensitive to just a tiny frequency window within delta.

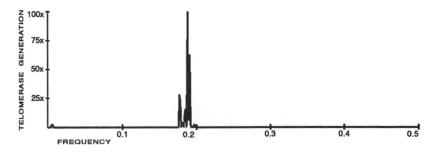

The resonant peaks for 10 telomere sequences clustered
around a frequency window of 0.19 Hz.

A research team inspired by the work of Marko Markoff, who has published more than 100 scientific reports on biological electromagnetism, found that delta frequencies between 0.5 Hz and 3 Hz stimulate the regeneration of nerve cells (Sisken, Midkiff, Tweheus, & Markov, 2007).

Delta is the wave that we see in EEG readouts when people are having a sense of connection with the infinite. They typically report mystical experiences in which the local self merges with the nonlocal self. Meditators with large amplitudes of delta feel connected to all of nature, to other human beings, and to the infinite. They lose the sense of being an isolated individual, or what Albert Einstein called the delusion of separateness. Instead, they experience oneness with all that is.

When our brains are producing delta, we are bathing our cells in a frequency that has the potential to produce a whole gamut of beneficial physiological changes at the level of our cells, from growing our telomeres and boosting our GH levels to regenerating our neurons and sweeping our brains clear of beta-amyloid plaques. We are not just having a nice subjective experience; in the delta state, we are creating an objective energy environment in which our bodies thrive.

People who are in transcendent states, experiencing oneness with nonlocal mind, show large amplitudes of delta brain waves.

Theta

Theta is the second slowest brain wave, with oscillations ranging from 4 to 8 Hz. It's the frequency most commonly observed in healers. Becker (1990) found that when healers were in the midst of an energy healing session, theta was the most common wave in their brains. Before starting the healing session, they might have had high beta or delta or other brain wave patterns indicative of ordinary consciousness, but once they placed their hands on or near a sick person and began the healing encounter, they reverted to theta.

This was true regardless of which healing school they belonged to or what set of beliefs they held. Some were qigong masters. Others were Native American shamans. Some were kabbalistic practitioners. Still others were Christian faith healers. Regardless of affiliation, their brains went into theta when they immersed themselves in the healing state (Kelly, 2011).

Healing session.

Theta is associated with many beneficial changes in the body. A group of researchers studied the effect of various frequencies on DNA repair. They found that electromagnetic fields between 7.5 Hz and 30 Hz were able to enhance molecular bonding (Tekutskaya, Barishev, & Ilchenko, 2015). Within that range, 9 Hz proved most effective.

There are many studies of human and animal cartilage cells, because repair of these cells is essential to wellness, as anyone who has had a sprained ankle or a pulled ligament can attest. A research group using pulsing electromagnets found that human cartilage cells are regenerated by the frequency of 6.4 Hz, right in the middle of the theta band (Sakai, Suzuki, Nakamura, Norimura, & Tsuchiya, 1991). This frequency also increases the activity of antioxidants, the molecules that neutralize the free radicals regarded as the most common cause of aging.

A research group at the Toho University School of Medicine in Japan looked at the EEG signatures of subjects practicing deep abdominal breathing. They found that their levels of the "feel-good" neurotransmitter serotonin rose, and theta as well as alpha and delta waves increased (Fumoto, Sato-Suzuki, Seki, Mohri, & Arita, 2004). Another study found that frequencies alternating between 5 Hz and 10 Hz produced a large reduction in lower back pain in 17 patients (Lee et al., 2006).

A pair of Russian scientists examined the effect of frequencies between 5.5 Hz and 16.5 Hz on DNA in a water solution. They found that the molecules were most highly stimulated at 9 Hz and that the effect was more than twice as great as it was on the untreated control molecules (Tekutskaya & Barishev, 2013).

Alpha

If you've undergone neurofeedback or biofeedback training, you've heard a lot about alpha. These trainings are designed to educate you to induce an alpha brain wave state at will. Alpha oscillates at 8 to 13 Hz.

Alpha is right in the middle of the frequency bands, between beta and gamma above and theta and delta below. Legendary brain pioneer Maxwell Cade believed that alpha serves as a bridge between the upper and lower frequencies. Beta reflects the activity of the conscious mind, while theta and delta represent the subconscious and unconscious minds. Cade believed that the alpha bridge connects the conscious mind with both the intuitive wisdom of the unconscious and the nonlocal resource of the universal field. A truly integrated person is able to generate large amplitudes of alpha.

It turns out that alpha also does good things for our bodies. It improves our levels of mood-enhancing neurotransmitters such as serotonin. When the alpha brain wave level increased in a group of exercisers, they gained a boost in serotonin, and their emotional state was elevated (Fumoto et al., 2010). In another study, Zen meditators received the same benefits from cultivating an alpha state (Yu et al., 2011).

Meditation produces beneficial changes in brain waves. The "alpha bridge" is the key to connecting our conscious minds with our unconscious resources.

A pioneering study exposed DNA to various frequencies. It found that the alpha frequency of 10 Hz resulted in significantly increased synthesis of the DNA molecule (Takahashi, Kaneko, Date, & Fukada, 1986).

Neurons in the brain's hippocampus also fire in this range (4–12 Hz), and at 10 Hz and higher frequencies, the synapses in the learning and memory circuits of the brain are enhanced (Tang et al., 1999). Other regions of the brain also use the 8–10 Hz band to communicate, with their neurons oscillating at those frequencies (Destexhe, McCormick, & Sejnowski, 1993).

Alpha, therefore, tunes the brain to peak performance, as well as facilitating gene expression and improving mood. The expansive emotional feelings reported by meditators after their regular sessions aren't simply subjective self-assessments. They are objective biological facts that can be measured in DNA, neurotransmitters, and brain waves.

Beta

Beta waves range from 13 to 25 Hz. There are two types of beta, and many modern researchers split beta into two different types of wave. Low beta, from 13 to 15 Hz, is also called SMR, which is short for sensorimotor rhythm. It's associated with the body's housekeeping functions.

High beta ranges from 15 to 25 Hz. It's always present in the thinking brain but increases when we focus on a task. Look up the route to a destination on your smartphone, write a blog post, take a language class, or cook with a complicated recipe, and your brain's amplitude of high beta increases.

Stress results in abnormally large amplitudes of high beta. When you're arguing with a friend, under an impossible deadline at work, hearing scary sounds in a dark house at night, remembering a childhood trauma, or thinking negative thoughts, your brain kicks into high beta. It's the signature brain wave of stress. It's associated with a rise in cortisol and adrenaline and a large number of adverse reactions in your body. Fear and anxiety produce high beta, and it inhibits many beneficial cellular functions. Your body ages much faster when your brain is bathed in high beta waves.

Gamma

Gamma is the most recently discovered brain wave. It is associated with the integration of information from all of the brain's regions, as well as with coherence as they all synchronize (Gray, 1997). Imagine having a flash of insight about a problem that has been bothering you for weeks. Imagine the satisfaction of doing a difficult task perfectly. Think about the synchronized brain function of a child at play, an artist painting, or a composer writing a masterpiece. That's gamma. It starts where beta leaves off, at 25 Hz, and goes up to 100 Hz and above.

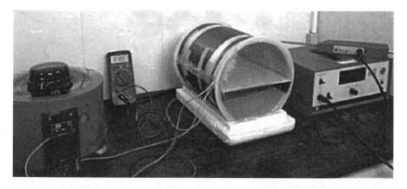

Researchers build an extremely low-frequency electromagnetic field generating system using a transformer, multimeter, solenoids coils, teslameter, and probe (Razavi, Salimi, Shahbazi-Gahrouei, Karbasi, & Kermani, 2014).

A team led by Li-Huei Tsai of MIT tested the effect of gamma waves on Alzheimer's disease. They had mice run a maze while they recorded the brain waves in the hippocampus, which is responsible for navigation and memory. When a mouse hit a dead end, its brain would display a sharp burst of gamma. The brains of mice genetically engineered to be prone to Alzheimer's didn't react the same way. They produced less gamma, with poor synchronization between groups of neurons.

The researchers then flashed light into the brains of the mice at a gamma frequency of 40 Hz. In just an hour, the levels of beta-amyloid decreased by half. "We were very, very surprised," says Tsai (Iaccarino et al., 2016).

Looking for a mechanism, she found that gamma had mobilized a class of brain cells called microglia. These are the scavengers of the brain, gobbling up malformed proteins and dead cells. After exposure to gamma, the size and number of the microglia doubled as they began to scoop up the beta-amyloid plaques.

Vikaas Sohal of the University of California says, "If gamma oscillations are part of the software of the brain, this study suggests that running the software can alter the hardware" (Yong, 2016).

A pilot study that used light to stimulate the hippocampi of five patients with the cognitive decline characteristic of Alzheimer's found that their symptoms improved (Saltmarche, Naeser, Ho, Hamblin, & Lim, 2017). Newer versions of this technology combine both 10 Hz (alpha) and 40 Hz (gamma) stimulation (Lim, 2014, 2017).

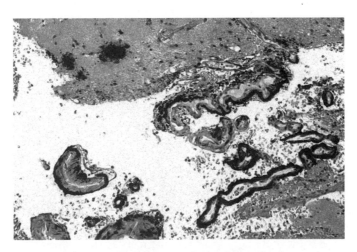

Alzheimer's disease produces plaques in the brain that impede neural signaling.

Gamma is associated with many other beneficial changes in our bodies. A frequency of 75 Hz is epigenetic, triggering the genes that produce anti-inflammatory proteins in the body (De Girolamo et al., 2013). On the lower end of the gamma spectrum, a frequency of 50 Hz results in the body increasing its production of stem cells, the "blank" cells that differentiate into muscle, bone, skin, or whatever other specialized cells are required (Ardeshirylajimi & Soleimani, 2015). The frequency of 60 Hz regulates the expression of stress genes, those that code for stress hormones like cortisol. The same frequency also activates a key gene called Myc that in turn regulates around 15 percent of all the other genes in the body (Lin, Goodman, & Shirley-Henderson, 1994).

High beta, the signature brain wave of a stressed-out consciousness, actually suppresses DNA synthesis. When bone cells were exposed to a beta frequency of 25 Hz, it inhibited their growth. Gamma frequencies of 75 Hz or more, however, increased their growth. A peak was reached at 125 Hz, with that frequency producing three times the growth rate of the beta frequency (Ying, Hong, Zhicheng, Xiauwei, & Guoping, 2000).

The previous studies are suggestive rather than definitive, because in many of them, the frequencies were produced by external devices such as pulsed electromagnetic field (PEMF) machines. Others, such as those linking brain waves to cell changes, demonstrate association between the two phenomena rather than causation.

The big picture, however, is that our bodies are sensitive to the frequencies generated by our brains, from the slowest waves of delta to the fastest waves of gamma, and that by understanding these links, we can use our brain waves to heal our cells.

MIND CHANGE = FIELD CHANGE = CELL CHANGE

The sheer number and variety of cell changes associated with brain waves is remarkable. Armed with the knowledge that the brain waves we generate are producing massive shifts in our body moment by moment, how can we nudge the process in the direction of optimal health?

Studies show that many spiritual practices change brain waves. Mindfulness produces a host of beneficial changes in brain waves. A meta-analysis including 56 papers and a total of 1,715 subjects found increased alpha and theta waves (Lomas, Ivtzan, & Fu, 2015). Other research shows that heart coherence produces alpha and gamma even while it calms the anxiety bands of beta (Kim, Rhee, & Kang, 2013). When you practice mindfulness meditation for just three months, you start to grow your telomeres (Jacobs et al., 2011).

Research I've done at Joe Dispenza's advanced workshops shows that thousands of people are routinely able to increase their levels of delta and gamma (Church, Yang, Fannin, & Blickheuser, 2016). I've hooked up meditators to EEG monitors at my EcoMeditation workshops and observed increases in gamma, alpha, theta, and delta brain waves while the monkey mind characteristics of beta disappear.

EEG expert Laura Eichman talked about what she observed in one participant at a workshop: "The changes I saw in Stephanie's brain waves were typical of everyone we measured. Ten minutes into the EcoMeditation exercise, people tune in to their heart energy and send it out to connect with someone else. I saw a huge increase in Stephanie's delta amplitude, and shortly after that, her gamma. Her higher gamma frequency bands were riding on her low delta.

"I had the screen readout on a standard 10-millivolt setting, which is fine to measure the usual brain activity. But Stephanie's brain was producing so much delta that I had to adjust the window all the way out to 20 millivolts. That still wasn't enough, I had to go out progressively further, to 30 and then to 40 millivolts to capture her brain activity.

"This link between the high and low frequency bands—delta and gamma—is one we've seen a few times in healers and psychics. Afterward, I asked Stephanie about her experience. It matched her brain map. She reported an 'inner knowing' that she was filled with light."

EcoMeditation combines tapping, mindfulness, heart coherence, and neurofeedback in a simple yet elegant package that integrates the benefits of all those methods. All of these are ways we can shift the energy fields in which our cells are reproducing.

The magic pill to increase well-being and happiness.

If I offered you a pill that could increase your levels of circulating stem cells, lengthen your telomeres, dissipate beta-amyloid plaques in your brain, improve your memory and attention levels, boost your serotonin, repair your DNA, regulate inflammation, boost your immune system, repair your skin, bone, cartilage, and muscle cells, power up your GH levels for cell repair, and enhance the neural connections in your brain, how much would you pay for it?

Though it's priceless, it's all free. EcoMeditation has been free on the Internet for over a decade. I've taught it to thousands of people all over the world. It's ironic that what might be the biggest medical breakthrough of our generation is freely available to everyone, from the poorest to the richest.

All of the beneficial brain wave states are available to us by simply touching our screens and following simple instructions. As we make this choice, our fields change, and the 810,000 cells that our bodies are creating each second are bathed in the health-promoting waves coming from our very own brains.

YOUR IDEAL BRAIN WAVE RECIPE

There are an infinite number of possible brain wave states. There is a brain wave state that you are accustomed to being in every day. It is the one your regular mental function produces. That's the way your very own personal brain processes information. It feels familiar to you, because you have a set range for the amplitude of each wave in which your brain normally functions. You are accustomed to a certain amplitude of beta relative to theta, alpha, and delta.

Your personal brain wave ratio is like a recipe. Your habitual mix is like the food you eat most frequently. You are familiar with the smell, taste, and texture of the dish, and you hardly notice you are eating it.

A peak state is different. It's like a gourmet meal with exquisite brain waves as the ingredients. Add more delta, and you feel one with the universe. Add more theta, and you experience a wave of healing. Increase the amplitude of alpha, and your conscious and subconscious minds start communicating with one another.

Perhaps your personal everyday recipe (expressed in μV, or microvolts) is this:

- Beta: 20
- Alpha: 25
- Theta: 30
- Delta: 100

That's a fairly normal set of numbers. There's nothing wrong with it, and most people's brains are somewhere in that range every day.

When you have a peak experience, the numbers change. The recipe your brain experiences when you enter an elevated state is different. Alpha swells from your usual 25 to 60 µV. Worry-driven beta shrinks from 20 µVto 5. Theta and delta balloon to 50 µV and 200 µV respectively. You have a profound inner experience of connection with the infinite field and feel one with all beings. This might be triggered by an experience such as:

- The first day of spring
- An inspirational movie
- Your favorite song
- A baby grasping your finger
- A foot massage
- A tender moment with a friend
- An inspirational talk
- Running a mile
- Receiving applause after a speech
- The perfect cup of coffee
- A new book from your favorite author
- Completing a long-overdue task
- Contemplating open space after throwing out clutter
- A smile from a stranger
- Dunking a basketball in the hoop
- Witnessing the birth of a puppy
- A perfect sunset
- Falling in love
- A walk on the beach

By accident, triggered by an external stimulus, you've experienced a new brain wave recipe, and it feels great. If at that moment of peak experience, I had you hooked up to an EEG, your brain wave recipe might look like this:

- Beta: 5
- Alpha: 60
- Theta: 50
- Delta: 200

Look at how different those numbers are from your everyday recipe. All that high-stress beta has disappeared. Your alpha has flared way up, as have theta and delta. You have a completely different ratio of waves as your brain processes information in a new way.

When we take a bite of a gourmet recipe, our palate is startled by how delicious the food is. We savor each mouthful. The recipe is unfamiliar and exotic. In the same way, the ratio of brain waves we experience during a peak state is one that is not familiar to us. It's special.

We might call it being in the zone or a transcendent state, or on a high or in an altered state, or channeling a discarnate being, or falling in love, or having a visitation by an angel, or feeling euphoric, or touching heaven, or living a magic moment, or having a peak experience, or seeing a spirit guide. Whatever label we give it, we recognize this novel experience as being special. We're sampling a recipe that is much more delicious than our normal fare. It doesn't feel like us, which is why we might think it's a divine visitation or a personality separate from our own.

Yet it's your brain that has created this recipe, even if only for a moment. The brain that creates that particular ratio of brain wave ingredients is able to create it again. It can be trained to do so at will.

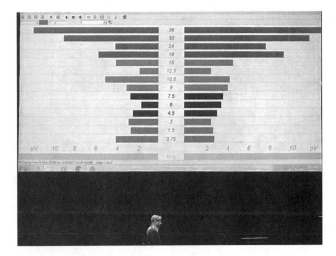

The habitual brain wave recipe of this workshop participant had lots of fear-induced beta, little theta and delta, and only a small alpha bridge.

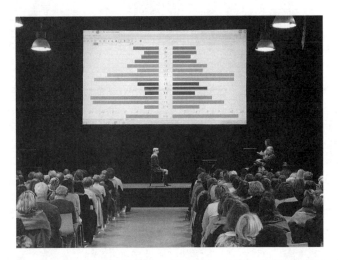

After treatment, we see large flares forming an alpha bridge, expanded theta and delta, and a disappearance of high amplitudes of beta.

When we first hook people up to EEGs during our workshops, we see the combinations of brain waves that represent their personal recipes. Often they are stressed and anxious, with a lot of high-frequency beta waves. They have little alpha, theta, or delta. To them, this state of being cut off from their unconscious and the universe, without an alpha bridge, is normal.

After treatment, the entire way their brains process information changes. They've sampled a new recipe and they like it. They have a big alpha bridge connecting their conscious and subconscious minds. They're in touch with the healing frequency of theta and the transcendent frequency of delta.

If we can persuade them to make this a consistent practice, with their brains enjoying the delicious new brain wave recipe every day, they become habituated to feeling good. It becomes the new normal. In time, their set point changes, and the gourmet recipe becomes their staple. Their bodies are bathed in the fields of healing every day.

Here is one example of a workshop participant who experienced a breakthrough when his brain flipped into this elevated state.

Hearing the Waves Breaking on the Distant Shore

Harold was in the middle of a profound crisis. A top official at the United Nations, he'd blacked out and fallen to the ground in the middle of a hostage negotiation three months before. His doctors told him he was stressed, and while they could find nothing wrong with his 52-year-old body, they advised him to relax and learn meditation. He'd made a complete recovery except for his hearing, which he had lost when he blacked out. Tests showed that he'd lost 80 percent of the hearing in his left ear.

He decided to enroll in a weeklong training I was offering at Esalen Institute in Big Sur, California. He had been visiting Esalen for various classes for 15 years, and the combination of massage, hot tubs, homegrown food, and oceanside views usually rejuvenated him.

When I met him, I was awed by his intelligence, humor, and expansive worldview. He had a satisfying long-term marriage, a successful son, a best-selling book, professional kudos, and every material benefit. Yet he was haunted by a gnawing sense that he'd made a wrong turn somewhere in his life. He wanted coaching to help him decide whether to take early retirement from his stressful job and to develop a robust health plan.

To help create the changes he envisioned, Harold volunteered to be my subject for a coaching demonstration in front of the whole group.

Before the training began, we used a panel of tests to assess the well-being of the people in the group. These tests included psychological evaluations of depression, anxiety, pain, happiness, and post-traumatic stress disorder (PTSD). We also measured Harold's physiological profile. The panel of tests included cortisol (the main stress hormone), salivary immunoglobulin A (SIgA, a primary marker of immune function), and resting heart rate. We hooked Harold up to an EEG during his session so we could monitor his brain waves.

Working with me in front of the whole group, Harold described his fears of growing older, of getting sicker, of becoming irrelevant. He recounted how shocked he felt when he abruptly lost consciousness during the hostage negotiation: "Suddenly, I hit the floor." While he was reconciled to the loss of hearing he'd suffered, he worried that it was the start of a progressive physical decline.

As I worked with him, Harold began to relax and tune in to his emotions. His breathing slowed and his muscles relaxed. His EEG readings showed flares of theta and delta waves, expanded alpha frequencies, and a reduction in beta. These were all indications that he was getting out of his anxious "monkey mind" and back in tune with his intuition and his bodily sensations. As his mind changed, his brain functions shifted.

We worked through a succession of his fears and disappointments and identified goals that he might achieve if he combined relaxation with creativity. Energy psychology helped him resolve all the jagged emotions left over from his health crisis, while coaching psychology clarified the opportunities before him and the fresh goals he could set for himself.

Eventually, I asked him, "How is that 80 percent hearing loss in your left ear?" He looked surprised, and said, "It's almost gone . . . maybe 15 percent loss now."

"How do you know it's an 80 percent hearing loss?" I wondered.

"The doctor told me," he affirmed. "It's a medical diagnosis."

"Let's work on that belief," I suggested.

We then focused on beliefs like *It's a medical diagnosis* and *The doctor said it, so it must be true.*

After coaching him through a process that questioned those beliefs, I asked him again about his left ear. He closed his eyes, focused intently on his hearing. Suddenly, his eyes popped wide open. Almost shouting, he exclaimed, "I can hear the waves breaking on the shore! I've been coming to Esalen for 15 years, and I've never been able to hear the ocean. Now I can!"

PRACTICE HABITUATES THE BRAIN TO BALANCE

During my EcoMeditation retreats, on the first morning, we teach people to attain these peak states. It isn't hard if you have the right combination of signals to the body. At first, it takes about four minutes to drop into the recipe. By the afternoon session, participants can do it in 90 seconds.

They feel wonderful and think they've arrived in heaven every time they close their eyes and start meditating. Yet that brain wave state is just the beginning. We then train them to evoke the magic recipe with their eyes open, at first in the meditation room. Once they become stable in the EcoMeditation state in that safe location, we start sending them into the environment outside.

They walk along the footpaths or through the gardens, learning to maintain that state. They come back into the meditation room and close their eyes again, increasing their amplitude of alpha. We then have them go outside again. We alternate inside and outside, eyes open and eyes closed, over and over again.

After the third day, they are usually able to maintain their new state with eyes open outside the room. At that stage, we've begun to change their set point and install a new normal. A doctor named Susan Albers describes it this way: "The morning following the class was the first time I had ever successfully meditated—in my entire life. All 52 years of it. I'm not someone who's calm, ever. And I was. What a revelation!"

Another participant, Maaike Linnenkamp, said: "EcoMeditation makes me calmer, more relaxed, and gives me a clearer mind. It was powerful for me to break the old thinking process and let go of the unpleasant memories that I usually dwell on. For the first time in my life, when I remembered bad events, I didn't become anxious. I just could not believe it when I talked to a friend about it later and still felt no anxiety. I feel very grateful and I will apply this technique on a regular basis."

Participants at an EcoMeditation workshop at Esalen Institute in California.

Susan, Maaike, and their friends have learned to take that gourmet brain wave recipe and turn it into their everyday brain food. They've trained their brains to be able to cook that delicious meal consistently. Just as it is hard to go back to bad wine once you've experienced fine wine, or start wearing harsh fabrics after you've enjoyed soft microfibers, or revert to your ancient cell phone after you've become used to the features of the latest model, it is hard to go back to the old normal recipe. Your previous brain state is the one that now feels foreign. You've upgraded your brain.

COHERENT BRAIN STATES TRIGGER GENE EXPRESSION

I have served as the chief investigator in many studies showing the effects of emotional healing on both physical and psychological symptoms. My latest work examines the epigenetic effects of stress reduction. The number and importance of the genes affected is astonishing.

After the first groups of U.S. veterans began returning from Iraq and Afghanistan, therapists told me they were encountering many clients with PTSD. Linda Geronilla, Ph.D., a clinical psychologist at Marshall University's medical school, shared with me that in just a few sessions of

EFT tapping with veterans, PTSD symptoms such as nightmares, flashbacks, and hypervigilance were gone.

Linda and I designed a study to determine if EFT was effective in treating PTSD. Our pilot study involved just seven veterans, but it was so successful that we were able to achieve statistical significance (Church, Geronilla, & Dinter, 2009). When you get statistical significance (which means that there is just one possibility in 20 that the results are due to chance) in a very small sample, it means you have a very effective treatment.

With a group of colleagues, I then launched a full-scale nationwide randomized controlled trial. We compared veterans getting standard care for PTSD, usually at a VA hospital, with a second group getting standard care plus EFT.

The study took several years to complete, but the results were the same. PTSD symptoms dropped by over 60 percent (Church et al., 2013). Once the study was published, Linda conducted a replication study, with almost identical results (Geronilla, Minewiser, Mollon, McWilliams, & Clond, 2016).

I wondered what was happening inside the bodies of these veterans, especially at the level of the genome. In 2009, I initiated a study of gene expression in veterans receiving 10 sessions of EFT. It took six years to complete, but eventually it showed that six stress genes were being regulated. Inflammation was being dialed down even while immunity was being dialed up (Church, Yount, Rachlin, Fox, & Nelms, 2016).

EFT PRODUCES DRAMATIC GENE SHIFTS

Beth Maharaj, an imaginative psychotherapist friend, designed a groundbreaking study for her doctoral dissertation. She had discovered a new type of gene test. While the earlier clinical trials required veterans to provide blood samples at a lab, the new test was saliva based. Participants had only to spit in a cup, and we could measure expression in hundreds or even thousands of genes.

Beth gave four subjects an hour-long placebo session, followed a week later by an hour-long EFT therapy session, and compared saliva samples before and after each session. She found that EFT produced regulation of an astonishing 72 genes (Maharaj, 2016). The functions of those genes proved to be fascinating. Among them were:

- The suppression of cancer tumors
- Protection against the sun's ultraviolet radiation
- Type 2 diabetes insulin resistance
- Immunity from opportunistic infections
- Antiviral activity
- Synaptic connectivity between neurons
- Creation of both red and white blood cells
- Enhancement of male fertility
- Building white matter in the brain
- Regulating metabolism
- Increasing neural plasticity
- Strengthening cell membranes
- Reducing oxidative stress

These shifts in gene expression were substantial, and when Beth retested participants a day later, about half of the effects persisted. That's a big payoff for just one hour of therapy.

MEDITATION REGULATES CANCER GENES

Inspired by Beth's example, my friend Joe Dispenza decided to test participants at one of his advanced workshops. I obtained saliva samples from 30 people, and when the results came back from the lab, we found that eight genes were significantly upregulated during the four days of meditation.

With a research team, I examined the data from over 100 EEG scans from another of Joe's workshops. We found that after practicing for four days, people entered a meditative state 18 percent faster and the ratio of anxiety-producing beta to integrative delta had improved by 62 percent (Church, Yang, et al., 2016).

As people's brains were being regulated by Joe's powerful meditation practices, their genes were also shifting. The functions of the eight genes we found changed tell a powerful story of physiological shift. They are involved in neurogenesis, the growth of new neurons in response to novel experiences and learning. They are also implicated in protecting our body against the influences that age our cells.

Several of these genes regulate cell repair, including the ability to move stem cells to the sites in the body where they can repair damaged or aging tissue. These genes are also involved in the building of cellular structures, especially the cytoskeleton, the framework of rigid molecules that gives our cells shape and form.

Three of these eight genes help our bodies identify and eliminate cancerous cells, suppressing the growth of cancer tumors. Their names and functions are as follows:

CHAC1 regulates the oxidative balance in cells. The hormone glutathione is key to reducing free radicals, and CHAC1 helps control the levels of glutathione in cells (Park, Grabińska, Guan, & Sessa, 2016). CHAC1 has several other functions. It also helps neural cells form and grow optimally (Cantagrel et al., 2010). It is believed to assist with the proper formation of the protein molecules that regulate oxidation and neuron formation.

CTGF (connective tissue growth factor) plays an important role in many biological processes (Hall-Glenn & Lyons, 2011). These range from the healing of wounds to the development of bones to the regeneration of cartilage and other connective tissue. CTGF helps new replacement cells migrate to the sites of wounding and damage in the body. It regulates the growth of new cells and the binding of cells to each other during the healing process. Decreased expression of this gene is linked to cancer and to autoimmune diseases such as fibromyalgia.

TUFT1 has a variety of functions in cell repair and healing (Deutsch et al., 2002). It helps regulate the functioning of a class of stem cells. During a child's development of teeth, TUFT1 acts to start the mineralization process of enamel. It is also thought to be involved in regulating oxygen levels in cells and in the differentiation of neurons.

DIO2 is important to the function of many types of brain and endocrine tissue (Salvatore, Tu, Harney, & Larsen, 1996). As well as being prevalent in thyroid tissue, it is highly expressed in other tissues, synchronizing local cells with thyroid gland function. It helps regulate metabolism by reducing insulin resistance, which in turn reduces the risk of metabolic disease (Akarsu et al., 2016), while also playing a role in craving and addiction. It helps regulate mood, especially depression.

C5orf66-AS1 is a gene associated with the suppression of tumors (Wei et al., 2015). It codes for a type of RNA that acts to identify and eliminate cancerous cells from the body.

KRT24 codes for the synthesis of a protein molecule that gives cells their structure. It also helps these molecules organize themselves in regular arrays (Omary, Ku, Strnad, & Hanada, 2009) and suppresses certain types of cancer cells such as those involved in colorectal cancer (Hong, Ho, Eu, & Cheah, 2007).

ALS2CL is one of a class of genes that suppress tumors, especially those contributing to a type of cancer called squamous cell carcinoma that affects the head and neck (Lee et al., 2010).

RND1 helps cells in the growth phase organize the molecules that give them their rigid structure. RND1 also catalyzes the growth of the parts of neural cells that reach out to connect with other neurons. It suppresses certain types of cancer cells such as those found in throat cancer and breast cancer (Xiang, Yi, Weiwei, & Weiming, 2016).

New technologies are allowing us to peer into the nuclei of our cells and the information flow in our brains and find out what happens during EFT, meditation, and other stress-reduction practices. What we are discovering is that the changes these techniques produce in the body are far from trivial. The picture emerging is that changes of mind produce profound changes in the matter of which our bodies are formed.

Bryce Rogow is a former Marine medic who served in four combat deployments in Iraq. He was there during some of the most bitter fighting and witnessed carnage and horror. After being discharged with PTSD, he set out on a quest for self-healing. Here's his story.

From a Combat Zone to Inner Peace

By Bryce Rogow

A lot of my friends say I'm a walking contradiction: on one hand a spiritual seeker; I've studied meditation at a Zen monastery in Japan, am a yoga teacher, and I've been learning mind-body medicine from some of the top healers around the world.

On the other hand, I'm a veteran of four combat deployments to Iraq as a corpsman, or medic, with the U.S. Marines. After getting out of the military, I was diagnosed with PTSD, and after some time of feeling lost and hopeless, I embarked on a journey of self-discovery and healing, intent on learning the most effective techniques for cooling the fires of mental and physical distress.

My first deployment with a U.S. Marine recon battalion (the Marines' version of Special Forces) led me to the second battle of Fallujah in November 2004, a massive assault on a city that has been described as the most intense urban combat U.S. forces have seen since Hue City in Vietnam.

All of us who deployed carry with us images that stay with us for the rest of our lives, images we have to learn how to live with.

For me, the first image of that kind came after my first buddy in my unit was killed while digging up an IED (improvised explosive device)—one of the homemade bombs insurgents would bury in fields and roadsides.

My method for preserving my own mental function, in addition to becoming addicted to the painkillers we medics had available, was to accept the fact that I was already dead, and so I would constantly remind myself that nothing that happened to me would matter, because I was already dead.

When I received my honorable discharge from the U.S. military in 2008, I was surprised to have survived the war. I expected a huge flood of relief when I was released from any possibility of future deployments, but that relief never came. I walked and drove around U.S. cities with the same tense fear I'd experienced in Iraq.

I spent a good deal of time heavily dependent on alcohol and drugs, including drugs such as clonazepam prescribed by well-meaning psychiatrists at the VA, drugs that were extremely addictive and led to a lot of risky behavior.

After getting out and realizing I needed to start helping myself, I decided that I wanted to learn meditation from an authentic Asian master, so I went to Japan to train at a traditional Zen monastery, called Sogenji, in the city of Okayama, Japan. Spending hours in the half-lotus position reminded me of the "stress positions" we used during enhanced interrogations after waterboarding became forbidden.

I am profoundly grateful to Shodo Harada-Roshi, a true modern Zen master, for facilitating that experience. However, after leaving the monastery, I realized that I would not be able to maintain that level of meditation on my own, that I would need faster and easier ways, and a better understanding of mind and body, to make meditative practices a useful part of my life.

> I was really amazed, then, to come across, one day while researching on the Internet, a man, Dawson Church, who had already put together such a program, a "meditation of meditations" he calls EcoMeditation.
>
> When I first came across his EcoMeditation, I simply read from the web page and followed the steps, and within two minutes found myself activating all these healing resources and entering a state of profound relaxation and well-being that I'd previously achieved only after hours, if not days and weeks, of meditation.

Bryce has become a passionate advocate for the use of EcoMeditation in the Department of Veterans Affairs. He believes that simple, low-cost self-help methods should be available to all veterans.

Thousands of people have now followed the seven simple steps at EcoMeditation.com and had the same profound and immediate experience of peace that Bryce had. As we investigate their physical changes, we find that their cortisol drops, along with their heart rate (Groesbeck et al., 2016). Their levels of immune hormones rise, as does their happiness. Depression, anxiety, and pain drop significantly. Inner peace reduces stress and produces beneficial changes in the body down to the level of gene expression.

YOUR INNER STATE IS YOUR GENETIC REALITY

Personal genetic testing is now widespread. Many people know what genes they have and understand their susceptibility for specific diseases based on their genetic profile. At workshops, I often get the question, "I have the XYZ gene. Doesn't that mean I'm destined to get XYZ disease?"

People get so worried about the results of gene tests. Yet as you see from the previous lists of genes, many are dramatically shifted by tapping and meditation.

It's not the genes you have that determine your destiny as much as what you do with them. Subject your body to high levels of stress over long periods of time and you upregulate the expression of cancer genes.

But make the opposite choice, and tap and meditate daily, and you reduce your stress. Along with it, your gene expression shifts. When those

810,000 cells that are being formed every second are birthed in an energy field of love and kindness, their gene expression is regulated by that field.

Mind to matter is not an abstract metaphysical proposition. It is a physical fact, as material as the bodies we live in. Thought by thought, moment by moment, our minds are creating the energy fields in which our cells reproduce. Positive thoughts provide our cells with an energy culture in which they thrive. Thoughts that nurture our cells as they regenerate become thriving molecular matter. Energy is epigenetic, regulating the processes of life and healing. When we elevate our consciousness to the infinite, generating the energy recipe of incandescence in our brains, our cells take form within the inspired energetic template we provide.

PUTTING THESE IDEAS INTO PRACTICE

Activities to practice this week:

- Practice altruism:

    Smile at strangers today.
    Thank people who help you in stores.
    Do an unexpectedly nice thing for someone
    close to you.

- Write a brief letter or e-mail to someone you love and send it to them.

- Listen to EcoMeditation on your mobile device as you walk, run, or exercise.

The Extended Play version of this chapter includes:

- Brain scan videos

- The database of energy healing research

- Audio interviews with EEG neurofeedback experts

- Additional case histories and references

To access the Extended Play version, visit:
MindToMatter.club/Chapter4

CHAPTER 5

THE POWER OF COHERENT MIND

I'm lying on the beach in Hawaii. It's a beautiful day, with a cloudless sky and a light breeze ruffling the ocean. Children are playing around me, and happy vacationers are splashing in the water. Snorkelers are ogling the turtle colony on the reef offshore, while kayakers and paddle-boarders ply the bay.

I'd flown to Hawaii to finish my book. The publisher's deadline was perilously close and I hadn't been making much progress at home, torn between the demands of single-parenting two young children and running a demanding business. Escaping to Hawaii seemed like a good way to give myself a window to complete the manuscript.

After working all morning, I decided to give myself a break. As I had pounded away on my laptop earlier, I could see the happy scene and the beach. My mind said, *You're in Hawaii! Why are you sitting here cooped up in this dark condo instead of playing on the beach?*

After those thoughts had driven me crazy for a few hours, I succumbed to their logic and headed for the beach.

Now, lying on the warm sand, my mind starts chattering again. *What are you doing here on the beach?* it demands. *The whole purpose of getting away to Hawaii was to write the book. You aren't writing a thing. You're just lying around doing nothing.*

How true, I reflect. I give a sigh, roll up my blanket, and head for the condo.

That's the double bind in which we live. Our inner critics give us hell regardless of which choice we make. When I was writing inside the condo, my inner critic savaged me for not enjoying the beach. As soon as I went outside, it began lambasting me for not writing. Damned if I do, damned if I don't. Nothing I could do could please my inner critic. Many of us are trapped on a similar hamster wheel of endlessly repetitive negative thoughts.

NEGATIVE THOUGHTS BESIEGE THE MIND

A study of psychologically normal people found that they had about 4,000 distinct thoughts each day. Of those, between 22 percent and 31 percent were unwanted and uncontrollable intrusive thoughts, while 96 percent of them were repetitive thoughts about daily activities (Klinger, 1996). The Cleveland Clinic's Wellness Program says that 95 percent of our thoughts are repetitive and 80 percent of them are negative.

Two thousand years ago, the Buddha identified the mind as the source of our suffering. In the Bhagavad Gita, Arjuna laments, "The mind is very fickle indeed O Krishna, turbulent, strong and obstinate." Most of us are trapped in the cycle of negative thinking, with no idea how to escape. But why did our huge and complex brains evolve to work that way?

THE EVOLUTIONARY VALUE OF NEGATIVE THINKING

Both repetitive thinking and negative thinking make sense from the perspective of evolutionary biology. For our distant ancestors, repetitive thinking handled routine life tasks in the background, while hypervigilant negative thinking gave them a survival advantage by keeping them attuned to possible threats from the environment.

The brain is designed to default to beta brain waves under survival conditions. Beta is the signature brain wave of fear. Fear was what kept our ancestors alive. Their degree of paranoid hypervigilant alertness was in direct proportion to their degree of survival. Miss the tiger in the grass, even for a second, and you got eaten.

Consider the tale of two teenage sisters 100,000 years ago. We'll call one Hug and the other Gug.

Hug is the happiest of people. As she carries water from the stream to the village each day, she sings for joy. She stops to smell the fragrant yellow roses. She pauses to listen to the sound of children laughing. She's filled with wonder as she gazes on the orange and grey hues cast by the rising sun. She notices the good in all the other people in the village.

Her sister, Gug, is the opposite. Suspicious and paranoid, Gug is always looking for what's wrong. Show her a silver cloud, and she'll point out the dark lining. She sees problems at every turn. She notices every imperfection in her fellow villagers. When she carries water from the stream to the village, others avoid her. Except for Hug, who searches for the good in everyone and tolerates Gug's company.

One day, they're ambushed by a hungry tiger hiding in the grass. Gug, always on the lookout for threats, spots the tiger a split second before Hug. She screams and starts running just a nanosecond before Hug sees the tiger and runs too.

Hug gets eaten by the tiger. She never makes it to puberty. But Gug reproduces, passing her threat-detection genes on to the next generation.

Multiply this by 1,000 generations, with each one getting a little bit better at finding the bad stuff. The ability to notice what's wrong in the environment has now been honed by natural selection to a fine art. That brings us to today, and to you and me. Even when absolutely nothing is wrong, the caveman brains we've inherited from Gug are diligently scanning the horizon for threats.

Our distant ancestors could make two kinds of mistakes. One was thinking that there was no tiger hiding in the grass when there was, and the other was thinking that there was a tiger in the grass when there wasn't (Hanson, 2013).

**Our brains evolved to be exquisitely sensitive
to environmental cues that signal danger.**

The second kind of mistake carries no immediate evolutionary penalty. Being attuned to threats, looking for the bad stuff, just makes you a miserable curmudgeon like Gug. It also guarantees your survival.

The first kind of mistake carried the death penalty. Miss the tiger in the grass just one time and you get eaten. People like Hug who lacked the ability to focus relentlessly on threats got weeded from the gene pool.

If she'd been watching me on the beach in Hawaii, Mother Nature would have given me gold stars for having such a well-developed ability to find the bad stuff everywhere I went. Unfortunately, caveman brain cares nothing for my happiness. Whatever my choice, my inner critic chews me to shreds.

The Orange Apron That Could Not Cut Keys

The Home Depot chain is famous for the orange aprons worn by staff. I walked into my local Home Depot one day to get a key cut. It was for my old RV, a 1983 Ford Econoline. The man who ran the key-cutting machine was at his station and I showed him the key.

He took it like it was an infected kidney and shook his head, saying, "I don't think we carry that style of key."

I pointed out that the Ford Motor Company had manufactured about three million of these vehicles, so they weren't exactly rare. He said, doubtfully, "It's a double-sided key," as though that represented an insurmountable difficulty.

"You cut the same key for me last week," I offered, helpfully.

He inserted the key into the laser reader, and after a scan, a red light flashed.

"No," he said mournfully, "we don't carry that one."

"Could you try it again?" I pleaded.

He punched the ON switch again, the laser scanned the key, and this time a green light appeared.

"We're really low on blanks," he said next, shaking his head.

"Can you just look?" I asked, politely.

He perused his stock, found the blank, and cut the key. All with the air of a man who has been let down by the world. His superpower could even make the laser malfunction.

The impatient part of me wanted to grab him by the shoulders and cheer him up. Buy him a copy of *The Power of Positive Thinking*. Give him a free pass to one of my workshops. Deliver one of my rousing keynote speeches.

The compassionate part of me extended itself into his consciousness. What might it be like to live in a mind that sees difficulties where there are none? Where your thinking defeats the simplest of enterprises before you even begin? What is it like to inhabit a mind predisposed to failure?

CAVEMAN BRAIN

Even though our ancestors left the savanna thousands of years ago, most of us still look much harder for what's wrong around us than for what's right.

When we wake up in the morning, our brains have been in theta and delta sleep states. We emerge into alpha, and it feels like we're in suspended animation as our brains gradually wake up to the day. Then beta kicks in and we start thinking. And worrying. The evolutionary mechanism that identified the tiger springs into action. A parade of paper tigers flows through our minds. We start thinking thoughts like this:

Is this the day that report is due on my boss's desk? Or is it next week?

What will I have for breakfast? Will it make me fat?

Did I hear my husband snoring last night?

What kind of mood are my kids in today? Will they make my life miserable?

I don't think the shoes I was planning to wear today are right for my outfit.

Did we run out of coffee?

I need to catch up on that disaster I watched on the news last night.

What's the weather like?

If Jane didn't leave a comment on my Facebook post, I'm going to be mad.

How much red is there in the commuter lane on Google Maps?

Once you wake up, your brain starts to drive you crazy with worry. Yet this is exactly what our brains evolved to do. When Gug woke up, she needed to be alert to a hostile environment from the second she opened her eyes. Might a tiger have crept up to the cave while she was sleeping? The Neanderthal who woke up grumpy, suspicious, and paranoid lived. Her sister who woke up happy, content, and peaceful missed those tiny survival cues that made the difference between life and death.

Today, without predators, we still wake up and immediately start to worry. Thoughts flood into our minds. The floodgates open and our minds churn in a torrent of anxiety. Before we've even walked out the front door to start our day, we've been consumed by anxious thoughts.

There are two basic survival questions: Can I eat it? Will it eat me?

Caveman brain takes a toll on our bodies. In an eight-year study of 68,222 adults published in the *British Medical Journal*, researchers found that even mild anxiety produces a 20 percent greater risk of death (Russ et al., 2012). The very skill that kept our ancestors alive—looking for the bad stuff and ignoring the good stuff—is killing us today. Our minds have become a major threat to our survival. Caveman brain is a fatal condition.

CARRYING THE Woman FOR a Day

There's a charming Zen story about two celibate monks who were on a long journey. One morning they came to a stream that was swollen with floodwater. On the bank was a young woman who couldn't get across. The older of the two monks hoisted her onto his broad shoulders, and both monks walked into the water and crossed safely to the other side. After thanking the old monk, the woman went on her way.

The two monks walked in silence till dusk, but there was tension in the air. The dam of emotional intensity in the younger monk eventually burst. "The rules of our religion forbid us to touch women," he said. "How could you have done that?"

"My son," said the older monk, "I picked her up and set her down this morning. You have been carrying her all day."

The angry inner ruminations of the younger monk had been raising his stress level long after the event was over. That's what we do when we obsess about the past or fear for the future. Using the system designed by Mother Nature to be engaged only when we are in true danger, we send stressful messages to our bodies with our thoughts, compromising our ability to regenerate and heal.

With Audrey Brooks, Ph.D., a research psychologist at the University of Arizona, I did a study of health-care workers. Professionally, they worked as chiropractors, nurses, psychotherapists, doctors, or alternative practitioners. We measured their levels of psychological distress before and after a one-day EFT tapping workshop. We assessed participants at five workshops, and the final study included 216 participants (Church & Brooks, 2010).

The health-care workers tapped together in groups.

We found that symptoms of anxiety, depression, and other mental health issues dropped an average of 45 percent in the course of the day. When we followed up six months later, those who had kept tapping had the lowest stress levels.

But one of our striking findings was just how stressed health-care workers are. On the scale we used for the study, a score of 60 represents such severe anxiety and depression that you need treatment. Their average starting score was 59. That's just one point less than the diagnostic threshold of 60. And that's the average; many individuals were more stressed than their patients. Being a health-care professional doesn't mean you can escape caveman brain.

The Whirlpool of Depression

By Naomi Janzen, EFT Universe trainer

I went through an 18-month period of depression after the end of a terrible relationship. I tried everything to shake it, but I could not. I felt trapped in an endless loop of anger and grief. I was being dragged around and around by this whirlpool of negative thoughts and feelings.

It used to exasperate me when I would read helpful pamphlets on depression that would say, basically, "Snap out of it."

I had a lot of tools. If anyone was capable of snapping out of it, it was me. But I'd wake up every morning at 3:11 A.M., when my defenses were down. I couldn't stop thinking about the man who had hurt me. The loop kept going. I was obsessed with justice I knew I would never get. The whirlpool dragged me around in a circle of repetitive thoughts.

If you have a friend who, maybe 20 years after a breakup, keeps talking about it, with nothing new to say, have compassion on them. They're in the whirlpool of looping anger and grief.

EFT rescued me from the endless loop, the whirlpool, and got me to dry land. Now my job is to help other people escape from their whirlpools!

The whirlpool that Naomi Janzen describes, in which the mind loops endlessly through a list of negative thoughts, is what kept her ancestors alive, but it's worse than useless today. These patterns rob us of peace of mind, drive our cortisol through the roof, and deprive our bodies of the resources they need to regenerate and heal. Even very smart people like Naomi often find, to their frustration, that they can't talk themselves out of the whirlpool. It takes a powerful psychospiritual tool like EFT to break the looping mental patterns of caveman brain.

SLOW-BURNING AND FAST-BURNING STRESS HORMONES

After completing the health-care workers study, I was intrigued by how quickly people could shed stress with EFT. I looked for a way of measuring changes in the body, and I found it in cortisol.

Cortisol is one of our two primary stress hormones, the other being adrenaline (also called epinephrine). You can think of adrenaline as our short-acting fight-or-flight hormone. When we're stressed, it kicks in immediately. In under three seconds, it speeds up our heart rate, contracts our blood vessels, and dilates our lungs. That gives our caveman the physical boost required to escape from danger.

Cortisol is our long-acting stress hormone. It rises and falls on a regular, slow curve throughout the day. It rises sharply in the morning, perking us up and getting us ready for an active day. It's at its lowest level around 4 A.M., when we're in deep sleep. It peaks at 8 A.M. When it starts declining, between 8 P.M. and 10 P.M., we become drowsy.

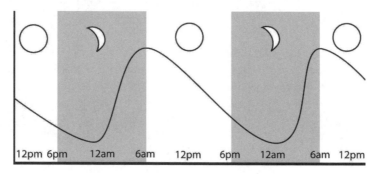

The cortisol cycle.

Like adrenaline, however, cortisol rises in just a few seconds when we're stressed. Stress disrupts the slow, even, daily cortisol rhythm. When you're running from a tiger, cortisol rises along with adrenaline. When you're worried, cortisol also rises.

Our bodies are designed to flourish with normal levels of cortisol synthesized along the smooth curve of the cortisol cycle. They are not designed to handle high levels of cortisol continuously. Chronic high cortisol leads to widespread body damage, including:

- High blood pressure
- Death of neurons in the brain's memory centers
- High blood sugar
- Heart disease
- Diminished cell repair
- Accelerated aging
- Alzheimer's disease
- Fatigue
- Obesity
- Diabetes

- Slow wound healing

- Reduced bone repair

- Fewer stem cells

- Reduced muscle mass

- Increased skin wrinkling

- Fat around the waist and hips

- Osteoporosis

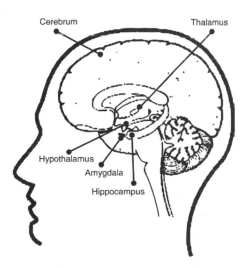

Cortisol kills neurons in the hippocampus, one of the structures of the emotional midbrain.

Over time, high cortisol disrupts cell metabolism so that excessive calcium enters brain cells and produces free radicals, the most harmful molecules in the body. Free radicals trigger a range of degenerative illnesses and rapid aging (McMillan et al., 2004). High cortisol also leads to dysfunction in our mitochondria, the "energy factories" of cells (Joergensen et al., 2011). We then feel tired and our energy levels crash. Cortisol kills neurons in the brain's hippocampus, which governs emotional regulation, memory, and learning (Sapolsky, Uno, Rebert, & Finch, 1990). Cortisol is accompanied by high beta brain waves, the signature waves of stress and anxiety.

CHRONIC HIGH CORTISOL

So when we get stressed for a few minutes, are we wrecking our bodies?

The answer is no. Bodies are designed to handle quick spikes of stress and then return rapidly to their normal baseline. Just two minutes after a stressful event, our body has already disassembled the fast-acting adrenaline molecules it built in response to danger (Ward et al., 1983). Slow-burning cortisol takes about 20 minutes to dissipate (Nesse et al., 1985). Your body is designed to generate cortisol quickly in response to an objective threat and dissipate it quickly when the threat is gone.

So if cortisol and adrenaline molecules dissipate rapidly, how can our levels stay high over time?

By *thought*—especially thought that triggers strong emotion. This sends signals through the neural pathways of negativity in our brains.

We cause chronic cortisol production by turning our attention to those factors in the environment that stress us out. Negative thinking drives high cortisol even when there is no tiger in the grass. Our brilliant brains are able to ruminate about the bad thing that happened in the past or the bad thing that might happen in the future. Even if it never happened and will never happen, we can nonetheless focus on it, picture it, contemplate it, imagine it, talk about it, and catastrophize about it.

The body cannot distinguish between an actual threat and a perceived threat. It has no way of knowing that the imaginary threat we are conjuring up in our minds using negative thinking is not an actual threat to our survival. Purely by thought alone, we can drive cortisol up and produce corrosive effects on our cells.

RESETTING STRESS HORMONE LEVELS

As I watched clients sigh and relax after EFT tapping sessions, I wondered what might be happening invisibly, inside their bodies, to their stress hormones. To answer this research question, I designed a study to examine their cortisol levels. With colleagues from the California Pacific Medical Center and the University of Arizona, I conducted the first study that examined psychological conditions such as anxiety and depression as well as cortisol levels before and after EFT (Church, Yount, & Brooks, 2012).

The study was ambitious and took several years to complete. It was conducted at five integrative medical clinics in California and included 83 subjects. It was a triple-blind randomized controlled trial, the gold standard of scientific proof. The results were provocative, and the study was published in a prestigious journal, the oldest peer-reviewed psychiatry journal in North America.

We assessed subjects' mental health, and also measured their cortisol, before and after a single therapy session. One group received EFT, a second group talk therapy, and a third group simply rested.

The results were striking. Psychological symptoms such as anxiety and depression declined in the talk therapy and rest groups, but they dropped more than twice as much in the EFT group. Cortisol dropped by 24 percent, showing that EFT was having an effect inside the body.

Devastated by the Loss of the Love of His Life

Dean, one of the participants in the cortisol study, was a 58-year-old male psychiatric nurse who had been randomized to the talk therapy group. Dean's scores on psychological distress were as high after the therapy session as before, and I was concerned about his well-being.

In the second treatment session, instead of talk therapy, we used EFT. We worked on a memory around which he had a high emotional charge: breaking up with his girlfriend. He told me that he thinks about the breakup every day.

He said that on the last day, he drove his girlfriend to the airport and put her on an airplane. He teared up as he remembered, "with stunned regret," the image of her walking down the jetway.

The adult event reminded him of a childhood incident. When he was five years old, he saw a television advertisement in which Gina Lollobrigida was touted as "the most beautiful woman in the world."

After watching the advertisement, little Dean went to the bathroom, climbed up onto a stool, and looked at himself in the mirror. He concluded that he was not good-looking and realized he never would be. When he described the memory, he experienced a sharp pain in his solar plexus, but after tapping, he felt much better at the end of the session.

When Dean's cortisol results arrived back from the lab (SabreLabs.com) a few days later, they showed that his cortisol levels had dropped from 4.61 ng/ml to 2.42 ng/ml, or 48 percent, after the tapping session. But after his earlier talk therapy session, Dean's cortisol had risen from 2.16 ng/ml to 3.02 ng/ml, an increase of 40 percent (Church, 2013). This echoes other research showing that therapies that engage the body are usually more effective than those that engage the mind alone.

Later, I had the opportunity to find out just what was happening inside the bodies of people taking a five-day residential EFT workshop. This particular workshop was held at California's Esalen Institute, the place where Gestalt therapy, Rolfing, humanistic psychology, and many other groundbreaking approaches were first developed.

Esalen Institute front gate.

The research team measured a comprehensive panel of physiological markers as well as psychological conditions such as anxiety, depression, and PTSD (Bach et al., 2016). As anticipated, large improvements in mental health occurred during the week.

However, the changes in physiological markers of health were extraordinary. Cortisol dropped by 37 percent. Salivary immunoglobulin A, an immune marker, rose by 113 percent. Resting heart rate dropped by 8 percent, and blood pressure was reduced by 6 percent. The blood pressure, cortisol, and heart rate figures showed that participants were much less stressed at the end of the week than at the beginning.

While an hour of EFT had reduced cortisol by 24 percent in the previous study, five days of tapping was associated with an even bigger stress-reduction effect. Participant pain dropped by 57 percent, while happiness increased by 31 percent. When we reassessed psychological symptoms six months later, most of the improvements had held. This close association between physical health and mental health is a pervasive finding in research in meditation, EFT, and other stress-reduction techniques.

At each moment, the body's processes, such as stress and relaxation, lie at a point on a continuum.

Tapping and meditation dial down stress. Stress isn't like a light switch, either on or off. It's like a dimmer switch, getting brighter or darker. When we relax, this nudges our cortisol levels and beta brain waves lower. When we get stressed, we move the needle in the opposite direction. Gene expression, hormones, brain states, and stress all operate on this type of continuum. Each strong emotion we have, positive or negative, moves the needle in one direction or the other.

COHERENT MIND = COHERENT MATTER

The caveman brain is not efficient. Addled by beta waves and intoxicated with cortisol, it's chaos. Imaging studies show that the four lobes of the brain fall out of synchrony and that groups of neurons fire chaotically rather than in harmony. In the scientific literature, the word for efficiency is *coherence*. When the brain is functioning at peak efficiency, an EEG scan shows coherence between brain regions and neural groups.

When our consciousness is disrupted by stress, our brains are not coherent. In this state, the creations of our minds are not coherent either.

But when we drop our stress, train our unruly minds to remain calm, and release negative thinking from our consciousness, our brains become coherent. In highly coherent states, our minds are able to create effects in the physical world that are astonishing.

THE POWER OF COHERENT LIGHT

Lasers use coherent light, while non-laser light sources such as LEDs or incandescent bulbs use incoherent light. Put another way, a laser is set up so that all the light rays are parallel to each other rather than going off in random directions. This characteristic of coherence makes lasers extraordinarily powerful. Light from a 60-watt incandescent light bulb can faintly illuminate objects two to four yards or meters away. It converts only about 10 percent of its energy into light, and that light is not coherent.

Organize that same 60 watts of light into a coherent laser, however, and it can cut through steel.

Coherent Laser Light

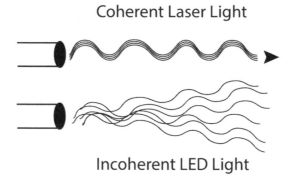

Incoherent LED Light

Coherent versus noncoherent light.

An ordinary handheld laser pointer of the kind used in lectures, with a tiny power source of just 5 thousandths of a watt, can illuminate a point 12 miles or 20 kilometers away (Nakamura, 2013). Using a trillion times more power (1 billion watts), scientific lasers can even bounce off the moon and reflect back to earth (Shelus et al., 1994).

Mental coherence is similar. When our brain waves are coherent, the quality of thought they produce is focused and efficient. We can turn our attention to problems, focus on them, and solve them.

BRAIN FOG

When our brains are not coherent, we aren't able to think clearly. We're afflicted by "brain fog," and our wooly brains can't think clearly. When we're upset, problems seem opaque, we're easily confused, and our cognitive abilities plummet. Brain researcher Joseph LeDoux calls this "the hostile takeover of consciousness by emotion" (LeDoux, 2003).

Laser used for astronomical observations at the Goddard Space Flight Center.

Brain studies have found that it takes less than a second for a statement or even a single word to trigger an emotional reaction (Davidson, 2003). By the time we recognize that we're under stress, our brains have already been triggered. We can be overwhelmed by emotional reactions in just a fraction of a second, producing brain fog and the inability to think clearly.

When that happens, our access to remembered skills and rational thinking is greatly impaired. We are unable to be objective and consider a problem realistically. Stress can result in a drain of more than 70 percent of the blood from the frontal lobes, the cognitive centers of the brain. As blood carries oxygen, this means that the brain is not getting its normal supply of oxygen either. We can't think straight when the blood and oxygen flow to our brains is reduced as a result of being stressed. The caveman doesn't have to be able to do long division in his head; he just needs to be able to escape from the tiger.

When that primitive survival response is triggered by thought and emotion, the result is a huge reallocation of biological resources. Blood flows out of the prefrontal cortex into the muscles. Suddenly, all those wise skills you have in your prefrontal cortex, your thinking brain, are no longer available to you. It's like a computer, which has masses of data stored on its hard drive. If you unplug the computer, all the stored information is still there, but you can no longer access it; there is no power to make it useable.

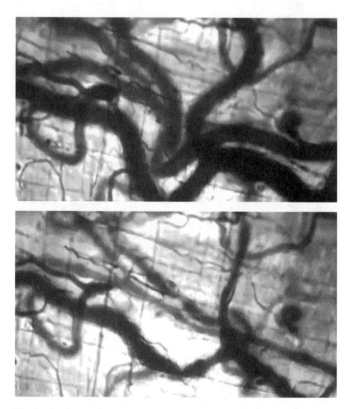

**Capillaries before (above) and 14 seconds after (below) a stress signal.
They can contract by over 70 percent.**

When you lose the blood supply to your prefrontal cortex, it's like a computer that's unplugged. All the resources that are stored in that part of your brain—the skills learned in therapy, the brilliant solutions you've read in books, the methods you've practiced in classes, the strategies you've learned from experts—all these are unavailable to caveman brain.

Come into coherence, however, and your resources come online. Like the laser pointing at the moon, you're able to perform inspired long-range planning. You think clearly about problems, you focus on your goals, your imagination is unlocked, and your creativity soars. That's the power of a coherent mind.

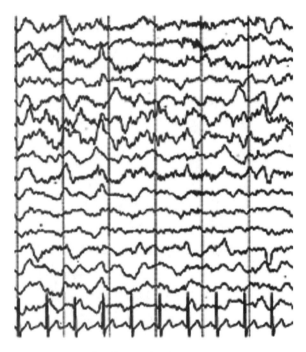

Incoherent brain waves.

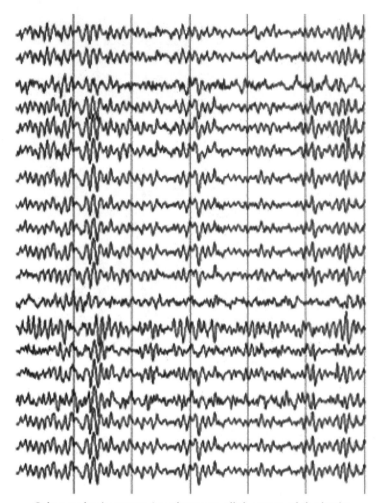

Coherent brain waves. In coherence, all the parts of the brain
are working together.

COHERENT MIND AND THE FOUR
FORCES OF PHYSICS

A coherent mind focuses the power of attention the way a laser
focuses the power of light. People who achieve high levels of coherence
are able to do extraordinary things. Remarkable research now shows that
a coherent mind can literally bend the forces of the material universe.

There are four fundamental forces in physics: gravity, electromagnetism, the strong nuclear force, and the weak nuclear force.

The strong force is what holds atoms together. The protons and neutrons in the nucleus of an atom contain huge amounts of energy, and the force required to hold them together is enormous, which is why it's called the strong force. It operates at very short distances between components of an atom.

The weak nuclear force is the one that gives rise to radioactive decay. In this process, the nuclei of atoms break down because they do not have enough energy to hold together. Energy and matter are released from these unstable nuclei over a period of time until they form a different, stable element that is not radioactive.

Different radioactive substances have different rates of decay. Some are very long while others are very short. The half-life of uranium-238 is very long, about 3.5 billion years. The half-life of another element, francium-233, is just 22 minutes.

These half-lives are so consistent that you can set your watch by them. Scientists who need precise measures of time use an atomic clock and reference their experiments by International Atomic Time, a scale that uses the combined output of 400 highly precise atomic clocks in various parts of the world. One second is defined as the period it takes for one cesium-133 atom to oscillate 9,192,631,770 times.

A cesium atomic clock constructed in 2004 for a lab in Switzerland that operates with an uncertainty period of 1 second every 30 million years.

A radioactive element often used in studies is americium-241. Discovered in 1944, it has a half-life of 432 years, emits what are known as alpha particles, and is stable at room temperature. It's also ubiquitous in our homes, where it powers most smoke detectors. It's safe, since its alpha radiation travels only 3 cm (under 1.5 inches) and is stopped by almost any solid object. If smoke particles enter the detector, they're hit by the alpha particles, triggering a drop in electrical current, which sets off the alarm.

The weak nuclear force is not affected by electromagnetism or gravity. In fact, it is 10 trillion trillion times stronger than gravity.

Given the stability of atomic radiation, so consistent that it powers atomic clocks, you might imagine that it would be very hard to change. Yet that is exactly what a number of researchers have tried to accomplish using the human energy field as the agent of change.

$QI = MC2$

A qigong master named Dr. Yan Xin projects qi, or life energy, to his patients. Scientists at the Institute of High Energy Physics, part of the Chinese Academy of Sciences, decided to put Dr. Yan's powers to a rigorous objective test.

They asked him to alter the rate of decay of a tiny 2-mm americium-241 disk inside a plexiglass container. One of the four fundamental forces of physics, the decay rate of radioactive substances is immune to high temperatures, strong acids, massive electromagnetic fields, or extreme pressures.

For the first eight sessions, Dr. Yan projected qi energy to the americium for 20 minutes while standing nearby. A second americium disk was used as a control. He was able to change the decay rate of radioactive alpha particles in the target disk while leaving the control disk unchanged. He could either slow down or speed up the decay rate, whichever was requested of him (Yan et al., 2002).

For the next three sessions, the researchers decided to study whether the effect diminished with distance. They placed Dr. Yan 100 to 200 meters away from the americium source. This made no difference in the results.

They then tested whether being in a distant city would weaken the effect. Over the next five years, they had him project qi into the target disk from progressively greater distances, starting 1,500 km away and eventually moving as far as 2,200 km away. A series of 39 additional trials showed that he was able to produce the same effect from a distance as he could standing in the same room.

These 50 separate experiments showed that Dr. Yan could lower the radioactive decay rate by 11.3 percent and raise it by up to 9.5 percent in the 20-minute course of the experiments. It normally takes 432 years for americium to decay, a rate of only 0.0006 percent per day, so the passage of time could not explain the results.

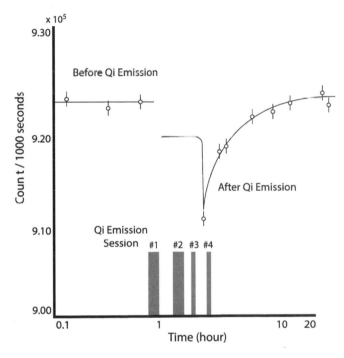

Readings from the spectrometer with Dr. Yan Xin in the same location as the americium source.

Nuclear physicist Feng Lu, one of the researchers, observed that "Dr. Yan's research transformed the accepted view of the nature of the world. The results of his research have demonstrated that the human potential is far greater . . . than that which has been previously thought."

In his book *The Energy Cure,* Dr. Bill Bengston describes his empirical tests of the healer Bennett Mayrick (Bengston, 2010). On one occasion, Bennett was hooked up to a device that measures the rate of radioactive decay. The technician instructed him to concentrate on making the radioactive material decay more rapidly. Bengston observed, "The technician gave a yelp. 'Something's wrong. This thing says the decay is occurring faster than I believe can be possible.'

"Ben playfully replied, 'Then I'll slow it down.'

"Soon the technician was mumbling something about the decay slowing to almost one-half its normal rate."

When Bengston asked Ben how he did this, Ben said that to speed up the decay, he imagined a cloud, which he then dissolved with his mind. To slow it down, he imagined a frozen rock.

My Eureka Moment

On June 26, 2017, I nervously unpacked my very own Geiger counter. For the past few months, I'd e-mailed colleagues—with far more experience than I—copies of the Bengston and Yan experiments and urged them to conduct replications. No one seemed interested.

The equipment required was simple and inexpensive, just a Geiger counter and a smoke detector containing an americium-241 disk.

The methodology was elementary. Either a healer could slow down the rate of radioactive decay or he could not. A Geiger counter can measure radiation as either microsieverts, a standard scientific unit, or counts per minute (CPM). CPM is a count of how many electrons are being released by the radioactive source.

I set up the equipment on my dining room table and figured out how to get a basic radiation reading. I discovered that the baseline in my house fluctuated between 12 and 22 CPM, with an average of 18 CPM.

I then placed the Geiger counter over the radiation source, a simple household smoke detector. The radiation readings rose to an average of 60 CPM. Just a couple of inches away, the readings were normal; a Geiger counter has to be very close to a smoke detector to measure any radiation since the devices are designed to be safe for household installation.

I performed the seven steps of EcoMeditation and then filled my mind with the same image that Ben Mayrick had used, a frozen rock. The Geiger counter didn't register any change.

Well, that's it, I thought. *It didn't work. That ability may be something only a few people, like Ben or Dr. Yan, possess.*

But I decided to continue meditating, my hands on either side of the smoke detector. I sent energy through my hands, just as I would with a client to whom I was offering healing.

The numbers began to rise. First to the high 60s and then into the 70s. By the time I'd meditated for a while, it rose to over 80 CPM. I ran the test for 10 minutes, and it averaged 80 CPM.

I then stopped meditating, and the numbers dropped back to 60 CPM. After another 10 minutes, I moved the Geiger counter two feet away from the smoke detector, and the background readings averaged the same 18 CPM as when I began.

The first experiment on June 26, 2017.

I paced around the house with questions exploding in my brain.

- Could I get the same result a second time?

- Why was I not able to lower the count, only raise it?

- Could other people do this? Is the effect more pronounced with gifted healers than it is with ordinary people?

- Can anyone be trained to do this? Is it a skill that can be taught? Does this ability improve with practice?

- Was my belief in energy healing enhancing the results?

- Would skepticism be a barrier to replicating them?

- What force could be producing the change in the radiation levels? How can I test this in a way that is methodologically impeccable?

- Did it happen because of my magic T-shirt? (just kidding)

I had so much energy that I couldn't go back to my office to do routine work. I jumped into my venerable relic of a car, a bright red 1974 Jensen Healey, and drove to the gym to exercise, screaming and shouting and punching the air around me. When life hands us such moments, it's worth celebrating!

I now knew that people other than Yan Xin and Ben Mayrick could produce the effect. The club of radioactivity changers had just expanded from two to three!

When my wife, Christine, came back from work that afternoon, I sat her down at the dining room table to see if we could boost the number of club members from three to four.

Ten minutes of measuring background radiation gave us an average of 17 CPM. When I put the Geiger counter on top of the smoke detector, a 10-minute test gave an average CPM of 60. When Christine placed her hands around the source and meditated for 10 minutes, the CPM dropped to 57, and when I asked her to visualize her youngest grandchild's face, it dropped to 52.

Christine was able to maintain 52 CPM for 10 minutes. When I asked her to raise the CPM by using Ben Mayrick's imagery, the dial didn't move upward for more than a few seconds before dropping again. She tried other imagery, but still was not able to raise it. This was interesting: I could raise it but not lower it, while Christine could lower it but not raise it.

After she stopped, I tested the unattended Geiger counter for 10 minutes and it averaged 61 CPM. Another 10-minute test, away from the smoke detector, gave us a background radiation count of 18 CPM. There were officially now four members of the club . . . and maybe millions more!

THE FIFTH FORCE

The ability to alter the rate of radioactive decay, one of the four fundamental forces of physics, raises several questions: If one force can be altered by a force that is not one of the other three, can any of those other three be altered? Can gravity or electromagnetism, forces far weaker than the two nuclear forces, be changed?

Joie Jones, Ph.D., late professor of radiological sciences at the University of California–Irvine, teamed up with Russian physicist Yuri Kronn to devise an ingenious experiment to determine if electromagnetism is susceptible to change. They pointed out that a "fifth force" is required to do this, and they called it "subtle energy" (Kronn & Jones, 2011).

They measured the electrical conductivity of various substances that were deliberately infused with subtle energy. They found that compared to baseline controls, electromagnetism was decreased by 25 percent.

An experiment with healing intention measured the magnetic fields around the targets of healing (Moga & Bengston, 2010). These were mice who had been injected with a substance that caused cancer. The healer sent intentional healing energy to them locally (with the healer present in the room) for 30 minutes on the first day of the study, and then nonlocally (with the healer in a distant location) for 12 weeks. Measuring devices in the mice's cages found an increase in the magnetic field to 20–30 Hz, followed by a decrease to 8–9 Hz, then a further drop to below 1 Hz. The effect then reversed.

Local healing and nonlocal healing produced the same effects. The researchers subsequently tested various healing modalities and found similar changes in the magnetic field during tai chi and healing touch sessions as well. They also reviewed five other studies that measured similar phenomena (Moga & Bengston, 2010).

This research suggests that at least two of the four fundamental laws of physics—electromagnetism and the weak nuclear force—can be altered by a coherent mind holding healing intentions.

Kronn and Jones found that their experiments could be done successfully in certain labs but not in others. They were puzzled as to why, and it took them some time to figure out the difference. It turned out that the labs where replications were unsuccessful were those in which experiments on dead animals were performed. Kronn developed an energy protocol, called "clean sweep," for those labs, after which they could successfully host replications (Kamp, 2016).

Kronn has found that scientists affect what they're studying. He says that "Your own energy will distort the energy pattern you are recording. Similarly, if you repeat an experiment and you don't want it to work, then it won't. Or, when one of my collaborators has a 'bad—out-of-tune—day,' we can't accurately test energy patterns" (Kamp, 2016).

When Christine and I were near the Geiger counter in ordinary consciousness, nothing much happened. But when we meditated, the readout changed. Similarly, Ben Mayrick used vivid mental imagery, while Dr. Yan projected qi energy into the americium sample, with the intention of either speeding up or slowing down its radioactive decay.

Changing matter in this way requires a coherent state of mind. When brain waves are incoherent, with anxiety-laden beta waves predominating and stress hormones such as cortisol and adrenaline infusing our cells, we're out of the state of flow. Our intentions lack clarity or power.

But when we slow ourselves down into a meditative state, with a broad alpha bridge connecting our conscious minds to high-amplitude theta and delta waves, we access the power of coherent mind. In this state, our intentions affect matter.

COHERENT MIND AND ACTIVE INTENTION

Led by Rollin McCraty, Ph.D., the Institute of HeartMath in Boulder Creek, California, has been studying the effects of coherent heartbeats for more than two decades.

Heart rate variability (HRV) readouts for anger (above) and appreciation (below) (McCraty, Atkinson, & Tomasino, 2003).

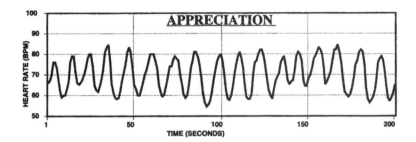

Heart coherence is a reliable marker of overall physical health, associated with pervasive effects throughout the body. It reduces cortisol secretion and expands the amplitude of alpha waves in the brain. It brings not only the brain but other organ systems such as circulation and digestion into coherence too, while also boosting the immune system (McCraty, Atkinson, & Tomasino, 2003).

McCraty writes: "The current scientific conception is that all biological communication occurs at a chemical/molecular level through the action of neurochemicals fitting into specialized receptor sites, much like keys open certain locks. However, in the final analysis, the message is actually transmitted to the interior of the cell by a weak electrical signal.

"From these and related findings, a new paradigm of energetic communication occurring within the body at the atomic and quantum levels has emerged—one which is compatible with numerous observed phenomena that could not be adequately explained within the framework of the older chemical/molecular model. 'Fight or flight' reactions to life-threatening situations . . . are too immediate and manifold to be consistent with the key-lock model of communication. However, they are comprehensible within the framework of quantum physics and an internal and external electromagnetic or energetic signaling system, which may also explain . . . the energetic communication links between cells, people, and the environment.

"Several of the brain's electrical rhythms, such as the alpha and beta rhythm, are naturally synchronized to the rhythm of the heart and this heart-brain synchronization significantly increases when an individual is in a physiologically coherent mode. This synchronization is likely to be mediated at least in part by electromagnetic field interactions. This is important as synchronization between the heart and brain is likely involved in the processes that give rise to intuition, creativity, and optimal performance" (McCraty, Atkinson, & Tomasino, 2003).

DNA CHANGE IN A COHERENT STATE

An ingenious HeartMath experiment used human placental DNA to test the effect of human intention in a coherent state. The degree of molecular twist in a sample of DNA can be measured by the molecule's absorption of ultraviolet light. This test can determine whether the molecule's double helix coils are more tightly or less tightly wound.

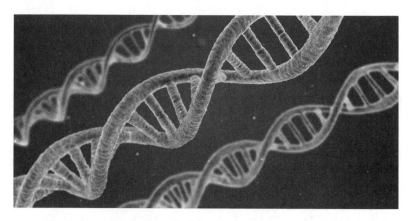

The DNA molecule has a double helix structure, and the degree of its twist can be measured by its absorption of ultraviolet light.

In the study, individuals trained in HeartMath techniques generated feelings of love and appreciation while holding a specific intention to either wind or unwind the DNA in an experimental sample.

The results were profound. In some cases, there was a change of 25 percent in the conformation of the DNA. Similar effects occurred whether participants were given the instruction to wind the helixes tighter or to unwind them.

When these participants entered that state of coherence but had no intention of changing the DNA, it changed no more than it did with a control group, which was composed of untrained local residents and students. When trained participants held the intention of changing the DNA but did not move into a coherent state, the DNA likewise remained unchanged.

In order to determine just how specific and local the effect might be, in one experiment with a highly trained volunteer, three separate vials of DNA were prepared. The volunteer was asked to wind the DNA spirals tighter in two of the samples but not in the third. Those were exactly the results measured under later UV analysis in the laboratory; changes showed up only in the two samples to which the volunteer had directed his intention.

This suggests that the effects are not simply the result of an amorphous energy field, but are highly correlated with the intender's intentions.

The researchers speculated that the effects might be due to the proximity of the samples to the participants' hearts, since the heart generates a strong electromagnetic field. They therefore performed similar experiments at a distance of half a mile from the DNA samples. The effects were the same. Five nonlocal trials showed the same effect, all to statistically significant levels.

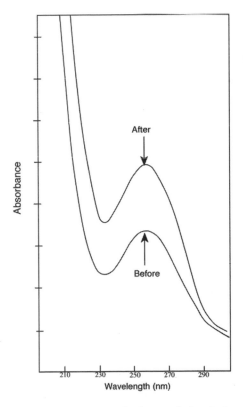

Ultraviolet absorption in DNA before and after being exposed to human intention (McCraty, Atkinson, & Tomasino, 2003).

These studies demonstrate that the DNA molecule can be altered through intentionality. The better participants were at generating a state of heart coherence, the better they were at affecting DNA with their intentions. Control group participants who were untrained and unskilled at heart coherence were unable to produce an effect despite the strength of their intentions. Both intention and coherence were required in order to alter the DNA molecules.

The researchers suggested that "an energetic connection exists between structures in the quantum vacuum and corresponding structures on the physical plane," and that "this connection can be influenced by human intentionality."

McCraty and his colleagues also speculated that the positive emotions affecting DNA might play a role in phenomena such as spontaneous remissions, the health and longevity rewards of faith, and the positive effects of prayer.

Legend holds that the Chinese medicine modalities of herbs and acupuncture are a secondary form of healing. Near the start of the 2,000-year-old book *The Yellow Emperor's Classic of Internal Medicine,* the basic text of acupuncture, the Yellow Emperor says, "I have heard that in early ancient times, there were the Enlightened People who could . . . breathe in the essence of qi, meditate, and their spirit and body would become whole."

In the distant past, the original acupuncturists believed, healing occurred by means of coherent intention and energy alone. This was a belief in the West as well. Romantic poet William Blake asked the question: "Does a firm persuasion that a thing is so make it so?" and replied to himself, "In ages of imagination this firm persuasion removed mountains" (Blake, 1968, p. 256).

The qi energy of traditional Chinese medicine has also been focused by Dr. Yan on living cells, not just on americium-241. When he applied five minutes of coherent mind to cancer cells and healthy cells, the DNA in the cancer cells disintegrated while the healthy cells were not harmed (Yan et al., 2006). In other studies, similar effects were noted in colorectal, prostate, and breast cancer cells.

The effect of human-generated healing energy has been measured in a large number of studies. A systematic review of 90 randomized controlled trials of healing methods—mainly qigong, healing touch, and Reiki—found that two-thirds of the higher-quality trials showed that the techniques were effective (Hammerschlag, Marx, & Aickin, 2014).

OKAY, IT HAPPENS. BUT HOW?

In science, *that* something is happening is usually observed before we understand *how* something is happening. EFT tapping studies showed *that* anxiety, depression, and phobias could be healed a decade before they showed *how* these conditions were being healed (cortisol reduction, brain coherence, gene expression). Medicine knew *that* aspirin cured pain a century before it understood *how*. *That* penicillin killed bacteria was discovered more than 30 years before science understood *how* it worked.

How are the intentions of a coherent mind able to affect matter?

We think of material realities as facts, but in the quantum world, all possibilities exist simultaneously and then condense into probabilities. Theoretically, any of the swarm of infinite possibilities present in the possibility wave can become reality. But only one possibility does. The swarm is then said to have "collapsed" into a particular reality.

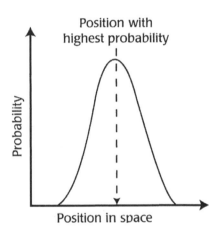

Distribution of quantum probability.

One of the factors that determine the direction in which the swarm of possibilities collapses is the act of observation. In a quantum universe, phenomena and space and time are affected by the observer. All possibilities exist in the quantum field; the act of observation collapses them into probability.

This is called the observer effect. When subatomic particles are observed, they collapse from an infinite number of possibilities to a single probability. Without the observer, they remain in a state of indeterminate possibility. Only when observed do they become a single defined probability. The scientific discovery that it requires observation to create material fact has profound implications for our understanding of the material world and the role of consciousness in creating it.

THE OBSERVER EFFECT

The observer effect is measured in a classic physics demonstration called the double-slit experiment. It has been repeated hundreds of times in the past century. It shows how the presence of an observer changes the outcome of what is observed.

While subatomic particles like electrons are supposed to behave according to the fixed laws of physics, they don't always cooperate. The double-slit experiment demonstrates that the act of observing a particle affects its behavior.

Electrons are fired at a barrier with two slits in it, and where they end up is recorded. If they behaved as particles, you'd expect to see two vertical areas of impact on the other side. It would be as if you'd thrown paint-covered tennis balls at the slits and they'd produced two vertical paint splashes on the wall.

But the electrons don't behave like tennis balls. Instead, they interact with each other to produce a wave. This also happens with photons of light, with water, and with sound.

What happens when you shoot a single photon through the double slits? It still forms an interference pattern, just as if it were traveling through both slits simultaneously.

However, if you place a detector near the slits and observe the process, the electrons behave like tennis balls. The wave interaction pattern disappears.

If you pass larger particles through the slits, they also behave like tennis balls. But on the level of the subatomic, electrons and photons behave like waves unless they are observed, in which case they show up as predictable tennis-ball particles. The act of observation completely changes the outcome of the experiment, collapsing waves into particles, energy into matter.

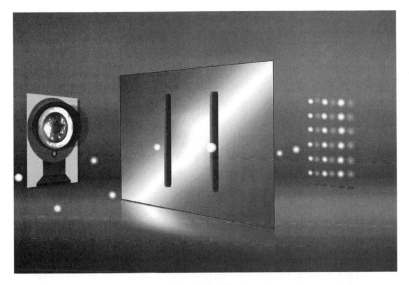

Setup of the double-slit experiment.

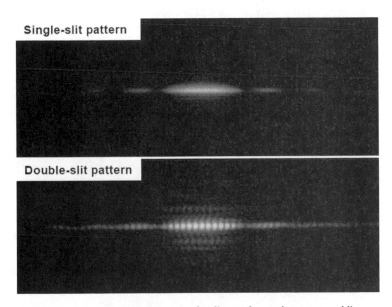

Single-slit pattern

Double-slit pattern

Interference patterns. *Top:* a single slit produces the expected line.
The double slit produces a wave pattern as observed electrons interact.

The double-slit experiment shows that subatomic particles can combine the characteristics of a particle and a wave and that the act of observation changes their behavior. Nobel prize–winning physicist Richard Feynman called it "a phenomenon which is impossible . . . to explain in any classical way, and which has in it the heart of quantum mechanics. In reality, it contains the only mystery [of quantum mechanics]" (Feynman, Leighton, & Sands, 1965).

Electrons and photons exist in waves of possibility. The act of observation triggers the collapse of the wave into a probability. Being measured by a machine produces the observer effect, and so does measurement by a human observer.

ENTANGLEMENT BETWEEN DISTANT PARTICLES

A second important principle from quantum physics is the phenomenon of entanglement. Physicists can produce entanglement by firing a laser through a crystal. Both photons of light and electrons of matter can be entangled. If two electrons become entangled, one will spin clockwise and the other counterclockwise. The act of measuring the spin determines the direction of rotation.

Once a pair of electrons has become entangled, they remain so regardless of distance. If a physicist in Paris measures one spinning clockwise, a colleague in San Francisco might observe its entangled partner spinning counterclockwise. No matter how great the degree of separation, the effect persists.

In a key experiment, researchers at the Delft University of Technology began with two unentangled electrons. Each electron was entangled with a photon, after which both photons were taken to a third location where they were entangled with each other. This caused both of their partner electrons to become entangled as well (Hensen et al., 2015).

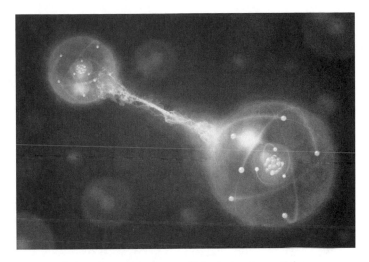

Entanglement between distant atomic particles.

An ingenious study performed by Dean Radin and Arnaud Delorme of the Institute of Noetic Sciences tested the effect of observation by human minds compared to robot observation. They had a double-slit experiment "observed" either by a robot or by human observers. The human observers participated online in a total of 5,738 sessions over two years. The results of the experiment showed that human observation real live minds—produces a greater observer effect than machine observation (Radin, Michel, & Delorme, 2016).

THE OBSERVER EFFECT AND ENTANGLED PARTICLES

The observer effect also shows up in entangled particles. In a study using two entangled photons, each had a possible position of being either horizontal or vertical. Left to their own devices in their own little universe, the two photons remain in an indeterminate state. But when an observer intrudes on this closed system by observing one photon, the possibility wave collapses into a probability and the photon becomes either horizontal or vertical. Its entangled partner then responds by taking up the opposite position (Moreva et al., 2014).

Physicist Werner Heisenberg said, "What we observe is not nature in itself, but nature exposed to our method of questioning" (1962).

Not until they are observed do entangled photons take up opposite polarities (Fickler, Krenn, Lapkiewicz, Ramelow, & Zeilinger, 2013).

"In the realm of possibility," says quantum physicist Amit Goswami, Ph.D., "the electron is not separate from us, from consciousness. It is a possibility of consciousness itself, a material possibility. When consciousness collapses the possibility wave by choosing one of the electron's possible facets, that facet becomes actuality" (Goswami, 2004).

So the scientific mind, rather than impartially witnessing objective phenomena, is itself influencing which of the infinite sea of potentials winks into existence as a phenomenon. Goswami continues, "The agency that transforms possibility into actuality is consciousness. It is a fact that whenever we observe an object, we see a unique actuality, not the entire spectrum of possibilities. Thus, conscious observation is sufficient condition for the collapse of the possibility wave."

IS SCIENCE THE OBJECTIVE MEASUREMENT OF MATERIAL PHENOMENA?

Science is usually thought of as the objective measurement of material phenomena. When a scientist reports that she has found a molecule that kills cancer cells and the results are published in a reputable journal, we believe that they are true. When a team investigates a social phenomenon such as emotional contagion and provides a statistical analysis demonstrating the effect, we confidently assume that it exists.

But what if all of science is swayed by the observer effect? What if scientists are finding things they expect to find, not just at the level of electrons and photons but stars and galaxies as well? What if the minds of scientists are shaping the matter they observe? What if the strength of their belief is producing all or part of the effects they're observing? What if the degree of belief scientists possess determines the outcome of their experiments?

Belief permeates and shapes the entire field of science. Scientists set out to measure something because they believe there is something to be measured. If they don't believe something is there, they don't look for it, so they have no way of finding it.

An example of this comes from the research into the spiritual states of AIDS patients. Early AIDS research focused on the disease as a biological phenomenon to be targeted at the level of matter. Only after hundreds of studies had been performed with that mind-set did a research team include a questionnaire that assessed the spiritual states of patients.

To their astonishment, they found that the beliefs patients held about God and the universe affected the progression of the disease. The quantity of AIDS virus in the bloodstreams of those who believed in a punishing God increased three times faster than those who believed in a benevolent God. Beliefs predicted whether patients would live or die more strongly than factors such as depression, risky behavior, and coping skills (Ironson et al., 2011).

Before that landmark study, the importance of spiritual belief was unknown. Not because it didn't exist, but because no one had thought to look for it.

The beliefs held in the minds of scientists shape the material reality they discover at every turn.

THE EXPECTANCY EFFECT

In an influential 1963 animal trial at Harvard University, researchers tested what is known as the expectancy effect. If you expect something to happen, you're more likely to perceive it happening. Professor Robert Rosenthal gave students two groups of lab rats. He told them that one group had been specially bred to be good at running mazes, or "maze bright." The others had been bred to be "maze dull." In reality, the rats had been randomly allocated between the two groups. The students conducted their tests and duly found the "maze bright" rats to outperform the others (Rosenthal & Fode, 1963).

Rosenthal then performed a similar experiment with teachers. He told them that tests showed that certain of their students were entering a year of academic flourishing. In reality, these students had also been selected at random. At the end of the year, the IQ scores of the designated students were higher than the control group (Rosenthal & Jacobson, 1963). Mind had produced matter, with belief making significant changes in performance in the material world.

The Freshman Whose Ignorance Could Precipitate Crystals

A grad student who supervised a chemistry lab at MIT described to me one of the procedures she and her fellow students were required to learn as part of the curriculum. They had to precipitate sodium acetate crystals out of a supersaturated solution. It was tricky to accomplish and required focused attention from the budding chemists. Most had to make many attempts and even then were not always successful. They knew that the procedure was difficult, and successful precipitation was akin to a rite of passage in the lab.

That semester, a first-year student joined the lab as an assistant. The first time he attempted the experiment, he was able to precipitate the sodium crystals immediately. The supervisor was very surprised. When the student tried it again, the result was the same. The freshman was able to precipitate the crystals effortlessly every time he tried. "He just has a knack for it," the supervisor exclaimed, with puzzlement tinged with envy. The student was so green that he hadn't yet received the memo that the procedure was fraught with difficulty.

Variability in the results obtained among individual scientists isn't supposed to happen in empirical sciences such as physics and chemistry. Molecules and atoms are supposed to behave the same way under the same conditions at all times. There is no room in the standard scientific paradigm for scientists' intentions, beliefs, or energy fields to be influencing the results.

Yet reports reveal that certain chemists are better than others at making elements behave and can use their intention to "will" them to conform (Sheldrake, 2012). Physicist Fred Alan Wolf speculates that "the laws of the universe may simply be the laws of our own collective minds" (Wolf, 2001). Neuroscience expert Robert Hoss says, "Solid matter is just an illusion. At our most fundamental level we may look something like this—an organized soup of subatomic particles popping in and out of existence within the infinite energy field of the universe" (Hoss, 2016).

THE MIND OF SCIENCE

The sciences can be classified by the scale and type of their subjects. First comes physics, which studies the most fundamental levels of matter such as atoms and subatomic particles. Then comes chemistry, which looks at how those particles assemble themselves into molecules and interact with each other. These sciences are called the physical sciences—or "pure" sciences or "hard" sciences—because they measure the cold, hard objective fact of physical matter. They're based on mathematics rather than the squishy unpredictability of living things.

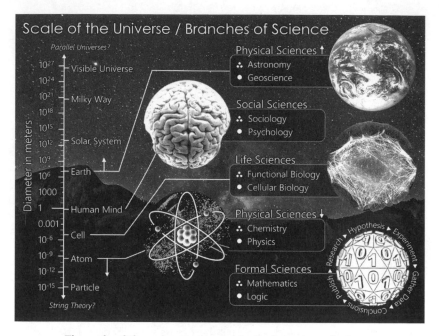

The scale of the universe mapped to the branches of science, with physical sciences as the foundation.

Biology and the other life sciences build on physics and chemistry to study living cells, tissues, and organisms. These interact in complex systems that are often unstable and evolving in unpredictable directions. Geology and astronomy also study solid physical matter. Geology examines the composition of the planet. Astronomy scales up by a large order of magnitude to look at the material structure and motion of stars, galaxies, and the universe.

Then come the "soft" sciences of the mind. Psychology examines individual behavior, while sociology studies the interactions of groups. Those in the hard sciences often feel superior to those in the soft sciences because they deal with the level of matter rather than that of mind. Physicist Ernest Rutherford, who in 1907 discovered that the atom was mostly empty space and that subatomic particles are bound together by electromagnetic fields, had a low opinion of the other sciences, sniffing contemptuously, "In science there is only physics. All the rest is stamp collecting."

THE REPLICATION CRISIS

When they publish their papers, scientists are required to provide a "methods" section. This outlines how the experiment was set up and does this so clearly that other scientists can run the same experiment in an attempt to replicate the previous study's findings.

A discovery published in a single paper may represent an actual effect. But when an independent research team comes up with the same result, it's likely that the effect found in the first study is real. For this reason, replication studies are important in science.

So much so that before it approves a new drug, the U.S. Food and Drug Administration (FDA) requires two studies demonstrating the drug's efficacy. When formulating standards for "empirically validated therapies," the American Psychological Association borrowed the same standard, requiring a replication of a study before declaring the therapy evidence based (Chambless & Hollon, 1998).

In the early 2000s, a giant biotech company, Amgen, set out to replicate some important studies. The company was pouring millions of dollars into research on cancer biology based on earlier research. If the effects found in the original studies were robust, then the next stage of development of cancer drugs would be built on solid ground. They asked their scientists which previous studies were most important to their work and came up with 53 "landmark" studies.

In 10 years of work, Amgen was able to replicate only 6 of the 53 studies. The researchers called this "a shocking result" (Begley & Ellis, 2012).

A few months earlier, another giant pharma company, Bayer, had published a similar analysis. This led to a sustained effort to determine how many key studies were replicable. An attempt to replicate five cancer biology trials was successful for only two (eLife, 2017). Epidemiologist John Ioannidis of Stanford University summarized the findings by saying, "The composite picture is, there is a reproducibility problem" (Kaiser, 2017).

What about the soft sciences? An international group of 270 researchers set out to replicate 100 studies published in 2008 in three top psychology journals. They found that they were able to replicate fewer than half of them (Open Science Collaboration, 2015).

The journal *Nature* conducted a survey of 1,576 researchers to identify their experiences with replication. It found that over 70 percent of them had failed when attempting to reproduce another scientist's research findings. Over half could not even replicate their own research (Baker, 2016).

There are many roots to the "reproducibility crisis" in science. A variety of factors stand in the way of successful replications. Among them are haphazard laboratory management, sample sizes too small to provide a high degree of statistical power, and the use of specialized techniques that are uniquely hard to repeat.

Selective reporting plays a big role, too, as positive results are usually reported while negative ones are swept under the rug. These are called file drawer studies because, metaphorically, they are thrown into the bottom drawer of a filing cabinet, never to see the light of day. An analysis of psychology studies estimates that 50 percent are never published (Cooper, DeNeve, & Charlton, 1997).

Another factor making studies hard to replicate is that beliefs can influence the results. Scientists have beliefs. They're human. They are not godlike intellects immune from glory seeking, egotism, jealousy, and territorialism. They have whims, preferences, and needs. They need successful research to obtain grants, jobs, and tenure. They fall in love with their work, the "Pygmalion effect" immortalized in the musical *My Fair Lady*. Scientists approach their work with as many presuppositions as any other demographic group has.

Scientists believe in what they're doing and look for effects they expect to find. The strength of their beliefs may skew their results, a phenomenon called the expectancy effect. To control for this, most medical research is carried out blind. The statisticians analyzing two groups of data don't know which sample is from the experimental and which from the control group.

Experiments in the physical sciences, such as chemistry and physics, are assumed to be independent of the observer effect, so they are blinded in fewer than one percent of cases.

The same is not true in the hard sciences, such as physics and chemistry. Surveys show that under one percent of studies in these fields are performed blind (Sheldrake, 1999; Watt & Nagtegaal, 2004). The researchers carrying them out know which of the samples is the experimental one, and the beliefs and expectations in their minds may well be producing the effects they observe in matter. The observer effect has been measured at the level of atoms and molecules in the physical sciences as well as on the scale of people and societies in the soft sciences.

MEASURING THE STRENGTH OF SCIENTISTS' BELIEF SYSTEMS

How strong are the beliefs of scientists? An interesting test comes from the work of Daryl Bem, a social psychologist at Cornell University, who performed experiments on precognition. In a series of nine experiments with over 1,000 participants, he found a statistically significant link supporting foreknowledge of future events (Bem, 2011).

Bem's critics so strongly believed that precognition was not true that they applied a radically more stringent approach. First, they analyzed each of the nine experiments separately, instead of combining the results to provide the largest possible pool of data (Radin, 2011). It's always more difficult to find an effect in a smaller data pool. They then used a statistical test very different from those normally used in psychology studies (Wagenmakers, Wetzels, Borsboom, & Van Der Maas, 2011).

The technique they used requires the formulation of two prior beliefs about the phenomenon. The first is the belief that it is true, the other that it is false. They set their level of belief that precognition cannot exist at 100,000 trillion to 1 (Radin, 2011). Unsurprisingly, this made the effect go away.

Bem's research team used this same method to re-analyze their own data. They found that even if you had a tiny belief that precognition might be true, the collective result of their nine experiments showed that it exists. How tiny? You needed only a prior belief there was 1 chance in 100 million that premonition might occur (Bem, Utts, & Johnson, 2011).

You didn't need to be a true believer in precognition to identify the effect. Even if you were a firm skeptic whose mind allowed just a sliver of belief—1 possibility in 100 million—the study validated precognition: "If one begins with the possibility that retrocausal effects might be real, even when that possibility is extremely small, then the strength of the existing evidence will substantially shift one's belief towards [precognition]" (Radin, 2011).

UNWAVERING FAITH

An independent team failed to replicate Bem's study (Ritchie, Wiseman, & French, 2012). This led to a large-scale research effort, involving 90 experiments in 33 different labs in 14 countries. This time, Bem used both the unconventional statistical methods of his critics as well the standard tests of probability and found that both supported the existence of premonition (Bem, Tressoldi, Rabeyron, & Duggan, 2015).

Most skeptics don't believe in premonition.

Bem's first experiment and the re-analysis of his data by his critics provides a fascinating but unintentional statistical comparison of just how strong beliefs among scientists can become. Bem's detractors could not tolerate a belief of just 1 possibility in 100 million that premonition might exist and set the threshold of their faith at an astonishing 100,000 trillion to 1 (Radin, 2011). That's the kind of unwavering certainty that the most hardened fundamentalist would be proud of.

The survey in *Nature* showing that 70 percent of scientists fail at replication didn't make much of a dent in their confidence in science. Their belief remained strong. Most still trust published papers. They're much more optimistic than they might be expected to be, based on the data: "Seventy-three percent said that they think that at least half of the papers in their field can be trusted, with physicists and chemists generally showing the most confidence" (Baker, 2016).

What we find when we examine the way science is conducted is that for better or for worse, it is heavily influenced by belief. The ideal of the scientist as an objective assessor of facts is at odds with reality. Scientists are believers, especially in their own work. They cannot separate mind from matter.

Science is not, in fact, the objective measurement of matter. It's a dance between the inner consciousness, or mind, of the scientist and the material world of matter. Change mind, and matter changes right along with it.

AT WHAT SCALE DO ENTANGLEMENT AND THE OBSERVER EFFECT OPERATE?

The consensus in physics up through the early 21st century was that entanglement and the observer effect occurred only on a micro scale. They were peculiar properties of the subatomic world, but for structures larger than an atom, good old-fashioned common-sense cause-and-effect Newtonian physics applied. Because entanglement requires communication between particles faster than the speed of light, Einstein detested it and called it "spooky action at a distance" (Born, 1971).

So for a century, physicists confined spooky action to the realm of the tiny. It could not possibly be operating at the large scales of things like cells and organisms. In 2011, however, researchers were able to entangle millions of atoms together at one time (Lee et al., 2011). In 2007, quantum effects were discovered in the way light is used by bacteria for photosynthesis. In 2010, this phenomenon was measured at room temperature, and in 2014, researchers discovered that this quantum coherence in living organisms is organized by fields (Romero et al., 2014).

On the human level, research has shown that our sense of smell is able to detect molecules based on their quantum energetic signature rather than just their shape (Gane et al., 2013). In the human brain, groups of neurons seem to have their own version of quantum entanglement. Widely spaced neural regions are able to fire in coherence, at the same time, in a process called phase locking, possibly synchronized by quantum communication (Thiagarajan et al., 2010).

Another important experiment seeking quantum effects in human brains examined seven pairs of subjects hooked up to EEGs. They enclosed one person from each pair in a soundproof room shielded from all known forms of electromagnetic radiation. At random intervals, 100 times during the course of the experiment, the brain of the member of the pair outside the room was stimulated briefly. When the two groups of brain wave samples were compared, they showed that the brains of those inside the shielded room responded to the stimulation of the partner outside (Grinberg-Zylberbaum, Delaflor, Attie, & Goswami, 1994).

In an experiment on a planetary scale, the Chinese government in 2016 launched the Quantum Experiments at Space Scale (QUESS) mission. Its goal is to use quantum coherence at distances of thousands of miles to provide ultra-secure data transmission.

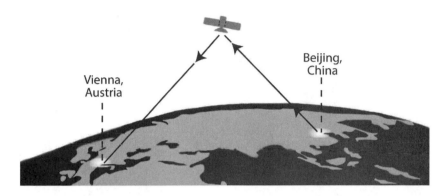

The QUESS teleportation system uses photon
entanglement to transmit data securely.

When data are transmitted through fiber-optic cables, the data get scattered or absorbed. Preserving the quantum state of photons over large distances is not possible using this technology. The goal of the Chinese project is to teleport quantum states using entangled pairs of photons.

Data are encrypted by polarizing a string of photons, which are then transmitted through space by bouncing the data off a satellite to a distant location on the planet. This eliminates the scattering that occurs when data are transmitted using fiber-optic cables and results in secure transmission.

GLOBAL CYCLES

The serious study of the effects of the fields of the earth, sun, and planets on human beings is a recent and exciting new branch of science. The interactions between these global fields and life-forms, and the effects that living beings are having on the planet's field, are just starting to be mapped.

The largest-scale project to gather data on these interactions is called the Global Coherence Initiative (GCI). It uses large, recently developed magnetometers to measure changes in the Earth's magnetic field. They are located all over the world. They measure "biologically relevant information that connects all living systems" (McCraty & Deyhle, 2016).

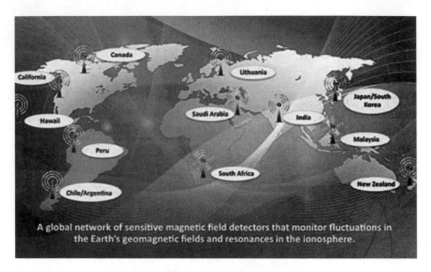

A global network of sensitive magnetic field detectors that monitor fluctuations in the Earth's geomagnetic fields and resonances in the ionosphere.

**The six operating and six proposed
Global Coherence Initiative (GCI) monitoring sites.**

The GCI sensors monitor changes triggered by shifts in the Earth's magnetic field, by solar storms, and by changes in the speed of the solar wind. They also test the hypothesis that collective human consciousness affects this information field, and they seek to determine whether "large numbers of people creating heart-centered states of care, love and compassion will generate a more coherent field environment that can benefit others and help offset the current planetary discord and incoherence."

Russian scientist Alexander Tchijevsky noticed a striking fact when looking at sunspot flares that occurred early in the 20th century. They coincided with the most violent battles of World War I (Tchijevsky, 1971). This led him to analyze earlier periods dating from 1749 to 1926. He looked at major historical events in the histories of 72 countries such as the onset of social revolutions and wars and found the same relationship going back centuries. He identified an 80 percent correlation between social upheaval and sunspot activity.

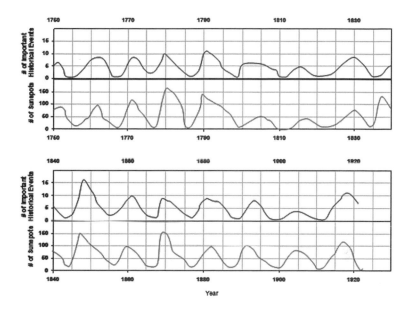

The upper line represents historical events and the lower line represents the number of sunspots during the same period.

This effect works in the opposite direction too. Solar activity has been related to periods of cultural flourishing and positive social evolution with leaps in the arts, science, architecture, and social justice (McCraty & Deyhle, 2016).

When a person is in a heart coherent state, they also radiate a coherent signal all around their body. When such a person comes together with others, that produces a group field effect (McCraty & Childre, 2010). This brings people nearby into coherence too. The goal of GCI is both to measure and to influence these interactions. Large numbers of people in coherence may be able to nudge the whole psychosphere of the planet toward positive evolutionary shifts.

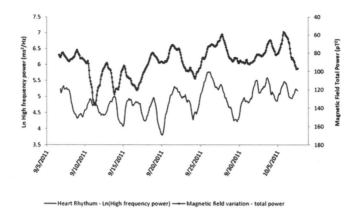

——Heart Rhythum - Ln(High frequency power) ——Magnetic field variation - total power

One participant's heart rate variability (HRV) and the magnetic field at the California GCI site over a 30-day period.

This process is expected to "greatly accelerate cooperation, collaboration, innovative problem-solving and intuitive discernment for addressing society's significant social, environmental and economic problems. This will become increasingly apparent as countries adopt a more coherent and inclusive planetary view. This planetary view will be critical for meaningfully and successfully addressing social and economic oppression, wars, cultural intolerance, crime and disregard for the environment" (McCraty & Deyhle, 2016).

Shifts in human consciousness can also be measured using random number generators (RNGs). These are computers that simply generate a continuous stream of zeros and ones at random. Because they're designed to produce random output, they should not, in principle, do anything else. At moments of peak collective experience, however, the streams of digits that they are constantly generating do indeed change. They deviate from randomness, sometimes so far that the results are statistically significant, meaning that there's only 1 possibility in 20 that the results are due to chance. At large sporting events, when the crowd is going wild, RNGs have been found to deviate significantly from baseline (Leskowitz, 2014).

MEASURING SHIFTS IN COLLECTIVE GLOBAL CONSCIOUSNESS

The Global Consciousness Project (GCP) is an international collective of scientists and engineers. It collects data from 70 host sites around the world and transmits the data to a central repository at Princeton University (Nelson, 2015).

When dramatic events engage large numbers of people around the globe and global consciousness becomes coherent, the behavior of the RNGs changes. It deviates from randomness. For around two decades, the GCP has been tracking these changes. It finds these correlate with significant global events that involve the awareness of large groups of people. Examples of these events include:

- 1998: The bombings of the U.S. embassies in Kenya and Tanzania

- 1999: The aerial bombardment of Yugoslavia by NATO in an effort to stop the massacre of Serbs

- 2000: The first visit by the pope to Israel

- 2000: The explosion on board the Russian submarine *Kursk*

- 2003: A global candlelight vigil for peace organized by Desmond Tutu and various organizations

- 2004: The Democratic Party convention

- 2004: The Beslan massacre in which 150 hostages died in Russia

- 2005: The Iraqi elections

- 2005: The earthquake in Kashmir, Pakistan

- 2006: The magnitude 6.2 earthquake in Indonesia in which over 3,000 people died

- 2008: The nomination of Barack Obama as president

- 2010: The passage of the Obamacare reform act

- 2010: The Israeli attack on a flotilla of pro-Palestinian activists that killed nine civilians

- 2010: The rescue of 33 Chilean miners after 18 days underground

- 2011: A global meditation called by New Reality Group, a group of "physicists and mathematicians that believe our very own consciousness defines our reality"
- 2013: A global meditation organized by the Peace Portal Activations group
- 2013: The death of Nelson Mandela
- 2015: International Peace Day

The GCP calculates the statistical probability of these changes occurring. It also tracks the cumulative possibility that these correlations are happening purely by chance. Those odds are one in a trillion (Nelson, 2015).

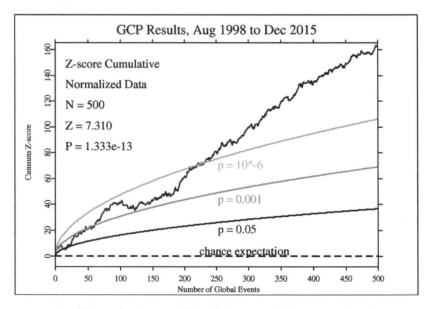

On this graph, the possibility of these correlations occurring by chance is indicated by the bottom dashed line. The three smooth curves represent increasing levels of statistical significance. The final result is the jagged top line (Nelson, 2015).

These large-scale measurements show that collective human consciousness interacts with the material world. Carl Jung believed that some elements of personal experience spring from a much larger consciousness shared by all humankind, which he termed the collective unconscious. He believed that "The collective unconscious contains the whole spiritual heritage of mankind's evolution, born anew in the brain structure of every individual" (1952).

Large-scale scientific projects such as the GCP and the GCI are now allowing us to measure the effects of shared experience. We are finding that what we experience collectively is having an effect on the material world. Group mind is affecting the matter of the entire psychosphere in which we live.

PERSONAL COHERENCE INFLUENCES GLOBAL COHERENCE

When we come into personal coherence, we feel much better emotionally, spiritually, and physically. Our cortisol levels go down, while the neurotransmitters serotonin and dopamine balance in our brains. We have high levels of all the brain waves that promote healing and low levels of anxiety-linked high beta. We feel good subjectively, and this translates into objective changes in the biology of our cells. Mind becomes matter as our brains are flooded with pleasure-inducing endorphins, intimacy-producing oxytocin, and the bliss molecule anandamide.

We're also then resonant with the corresponding global frequencies. We aren't living our lives as isolated human beings but as resonant nodes that are part of a great universal whole. As we increase our personal coherence, we add our measure to the sum of coherence being generated by everyone else on the planet resonating in synchrony with those energies.

In this way, we play a small but significant part in nudging the whole planet into flourishing. The following story by Joe Marana is an example of the synchronicities that sometimes tie geological and personal events together.

My Sister's Love FROM BEYOND THE Grave

By Joe Marana

I had lent a cassette set of Wayne Dyer's audio program *Real Magic* to a friend.

It contains six cassettes. When they were returned to me, they were all rewound except for one cassette. I was a little bit annoyed and thought, *Why didn't he rewind this one?*

Then I thought, *Maybe there's a message here for me.* So I went over to my elaborate stereo system with its fancy cassette player, dropped the tape in, and hit the play button.

I heard Wayne Dyer's voice saying, "What if you hadn't heard from your sister in three years and you're thinking about how nice it would be to talk to her?"

I was stunned. It was the three-year anniversary of my sister's death, and I had been missing her terribly.

When the mail arrived that day, it included a letter from a lady from Paraguay named Juanita Lopez. She has multiple sclerosis, and a few times each year I send her money. Each time, Juanita would write back and give me a detailed list of what she'd spent the money on. Shoes for her niece. New thatch on her roof. A water purifier.

I opened the letter. At the very top, in block capitals, in handwriting completely different from Juanita's, it said, "I am your everlasting sister and I remember you every day and send you love."

I fell to the ground, and I couldn't stop sobbing for a long time.

I fired off an airmail letter to Juanita asking, "Why did you say that?"

The next day, there was an earthquake in Paraguay. It killed four people, and one of them was Juanita Lopez. So I never got a reply.

I shared this story with a scientist from the Institute of Noetic Sciences, and he said that the most likely explanation is entanglement. The letter had been mailed before I heard the message from Wayne Dyer. Yet somehow they were all connected.

To add to the synchronicities, I heard Joe's story on a radio show while I was parked outside a hotel in my car, waiting for my wife, Christine, to check us out. I had just finished keynoting the annual conference of . . . (you guessed it) . . . the Institute of Noetic Sciences.

ENTANGLED LIVES

Entanglement might be at work in distant healing and nonlocal communication. People who are emotionally close are also neurologically close, no matter the distance. Research teams at Bastyr University in Seattle and the University of Washington examined the EEG signatures of people with close emotional bonds. They found that when a partner was shown an image, the other partner, even though distant, immediately developed the same pattern of EEG brain function (Standish, Kozak, Johnson, & Richards, 2004).

A gifted faith healer might be considered, in quantum terms, to be an observer who routinely collapses space-time possibilities into the probability of healing. A prayer is an intention that might also collapse the swarm of possibilities present in the possibility wave in the direction of a certain probability.

In *The Intention Experiment,* her book about large international experiments that gauge the effect of human intention on physical matter, Lynne McTaggart states that the observer effect implies that "living consciousness is somehow central to this process of transforming the unconstructed quantum world into something resembling everyday reality," and that "reality is not fixed, but fluid, and hence possibly open to influence" (McTaggart, 2007). According to Bill Bengston, "This suggests that human consciousness, individually and collectively, produces what we call 'reality'" (Bengston, 2010).

Robert Hoss, an expert on the neuroscience of extrasensory phenomena such as near-death experiences and precognitive dreams, asks a provocative question: If it is only the act of observation that is collapsing the waves of energy into the particles of matter that make up the world around us, *who or what is doing the observing?* Who is the grand observer catalyzing the creation of all the matter in the physical world? Hoss believes it is consciousness: the great nonlocal consciousness of the universe itself. That is, the universe itself is consciousness, continually creating matter out of mind (Hoss, 2016).

This view has increasing support from mainstream scientists. Gregory Matloff is a veteran physicist at the New York City College of Technology. He argues that our individual local minds may be linked to the nonlocal mind of the cosmos through a "proto-consciousness field" that extends through all of space. In this model, the minds of stars might be controlling their orbital journeys through matter. The entire universe may be self-aware. His views are shared by many others (Powell, 2017).

When we as human beings release the fixation our local minds have on local reality and instead align our local consciousness with the nonlocal consciousness of the universe, we bring local mind into coherence with nonlocal mind. In this coherent state, what we create with local mind is a reflection of nonlocal mind. We're no longer limited by our old, conditioned thinking, so we no longer create the same present-day reality out of the stale experiences of our past.

Instead, we think outside the box. We see possibilities we were blind to when trapped in local mind. We explore the potential of our lives found in the expansive awareness of nonlocal mind. We perceive ways in which the world can change that we simply don't see when stuck in a noncoherent personal reality field. The observer effect demonstrates that reality is plastic. Bringing the power of coherent mind to our experience, our perception creates events that are extraordinary.

In my own life, I find it easy to get sucked into the conventional view that "facts are facts" and that the outside world just is the way it is. To correct this tendency, I practice framing my experiences, good or bad, in ways that support my goals. When I'm acting with awareness, I use my mind to create and maintain a "reality field" that is congruent with what I want.

Maintaining the Reality Field

I had a career change at the age of 45. I'd left the book publishing world a few years earlier and purchased a small hotel. While I raised my two children, I lived a semiretired life.

I was also bored to tears, feeling cut off from the world of healing and ideas I'd participated in as a publisher.

To get back in the game, I decided to publish an anthology called *The Heart of Healing,* a reprise of a successful anthology I'd published in the 1980s.

I sent letters of invitation to 30 of the best-known names in healing, people like Larry Dossey, Deepak Chopra, Donna Eden, Bernie Siegel, and Christiane Northrup.

Inside each letter was a stamped blue postcard. I asked each person to check a box saying yes or no and write a line explaining why they were responding that way.

For the following month, I ran out to my mailbox eagerly each day, awaiting the return of blue postcards. The first one came from Bernie Siegel with a yes! I went back to my office and told my assistant how relieved I felt that at least one person, Bernie, hadn't forgotten me after 15 years!

Then came one from Larry Dossey with a no.

I ran back into my office. I waved the postcard above my head excitedly. After seeing the no, my assistant looked at me with a puzzled frown.

"I've opened a dialogue with Larry Dossey!" I exclaimed.

That's how I framed every no. That blue postcard didn't represent a closed door, it was the start of a dialogue. I maintained my reality field of a successful anthology even when faced with evidence to the contrary.

Eventually, almost all the no's did appear in the anthology, which went on to win an award for best health book of the year. As for Larry, he has become a friend and sent me one of the very first endorsements for *Mind to Matter.*

CULTIVATING COHERENT MIND

We can retrain our scattered and chaotic minds to function coherently. EEG scans show that this produces flares of gamma waves, signaling increased creativity as well as orchestration of all the regions of the brain. Add to that synchronization entrainment with the nonlocal mind of the universe and our intentions have the focused power of a laser.

As Christine and I discovered with the Geiger counter, the ability to use intention to affect molecular matter isn't a superhuman anomaly. It's something a trained and coherent mind can easily accomplish. Entanglement and the double-slit experiments demonstrate that consciousness is influencing the material world around us every day.

Stanford University professor William Tiller reminds us of the difference between incoherent light in an incandescent bulb and the power of organized light in the form of a laser. He says: "Just like the light bulb example, vast unutilized potential exists within us, the basic ingredients are already there but they are relatively incoherent with respect to each other. Our task is to transform the largely incoherent ingredients into a completely coherent system" (Tiller, 1997).

Think deliberately. Use this remarkable gift of consciousness to direct your thoughts rather than being pushed around by reality. Even adverse circumstances can propel us to greatness if we've mastered our minds, deliberately filling them with love and purpose rather than doubt and fear.

A coherent mind has the power of a laser, able to cut through steel. Consciousness, holding an elevated reality, organizes our neural pathways. It brings our brain waves into coherence, along with our hearts and every other system in our bodies. It rewires our neural networks. In this state, we're able to operate at levels that transcend the known laws of physics.

We then join naturally together with other people, aligning with the large social energy fields of positive resonance. Synchronicities become the norm rather than the exception. As philosopher C. S. Lewis exclaimed, "Miracles are a retelling in small letters of the very same story which is written across the whole world in letters too large for some of us to see" (Lewis, 1970).

Cultivating coherent local mind starts with aligning our consciousness with the fields of love and creativity found in nonlocal mind. That's why meditating first thing in the morning, while your brain is in an alpha state, before beta kicks in, is so effective. Trying to quiet the mind after the floodgates of thought have already opened is hard. Extending the alpha state you've been in when your eyes were closed during sleep is much easier.

When I wake up in the morning, I want to stretch out that alpha connection as long as possible, so I meditate immediately. I then start my day with coherent mind rather than caveman brain. These positive mental states have profound effects on health and longevity. Optimists have half the mortality rate of pessimists, and lowering your stress can add 10 years to your life span (Giltay, Geleijnse, Zitman, Hoekstra, & Schouten, 2004; Diener & Chan, 2011).

A mind attuned to the infinite is a wonderful place to live. It nudges the matter of our bodies toward health and well-being. It unlocks our creativity. It shifts our family and community relationships to a state of love, compassion, and pleasure. It nurtures the natural world and influences the psychosphere of the entire planet. Our minds, organized into coherence, can illuminate the realm of miracles.

PUTTING THESE IDEAS INTO PRACTICE

Activities to practice this week:

- Continue to practice EcoMeditation for at least 10 minutes each morning and evening.

- Touch the people in your household every day deliberately. This can be:

    An encouraging squeeze on the shoulder
    A pat on the back
    A longer hug than usual

- In your journal, take a look at the entries for the past few weeks. Do you notice any synchronicities? Mark them with an *S*.

The Extended Play version of this chapter includes:

- Audio interview with Bob Hoss

- Statistics on the causes, symptoms, and impact of stress

- The Global Consciousness Project (GCP)

- The Global Coherence Initiative (GCI)

To access the Extended Play version, visit:
MindToMatter.club/Chapter5

CHAPTER 6

Entraining Self with Synchronicity

Molokai is often called the most Hawaiian island. Though 260 miles square, it boasts not a single traffic light. There are two gas stations serving the 7,000 inhabitants, along with one modest grocery store. Visitors stay at an establishment called the Hotel Molokai—"the" hotel because that's the one and only hotel on the island. Visitors can buy postcards entitled "Molokai Nightlife." They're solid black.

My wife, Christine, and I visited Molokai for the first time a few years back. We had 10 days to relax there, and we had a strong intention of connecting with some of the local residents and events. Synchronistically, the day before we flew from Maui to Molokai, we met a musician and shaman from Molokai named Eddie Tanaka. He offered to show us around when he got back to the island a few days after we were due to land there.

On our first day, after driving the oceanfront road for a few miles, we decided to take a walk and try to find a trailhead. We got ready to leave our condo, then got distracted and pottered aimlessly around the living room instead. About 45 minutes later, we finally wandered downstairs to start our planned walk.

My eye was caught by a bumper sticker on a car in the parking lot. It said: "Don't change Molokai. Let Molokai change you." I took a photo with my phone to share on the Love Bathing Facebook page where Christine and I record our travels.

The owner of the car walked by and noticed me photographing her car, and we fell into conversation. She was a retired accountant named Joy, and she turned out to be a fountain of information. She told us where the nearest trails were and about the community sing-alongs where people connect. She shared the locations of heiaus, Hawaiian sacred sites that we love to visit, soaking in the energy fields of these ancient places of worship.

A restored Hawaiian heiau, or ancient temple.

It turned out that Joy and her husband lived in the condo below ours. She knew Eddie and often played ukulele with him. She told us about his distinctive house, with a front wall topped with hundreds of glass bottles. We'd driven past it that morning.

Joy invited us to a community sing-along at the Hotel Molokai the following day, where we met her friends. People welcomed us warmly. At the end of the performance, everyone held hands in a big circle and sang "Hawaii Aloha" together. My heart was so touched that I cried all the way through the beautiful song. We enjoyed 10 days in which we "talked story" with Joy, Eddie, and our other new friends.

But the synchronicities had begun long before that. The year before, the 20-something daughter of a friend of ours took a whole year off work to explore the Caribbean, "looking for the perfect island." I envied her and imagined taking a year off to do that myself. Because of my speaking engagements and my life mission of training people in advanced healing methods, it was impossible.

Then one morning after meditation, I realized, *You don't have to move your body all over the place in a search for the perfect island. The universe already knows! Just ask your inner guidance.* I asked the question, and a still small voice said, *Check out Molokai.* I'd been visiting the Hawaiian Islands for 20 years and it had never occurred to me to visit Molokai before that morning meditation. That nudge led to booking the 10-day vacation.

Christine and I had a wonderful time. Molokai has miles of sandy beaches, and they are usually deserted. Often ours were the only footprints in the sand. On our hikes, we discovered remote *heiaus* so overgrown with vegetation that they were invisible till we stumbled upon them. Magic was in the air every day.

Miles of sandy beaches on Molokai, with a rainbow
thrown in for good measure.

Since I was a toddler, I've been fascinated by rainbows. On a number of occasions, I've driven my car for miles, whimsically trying to locate the base of a particularly vivid rainbow. But I've never found a rainbow's end.

One afternoon, as Christine and I drove around a bend on the rugged west side of Molokai just after a rainstorm, there it was. The rainbow ended on the road just in front of the car. Or rather, one of the rainbows—there were two others ending in the steaming foliage on either side of the road. I'd been granted more than I'd wished for.

We left Molokai feeling loved, rested, and renewed. The morning before our flight left, we went to our last sing-along, at an old coffee plantation, where a sizable percentage of the island's population had turned out to enjoy the homemade entertainment. I left with tears in my eyes, feeling as though I'd found a second home.

None of the connections we made on that first day on the island would likely have happened unless . . .

- We decided to go on a walk our first morning.

- We got distracted and left 45 minutes later than planned.

- I stopped to look at a bumper sticker and stayed long enough to take a photo.

- Joy walked by at that exact moment.

We would never even have been on Molokai if I had not tuned in to my intuition.

Sure, all of this could have happened quite by chance. Yet synchronicities like this happen to Christine and me all the time. Since we met, we've kept a relationship journal in which we record events and epiphanies in our lives.

A few years back, we were struck by just how many unlikely synchronicities happen to us and how things we think about seem to manifest as if by magic. We began writing a big *S* in our journal to identify those entries and to remind ourselves to be grateful for a happy and harmonious life. Journal entries from our time in Molokai contain *S* after *S* after *S*.

GOD'S WAY OF REMAINING ANONYMOUS

Ours is not the first generation to notice synchronicity. It's fascinated human beings for millennia. Two thousand years ago, the father of modern medicine, Hippocrates, observed, "There is one common flow, one common breathing, all things are in sympathy. The whole organism and each one of its parts are working in conjunction for the same purpose. . . . The great principle extends to the extremist part, and from the extremist part it returns to the great principle, to the one nature, being and not-being" (Jung, 1952). Roman emperor and philosopher Marcus Aurelius believed, "Everything is connected and the web is holy."

In the early 20th century, the great Swiss psychiatrist Carl Jung became intrigued by the phenomenon of synchronicity. He defined it as "a meaningful coincidence of two or more events, where something other than the probability of chance is involved" (Jung, 1952, p. 79).

One of his most quoted examples of synchronicity occurred during a therapy session. A young woman who was a patient of Jung's but who was not making progress in her therapy recounted a dream. In it she saw a piece of jewelry shaped like a golden scarab beetle. In ancient Egyptian cosmology, scarabs are the symbol of rebirth.

While they were discussing the dream, Jung heard a rapping at the window. Opening it to investigate, he found a beetle of the scarab family. He gave it to the woman, a symbol of her potential to move past her obstacles and renew her life. Jung wrote, "Synchronicity reveals the meaningful connections between the subjective and objective world."

Albert Einstein was a frequent guest at Jung's house during the time he was developing his theory of relativity. Their conversations about the relativity of time and space played a role in the development of Jung's concepts of synchronicity. Einstein quipped, "Synchronicity is God's way of remaining anonymous."

SYNCHRONICITY AND DREAMS

Dreams are often harbingers of synchronicity. Jung analyzed his patients' dreams, paying particular attention to the symbols they contained. He looked for connections between dream images and waking life, like the scarab beetle. These turn up with surprising frequency.

Dreams can change the course of our lives. They're often filled with symbols and events that contain synchronous links to the real-life challenges we face. They give meaning to our experience and can provide information far beyond the abilities of the waking mind.

One category of synchronous dreams are those that carry information about our health. In dreams, people often gain knowledge about their bodies that transcends the scope of ordinary consciousness.

Radiologist Larry Burk, M.D., has been collecting and studying breast cancer dreams for years. Analyzing stories from women around the world, he finds that many of these dreams are life-changing experiences (Burk, 2015). They also share common characteristics. Among these are that the dreamer senses that the dream is important (94 percent of cases). In 83 percent of cases, the dream is more intense and vivid than other dreams. Most dreamers experience a feeling of dread, and in 44 percent of cases, the words *cancer* or *tumor* appear.

In over half the cases Dr. Burk has collected, the dream resulted in the woman seeking medical consultation. Dreams led directly to diagnosis and frequently highlighted the precise location of the tumors.

The Debris Hidden
under the Ledge

One of the participants in Dr. Burk's study is named Wanda Burch. She had a series of dreams about a tumor and followed up by getting a physical exam and mammogram. Neither definitively showed the existence of a tumor. Her physician, Dr. Barlyn, was an open-minded clinician and willing to consider her story. As she tells it:

"Dr. Barlyn listened to my dream and handed me a felt-tip marker. 'Draw the location on your breast.' I drew a dot far underneath the right side of the left breast and told him that another dream had shown me a ledge, with the 'dream debris'—or tumor—hidden underneath the ledge. Dr. Barlyn inserted the biopsy needle in the area I designated and felt resistance, an indication of a problem. The surgical biopsy gave Dr. Barlyn the details of a fast-moving, extremely aggressive breast cancer whose cells were not massing in a fashion that allowed them to be seen on a mammogram."

This led Wanda to successful treatment and to sharing her story with other women in the form of a book called *She Who Dreams* (Burch, 2003).

A friend of Dr. Burk's was not as fortunate in her interaction with her doctor. Sonia Lee-Shield had a warning dream and described her symptoms during a consultation:

"I had a dream that I had cancer. I went to the G.P. complaining of a lump and spasm-like feelings on my sternum. The G.P. concluded it was normal breast tissue, and the feeling in my sternum was dismissed, a devastating mistake. A year later, a different doctor diagnosed stage 3 breast cancer."

At that late stage, treatment was unsuccessful, and Sonia did not survive. Her tragedy gave Dr. Burk the impetus he needed to publicize the importance of synchronous warning dreams. He has found cases in which the diagnosis of many other types of cancer was preceded by dreams. These include skin, lung, brain, prostate, and colon cancers (Burk, 2015).

Dreams are filled with symbolism uniquely meaningful to the dreamer.

The dreams of cancer patients like Wanda and Sonia demonstrate the intricate dance of mind and matter. Consciousness, speaking to the mind in dreams, highlights problems in the body. It not only shows that a problem exists, but it can also pinpoint exactly where the problem is. Consciousness is able to present refined levels of information beyond the most sophisticated scans and instruments available to modern medicine.

Dreams don't just warn us of malfunctions in our bodies and our lives. They can also play a role in healing. There are many accounts of people who've had dreams in which they healed their bodies or facilitated healing for others. The dream messages were corroborated by subsequent medical diagnoses. The following case history describes a dream a therapist had about her client. It comes from a provocative collection of stories called *Dreams That Change Our Lives* (Hoss & Gongloff, 2017).

MOTHER MARY AND THE ORBS

By Carol Warner

I was seeing a client and her daughter, whom I will call Jennifer. Jennifer had been brutally beaten and sexually abused by a male relative who had been living with them. She had not disclosed this early on because he had repeatedly threatened to kill her mother and her. When, after many years, she did disclose, the man was arrested but then acquitted. Inexplicably, the judge blamed the mother.

Jennifer entered into a downward spiral. She ended up in a relationship that replicated her years of beatings; she got into drugs, ran away, worked at a strip club, and was raped again. Jennifer was emotionally unreachable, and her mom's grief was enormous.

After some time, her mom moved to another city to start a business, so we no longer met for sessions, but one day she called and said Jennifer had asked to return home. She said she was ready to start her life over and "face her past." Mother wisely insisted on therapy as a condition of Jennifer's return home. Jennifer said she only trusted me—and I lived three hours away!

Since Jennifer had lost her driver's license, her mother, in an extraordinary offer, agreed to take one day off her job weekly to drive Jennifer the six-hour round trip to my office to see me. In our first meeting, I asked Jennifer if she had received a gynecological exam. She had never had one. I strongly encouraged Jennifer to see a gynecologist for a thorough exam.

In our next meeting, Jennifer and her mom came together to my office, long-faced, with very sad news. A biopsy revealed several large spots of ovarian cancer, a cancer with a very poor prognosis.

Shocked, Jennifer went for a second opinion. This gynecologist said she could easily see three large spots of cancer on Jennifer's ovaries. The second biopsy also revealed cancer. The prognosis was terminal. Jennifer's estimated life span was now only six months. Mother and daughter were devastated.

Jennifer commented how "my life has been shit" and how ironic it was that now that she was making a fresh start, she would likely die. Her mother was heartbroken, and felt hopeless and helpless. I, too, was stunned and extremely saddened. I had a heartfelt connection with them.

That night I included Jennifer and her mom in my prayers. I asked God to help them. During the middle of the night, I had the following dream:

Mary, mother of Jesus, is descending from the sky. She is luminous, glowing, surrounded by the most beautiful ethereal blue light imaginable. As she floats down toward me, I see that she is dressed in a beautiful blue gown, perhaps with gold specks in it. She emanates an incredible aura of peace and love. As I watch Mary, her arms are outstretched, and three glowing globes of golden-white light issue forth from her hands. Somehow, I have the knowledge that each of the globes of light goes to one of the three cancerous spots on Jennifer's ovaries. I watch as each globe surrounds a spot completely and envelops it. As I watch this amazing sight, I awaken with absolute certainty that Jennifer is now totally healed of her cancer.

I experienced this absolute certainty both in the dream and upon wakening. As the day went on, I thought often about the dream. In my day consciousness, I was having doubts. I wondered whether to tell Jennifer the dream. I did not wish to give her false hope. I decided to tell her, while cautioning that I did not know what the dream meant. It seemed to me I had no right to keep this dream from Jennifer, since it was about a visitation from Mary to Jennifer.

When I spoke next with Jennifer, her eyes grew wide as I told her the dream. Despite my cautions, she said she knew it was true, that Mary healed her.

Jennifer went back to the same doctor who had told her the spots were visible. The doctor expressed disbelief that just one week later, there was now absolutely no trace of cancer. Two repeat biopsies verified that the cancer was gone. We were all thrilled and awed at what had happened. Fifteen years later, she is cancer-free.

It is not surprising that dreams can play a role in healing. The most vivid dreams occur in REM (rapid eye movement) sleep. In this state, our eyes are moving around rapidly, just as they might do while we're looking at things when we're awake.

The dominant brain wave frequency in the REM dreaming state is theta. Theta is also observed in the brains of healers at the height of the healing experience (Oschman, 2015). The EEG frequency window of healing corresponds with that of dreaming. In both dreams and healing, the brain is in a theta state. Brain and consciousness are sharing an experience, one measured in matter, the other in mind.

PRECOGNITION AND THE ARROW OF TIME

Another anomalous experience that has been extensively studied is precognition, the ability to sense events before they occur. While there are over 100 studies of precognition, a series of decisive experiments was carried out by Daryl Bem.

Bem used standard psychological tests, such as giving students a long list of words and asking them to remember as many as possible. Later, words were randomly selected from the list and given to the students to type out. Their recollection of the typed words was compared to their recall of those they weren't asked to type. They had significantly better recollection of words they were later asked to type.

Another experiment showed two curtains on a computer screen. In a series of 36 trials, students were told that an erotic image was behind one of the curtains and asked to guess which one it was. Chance would have dictated a 50 percent probability of success, but they scored 53.1 percent, significantly above chance.

Bem's meticulously designed and conducted studies took 10 years to complete and involved a large sample of over 1,000 participants. His results were echoed by an analysis of 101 studies of precognition spanning 75 years performed by Dean Radin of the Institute of Noetic Sciences (Radin, 2011). They were performed in 25 different laboratories located in various countries, including the United States, Italy, Spain, Holland, Austria, Sweden, England, Scotland, Iran, Japan, and Australia. The analysis showed that 84 percent of them reported statistically significant results.

Bem later replicated his initial work on an even larger scale (Bem, Tressoldi, Rabeyron, & Duggan, 2015). His studies produced a storm of criticism among skeptics and those who simply couldn't believe that precognition might exist. Human beings tend to stick firmly to their worldviews regardless of the findings of science.

Yet quantum physics does not require the arrow of time to move only in a forward direction. Many equations work both forward and backward. Einstein said, "The distinction between past, present, and future is only a stubbornly persistent illusion" (as cited in Calaprice, 2011).

ATHEISTS AREN'T EXEMPT

What we have come to call anomalous experiences, such as precognition and out-of-body states, are far from uncommon. In a poll of students at American, Chinese, and Japanese universities, many report anomalous experiences, while over 30 percent report having them frequently (McClenon, 1993). At least 59 percent had experienced déjà vu, and many described out-of-body experiences.

Being religious or believing in the supernatural was not a requirement for such experiences: atheists and agnostics had them too. The researchers analyzed whether believers were more prone to anomalous experiences and found that they were not. Even famed skeptic and editor of the *Skeptic* magazine, Michael Shermer, described an event that shook his belief system "to the core" (Shermer, 2014).

THE BROKEN RADIO THAT PLAYED LOVE MUSIC

June 25, 2014, was the wedding day of Michael Shermer and Jennifer Graf. She was from Cologne, Germany, and had been raised by her mother and grandfather Walter.

Three months before the wedding, Graf shipped her possessions to Shermer's home in California. Many of the boxes were damaged and several heirlooms lost. One that arrived intact was Walter's 1978 Philips radio, and when it was unpacked, Shermer inserted batteries and set out to "bring it back to life after decades of muteness."

His attentions were in vain. He even opened it up to see if there were any loose wires inside that he could solder, but the radio refused to emit even static.

On her wedding day, Graf was feeling lonely. Her beloved grandfather was not there to give her away. She and Shermer walked to the back of the house, where music was playing in the bedroom.

They looked at their computers and phones to locate the source of the music. They even opened the back door to see if was coming from a neighbor's house.

Then Graf opened the drawer of Shermer's desk to reveal her grandfather's radio. It was playing a love song. The couple sat in stunned silence, broken only by Graf's sobbing. Shermer's daughter also heard the music.

The following day, the radio fell silent, and has never worked since.

In the survey of anomalous experiences, even students in the hard sciences were disposed to them. Ethnic background didn't make a big difference; anomalous experiences were common in both white and black American students. As Jung observed, "Synchronicity is an ever-present reality for those who have eyes to see."

Jung witnessed a snake swallowing a fish on the shore of the lake at Bollingen and afterward had the image carved into a rock in his garden.

Jung continues to tickle us with synchronicity from beyond the grave. One of the most comprehensive texts on the subject is *Synchronicity: Nature and Psyche in an Interconnected Universe* by prominent Jung scholar Joseph Cambray (2009). David Rosen, editor of Cambray's book, shares a striking synchronicity related to working on the text:

"In my backyard there is a Japanese garden with a pond containing numerous koi. Shortly before Joseph Cambray arrived [to deliver the lectures that became the synchronicity book], a snake caught and swallowed a koi. When I saw figure 1 of 'Jung's carving of a snake swallowing a fish,' I wondered if this was an example of synchronicity. . . . I had not observed such an event before or after this occurrence (Cambray, 2009)."

WHAT CAN EXPLAIN SYNCHRONICITY?

That synchronicity happens is well established. *How* it happens is another question. What could possibly be coordinating processes in so many different dimensions of reality? How can a biological phenomenon such as the proliferation of cancer cells be linked to a state of consciousness such as a dream or premonition?

Cancer cells are matter. They are physical units inside living bodies. They grow and divide at a rapid pace, exempt from the signals that cause normal cells to self-destruct when they are old or damaged. Cancer cells lose the molecular bonds on their membranes that keep them in place, allowing them to detach from the surrounding tissue. They then migrate to distant parts of the body. In stage 3 and 4 cancers, rogue cells metastasize throughout the body. They are matter gone wild, molecular clusters on a path of self-destruction.

Dreams are pure mind. They are completely subjective, with a meaning unique to the dreamer. They are filled with images that engage our emotions and senses. They engage the full spectrum of our consciousness whenever we sleep. How can a subjective experience such as dreaming connect with an objective reality such as cell proliferation?

Synchronicity ties the subjective and objective together. It connects the immaterial world of mind and energy with the material world of matter and form. The worlds of mind and matter resonate together in the course of synchronous events.

RESONANCE IN SMALL AND LARGE SYSTEMS

There are many videos online showing pendulums coming into resonant coherence. There is a link at the end of this chapter for a video showing 64 metronomes being activated one after the other. At first, they all swing independently and randomly.

In the first image, 32 metronomes begin ticking independently. Within three minutes, resonance produces coherence and all the metronomes tick together.

Then, slowly but surely, a remarkable change occurs. Two of the pendulums begin to swing in synchrony. A short while later, a third one joins them. The fourth one comes into coherence quicker than the third. Within three minutes, the entire collection is swinging away together, precisely in sync.

This type of resonance was described in 1665 by Dutch physicist Christiaan Huygens. Eight years earlier, he had patented the pendulum clock. While recovering from an illness during which he had plenty of time to observe his surroundings, including the two pendulum clocks in his room, he noticed an odd phenomenon: regardless of the position in which the pendulums began, they would slowly entrain to swinging in unison.

Resonance is a property of all systems, from the very small to the infinitely large. At the atomic level, we find molecules with similar properties resonating together (Ho, 2008). At the cellular level, cells use resonance to communicate, propagate, and heal (Oschman, 2015).

Ascending the scale, we find resonance operating in organisms, from tiny ones such as viruses to large ones such as human beings. Scaling up even bigger, resonance is found at the level of the entire planet.

Getting still larger, we find resonance in "the music of the spheres," at the level of solar systems, galaxies, and the universe. From the infinitesimally small to the unimaginably large, resonance is the song sung by matter.

Not only do similar systems resonate together, they resonate with other systems as well. The very large can resonate with the very small. Our human bodies can be entrained by the resonance of Earth, picked up by the brain's pineal gland, 30 percent of whose molecules are metallic and hence magnetically sensitive (Oschman, 1997).

FIELD LINE RESONANCES

Our planet has an electromagnetic field of its own, just like a big magnet. It has a north and a south pole, and the lines of force generated by this enormous magnet radiate out hundreds of thousands of miles into space.

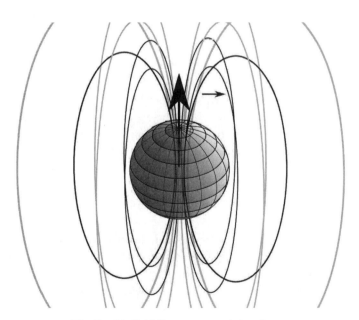

The Earth's field lines surround the planet.

Imagine these lines as strings on an instrument such as a violin. When you pluck a string, it resonates. In a similar way, the field lines of Earth resonate when they are plucked. As the solar wind sweeps by the planet at a speed of two million miles an hour (3 million km/h), it is constantly plucking those strings.

Several common "notes" are played on Earth's geomagnetic strings. Some of these notes play all the time, like a continuous chord, while others sound intermittently, like a string that is plucked occasionally. For this reason, field line resonances are divided into continuous and irregular pulsations (Jacobs, Kato, Matsushita, & Troitskaya, 1964; Anderson, Engebretson, Rounds, Zanetti, & Potemra, 1990).

One of the most important continuous geomagnetic pulsations that scientists measure is in the frequency window of 0.1 to 0.2 Hz. Another is in the range of 0.2 to 5 Hz. Irregular pulsations in the lowest frequency range are from 0.025 to 1 Hz.

The lowest of Earth's continuous geomagnetic frequencies, 0.1 Hz, is exactly the same frequency as the rhythm of the human heart when in coherence. If we practice a relaxation method like the Quick Coherence Technique developed by the HeartMath Institute, our heart begins to beat in coherence. In that state, our individual human heart is sounding the same note as the slowest of the frequencies of Earth's magnetic field (McCraty, 2017).

The 0.1 Hz frequency also happens to be the frequency of human cardiovascular systems. The same frequency is used by a variety of animals and even individual cells to communicate and entrain the systems that surround them, just like metronomes in synchronous alignment.

If you've ever held a guitar or violin on your lap while someone else was playing an instrument in the same room, you'll have felt the vibration that the music sets up. The strings and sound box of your instrument vibrate in harmony with the instrument being played nearby, even though no one is plucking the strings of the instrument you hold.

That's resonance. Resonance entrains objects tuned to similar frequencies even at a distance.

Certain of Earth's field line frequencies resonate with exactly the same frequencies that occur in the human brain and heart. As the planet plays its chords, our brains and bodies are humming along and possibly even using that constant music to regulate biological processes.

SCHUMANN RESONANCES

Have you ever blown air out of your mouth across the opening of a bottle? It makes a low-frequency whistling sound. Sound waves bounce back and forth between the sides of the bottle, traveling through the air inside. The pitch produced depends on the volume of the bottle.

A German physicist named Winfried Schumann used mathematics to postulate that a similar effect occurs on a global scale. In this case, the volume determining frequency is not that of a bottle but of the space between the surface of the planet and the edge of the ionosphere.

The ionosphere is a bubble of plasma that encircles Earth. One of the properties of plasma is that low-frequency magnetic waves bounce off it. Like a mirror, the inside of the plasma bubble reflects waves.

That is how radio works. A signal is sent up, it bounces off the ionosphere's mirror, and it is then captured at a distant location by a person with a receiver tuned to that frequency. When magnetic pulses are introduced into the cavity between the planet's surface and the top of the plasma bubble, some are dissipated while others aren't. Only resonant waves propagate consistently, like the whistle you hear when you blow across a bottle. These are the Schumann resonances.

Schumann resonances bounce off the plasma bubble surrounding the planet.

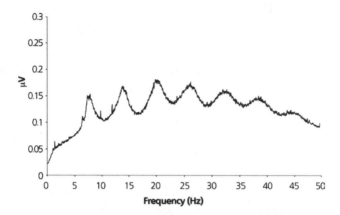

**Schumann resonance data recorded from sensor
site in Boulder Creek, California. Note that the
frequencies correspond to those of human brain waves.**

In 1960, long after Schumann predicted mathematically that such waves must exist, they were measured experimentally. The primary Schumann resonance is 7.83 Hz. Harmonics are resonant multiples of the original frequency, and Schumann's wave produces harmonics at 14.3, 20.8, 27.3, and 33.8 Hz.

These frequencies are also found in the waves originating in our brains as they process information: 7.83 Hz is in the theta band, in the exact same frequency window measured in brain waves during peak healing moments (Oschman, 2015; Bengston, 2010).

The next harmonic of the Schumann resonance, 14.3 Hz, is in the frequency range of low beta brain waves, typical of the housekeeping functions of the body. The third harmonic of the basic Schumann resonance, 27.3 Hz, is in the same frequency range our brains use when we're focused on a task and thinking hard. The harmonic of 33.8 Hz falls within the frequency range of gamma, the waves produced by our brains at moments of integration and insight.

It's striking that the primary resonance of Earth's plasma sheath as well as its harmonics fall into the same frequency windows as the primary human brain waves. Our mental states, generated by the fields our brains produce as they process information, resonate with the frequencies of the planet on which we live. When we increase a particular wave, such as the surge of theta that accompanies energy healing treatments, we increase our resonance with that planetary information signal. Planet and healer are entrained in an intense energetic union.

BODIES AND BRAINS ENTRAINED
BY EARTH'S FREQUENCIES

Dr. Franz Halberg of the University of Minnesota Medical School coined the term *circadian rhythms* to describe the body's daily cycles (Halberg, Tong, & Johnson, 1967). Until his death in his late 90s, he conducted research in his lab seven days a week. In 2017, research on the genetics of the body clock won the Nobel Prize in medicine.

Halberg believed that the reason that the delta through gamma frequencies are pervasive in our brains and our bodies is that we evolved on planet Earth, entrained in its frequencies. Studies conducted by his Halberg Chronobiology Center and by other researchers have demonstrated links between Earth's field lines and Schumann resonances and markers of human health (Selmaoui & Touitou, 2003; Brown & Czeisler, 1992).

Human emotions, behavior, health, and cognitive function are all affected by solar and geomagnetic fields (Halberg, Cornélissen, McCraty, Czaplicki, & Al-Abdulgader, 2011). Earth's field is hypothesized to be a "carrier of biologically relevant information that connects all living systems" (McCraty, 2015).

Rollin McCraty, director of research at HeartMath, says, "We're all like little cells in the bigger Earth brain—sharing information at a subtle, unseen level that exists between all living systems, not just humans, but animals, trees, and so on" (McCraty, 2015). Information is flowing throughout this living matrix of the "Earth brain," synchronizing the activity of all life-forms, down to the level of cells and molecules.

The human brain is attuned to electromagnetic fields.

The human brain, an electromagnetic organ pulsing with neural connections and impulses, is exquisitely sensitive to electromagnetic fields: "Changes in the Earth's magnetic field have been shown to affect human heart rhythms and have been associated with the following: changes in brain and nervous-system activity; athletic performance, memory and other tasks; synthesis of nutrients in plants and algae; the number of reported traffic violations and accidents; mortality from heart attacks and strokes; and incidence of depression and suicide" (HeartMath Institute, n.d.).

Given the pervasiveness of these frequencies on a planetary scale and the fact that we evolved in them over the course of hundreds of millions of years, it's hardly surprising that our bodies, minds, hearts, and cells are entrained to them.

HOW ANOMALOUS EVENTS ASSEMBLE INTO SYNCHRONICITIES

A team of Dutch researchers performed a systematic review of 175 studies of biological fields. They suggest that coherent quantum frequencies regulate the processes of living organisms. They found that electromagnetic fields influence neural systems and consciousness and may represent "a universal electromagnetic principle, that underlies the observed life-sustaining effects and also may have been instrumental in the creation of biological order in first life and quantum consciousness" (Geesink & Meijer, 2016).

Parallels between quantum mechanics, biological systems, and consciousness were drawn by many of the movement's founders, including Albert Einstein, Erwin Schrödinger, Werner Heisenberg, Wolfgang Pauli, Niels Bohr, and Eugene Wigner. These pioneers perceived energy, space, time, consciousness, and matter not as separate entities but instead as interacting in a vast synchronistic dance.

Geesink and Meijer found that the human electromagnetic (EM) field "communicates bi-directionally with a global EM field, via wave resonance [and] comprises a universal consciousness, that experiences the sensations, perceptions, thoughts and emotions of every conscious being in the universe" (2016, p. 106). Connect the dots between all the scientific findings and synchronicity suddenly doesn't seem mysterious at all.

Frequencies may function as the resonators that entrain micro and macro events in synchronicity. Though we can't see these frequencies, they permeate both mind and matter. We swim in them as a fish swims in water, unaware of the existence of the fundamental fields that shape consciousness and everything in the material world.

I believe that the intercommunication between these levels of reality provides a plausible scientific explanation for synchronicity. Multidirectional intercommunication throughout the emosphere, psychosphere, and magnetosphere allows information to pass rapidly throughout all levels of reality, those of both mind and matter. Fields link us continuously, even if we are unaware of their existence. That linking is how all the unlikely components of anomalous events are able to assemble into synchronicities.

THE BOY WHO FLEW FOR Peace

The 1980s were a time of huge international tension. The United States and the Soviet Union glared at each other across a vast arsenal of nuclear weapons. If either fired first, the result would be mutually assured destruction, which bears the appropriate acronym of MAD.

The two empires fought proxy wars in Asia and Africa. Their European allies (NATO for the United States and the Warsaw Pact for the USSR) lived tensely together. Some states were split in two, such as East and West Germany. If the Cold War turned hot, they would be the front lines.

Any incident had the potential to set off the powder keg, and the leaders of the two countries maintained a hotline from one capital to the other to head off disaster.

In 1983, a South Korean airliner, flight KAL 007, was shot down by a Soviet MiG fighter. All 269 passengers on board were killed.

Ronald Reagan was the U.S. president at the time. The Soviet Union was in flux as two hardline presidents, Yuri Andropov and Konstantin Chernenko, died in office. The youngest man to hold the job, Mikhail Gorbachev, was installed in 1985.

In Reykjavik, Iceland, in 1986, Regan and Gorbachev met in a summit. Their goal was to reduce the number of nuclear warheads each possessed. At the last minute, the talks collapsed.

A teenager in West Germany named Matthias Rust was following the negotiations closely "because if there was a conflict, we all knew we would be the first to be hit" (Dowling, 2017). Just 18 years old, Rust had been taking flying lessons, learning to fly the venerable Cessna 172. The aircraft had been designed in the early 1950s, using pre–World War II technology such as an air-cooled engine and wings above the fuselage.

Deeply affected by the failure of the peace talks, Rust hatched a plan to build a metaphorical "bridge of peace" between East and West. He booked his Cessna for three weeks, not telling anyone what he planned to do. He took off from Uetersen Airfield, near Hamburg, on May 13, 1989.

He flew to Iceland, where he prepared for the next leg of his journey. He visited Hofdi House, where the failed talks between Gorbachev and Reagan had taken place, and later reported, "It gave me motivation to continue."

He then flew to Norway and on to Finland, the country closest to the Soviet Union, and the one with the most porous border.

Before he took off again, on May 28, he filed a flight plan with the authorities, telling them he was bound for Stockholm, Sweden. But after leaving the air traffic control zone, he turned off the plane's transponder, the device that allows any plane to be tracked, and headed for the Soviet border.

Soon he was spotted by Soviet radar in Latvia. As he approached the border, he entered the air above the most sophisticated air defense system in the world. Missiles and fighter planes stood ready to repel attackers 24/7. The fleet included extraordinary craft such as the MiG-25, which can fly nearly three times the speed of sound, and the largest fighter plane ever constructed, the Tu-128, which fires missiles 17 feet (5m) in length and is the size of a World War II bomber.

The day of Rust's flight happened to be Border Guards Day, a national holiday on which most of the men guarding the border were off on vacation.

Nonetheless, radar detected Rust's plane and directed MiG fighters in close to identify it visually, since its transponder was not responding. They reported that it was a Yak-12, a Soviet training plane that looked similar to the Cessna 172. Clouds then concealed Rust's whereabouts, but the next wave of MiGs spotted him again. One pilot flew in close, then reported to headquarters that the aircraft was actually a West German intruder.

Upstream in the command chain, that pilot's superiors were convinced that the pilot was mistaken: how could a West German plane have made it all the way across the border?

Because of the negative publicity from the attack on KAL 007, Soviet commanders were cautious. They wanted the order to shoot Rust down to come from the highest level, in this case Defense Minister Sergei Sokolov.

Other ground commanders still believed that Rust's plane was a Yak-12, and near Moscow he entered an air control zone in which Yak-12 pilots were training in their aircraft.

To navigate, Rust had only simple maps he'd purchased off the shelf in West Germany. Late in the day, he identified Moscow. After seeing the onion domes of Saint Basil's Cathedral, he scouted for a safe place to land.

He found a clear runway on the eight-lane Bolshoy Moskvoretsky Bridge, connecting Red Square with the districts to the south of the city. Normally, the bridge was a tramway route, but that morning one section of cables had been removed for maintenance. There was just enough room for him to land.

After Rust touched down, Muscovites surrounded the plane. Everyone was friendly. A British doctor, Robin Stott, had just decided to get some fresh air and walked out of his hotel for an evening stroll, taking his video camera with him. Hearing the noise of the plane's engine, he pointed his lens at the sky in time to video the landing and its aftermath. KGB agents arrived but stood around talking to each other, unsure of what to do next.

They eventually detained Rust and took his Cessna to a nearby airport for examination; no one could believe that a teenager had just penetrated the air defense system of the mighty Soviet Union. After nearly a year in jail, Rust was returned to West Germany.

The military confusion that facilitated Rust's flight gave Soviet leader Mikhail Gorbachev an excuse to get rid of hardliners who opposed his reforms, including Sokolov. Gorbachev's reforms, such as the economic revolution called perestroika and the opening of society called glasnost, gained momentum. The Soviet Union collapsed three years later.

Rust's Cessna is now on display in a German museum.

Matthias Rust could never have known what the full effects of his action on the consciousness of other people would be. He just followed his vision and made a personal statement so dramatic that the world took notice. He never flew a plane again.

Rust's story is an example of how the personal and the global come together. Global stories are often dramatized by personal stories. Like the man standing in front of the tank during the Tiananmen Square protests in China the same year as Rust's flight, one individual's actions often highlight momentous events. Huge information fields involving millions of people can come into focus through the lens of a single person.

Notice how many synchronicities had to be in place for Rust's trip:

- Most of the men normally guarding the Soviet border were off duty, celebrating Border Guards Day.

- The first Soviet fighters to spot Rust's plane took it for a Soviet training plane.

- Low clouds obscured most of Rust's journey.

- The Soviet pilot who correctly identified his plane as a West German aircraft was not believed by his superiors.

- The Soviet authorities were cautious because of the huge negative publicity recently generated by shooting down a South Korean civilian airliner.

- The defense minister, Sergei Sokolov, was unavailable because he was attending a high-level meeting.

- Ground controllers assumed Rust's was a Soviet training plane whose transponder had malfunctioned.

- Rust accidentally flew over a training range where similar aircraft were practicing.

- The tram cables spanning the bridge on which Rust landed had been removed that morning for maintenance.

- Peace activist Dr. Robin Stott had decided to walk outside to get some fresh air just before Rust landed.

- Stott happened to take his video camera with him.

- Stott heard the sound of the plane's engine and was able to train his camera in the right direction just before it landed.

At pivotal moments in history, synchronicities can abound. Many highly unlikely events stack up, one on top of the other, which nudge the future in a certain direction. As we read the accounts of great social, political, or military changes, they're often laced with huge numbers of improbable synchronous events.

Though we perceive the world as stable, it is actually changing rapidly. Of those companies that were in the Fortune 500 list of the world's largest companies in 1950, only 10 percent appear there today. Even the best-organized and most information-rich organizations in the world aren't usually able to maintain their positions as the cosmos swirls and changes around them.

SPONTANEOUS SYNCHRONIZED ORDER IN NATURE

Cornell University mathematician Steven Strogatz says that a tendency toward spontaneous synchronized order is a primary characteristic of nature, from the subatomic scale to the most distant reaches of the universe (Strogatz, 2012). From inanimate molecules to complex living systems, spontaneously arising order may be a fundamental tendency in all of nature.

Strogatz points to examples such as the synchronization of schools of fish, flocks of birds, and the internal clocks of the human body. He even shows how waves of movement propagate through flocks of birds and schools of fish. There's no leader, master plan, or supercomputer coordinating these millions of intricate movements. Organization arises spontaneously from within the flock, herd, or cell, synchronized by nature.

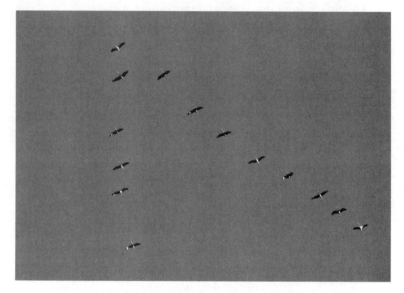

Flocks of birds move in spontaneous synchrony.

Strogatz notes that spontaneous order arises at every level of the universe, from the smallest to the largest. It extends from superconductivity in elements to the nuclei of individual cells, to the flashing tails of fireflies, to the tissue that signals our hearts to pump, to traffic patterns, and to the farthest edges of the cosmos. The clock genes in the human body entrain with the diurnal cycle of the planet and even with the bodies of other human beings nearby.

Spontaneously arising order is also evident in the functioning of our cells. Each cell undergoes some 100,000 metabolic processes per second. Groups of millions of cells, sometimes in distant regions of the body, coordinate their activities. They use fields to do this.

Fields are a far more efficient method of coordination than chemical or mechanical signaling. If you are walking up to your locked car and want to unlock the door, you can insert the key in the lock and turn it. That's the mechanical approach to getting the job done. But it's much faster to press the button on your remote and use the field approach instead.

Our bodies communicate through fields in a similar way.

Strogatz uses many examples of resonance drawn from human behavior, including fads, mobs, and stock trading. One of his examples is the unexpected saga of London's Millennium Bridge.

The Millennium Bridge

The Millennium Bridge over the Thames River was intended to be a marvel. Opened on June 10, 2000, it was the first crossing to be constructed over the venerable river in a century.

The bridge's designers extolled it as "a pure expression of engineering structure," comparing its sleek lines to a blade of light. Engineers called it "an absolute statement of our capabilities at the beginning of the 21st century." At the opening ceremony, thousands of enthusiastic spectators swarmed all over the bridge.

Then something unexpected happened. The bridge began to sway slightly from side to side.

The wobble became more pronounced. Pedestrians didn't know what to do. They began to walk with wide strides to counteract the bridge's motion. Like entrained pendulums, they stepped to the left and then to the right.

The wobble increased, and the people scrambled off the bridge as soon as they could. It was closed immediately.

Why did the bridge fail, after the brightest design and engineering minds in the world had done their utmost to make it perfect?

When they first felt the first tiny sway, the pedestrians on the bridge adjusted their behavior to compensate. This unintentionally brought them into resonance. They began to walk together, exacerbating the movement of the bridge.

In an example of what scientists call emergent systems, there was no plan or leader guiding the Millennium Bridge wobble. It took place as an emergent response to resonance.

The bridge's problems were soon solved by installing dampers to cushion the bridge's movement, and the bridge reopened. But the event remains an example of how resonance can trigger unexpected consequences in complex systems.

The Millennium Bridge.

JUNG, EMERGENT PROPERTIES, AND SELF-ORGANIZATION

One of the first scientists to study self-organizing systems was Nobel laureate Ilya Prigogine. He explored ways in which order can emerge out of apparent chaos. His work contributed to the establishment of the Santa Fe Institute, which studies complexity and chaos theory.

One branch of the Santa Fe Institute's work examines systems that have self-organizing features, also known as emergent properties. They are termed *emergent* because they don't originate within the systems themselves but are stimulated by forces in the external environment. In the book *Emergence: The Connected Lives of Ants, Brains, Cities, and Software,* researcher Stephen Johnson writes, "In these systems, agents residing on one scale start producing behavior that lies one scale above them. . . . The movement from low-level rules to higher-level sophistication is what we call emergence" (Johnson, 2002, p. 18).

There are five characteristics of emergent structures (Corning, 2002). They are:

- Radical novelty: they spontaneously develop new features.

- Coherence: they maintain themselves over a period of time.

- Higher holistic order: they exhibit the property of wholeness.

- Dynamic process: they evolve.

- Apparent: they can be perceived.

One example of emergence is the evolution of distinct neighborhoods in large cities. Like-minded people get together and organize the businesses, social clubs, schools, and religious institutions most relevant to them. The process is organic and bottom-up, resisting the top-down control systems of zoning laws and planning commissions.

These types of "emergent intelligence" organize without consciousness and in response to changing stimuli. Assimilating and responding to information, emergent systems adapt and self-organize into new patterns. Physicist Doyne Farmer said: "It's not magic, but it feels like magic" (Corning, 2002).

A Nova Science television program on emergence uses the example of an ant colony: "Ants are not mental giants, and they can't see the big picture. Yet out of their simple behaviors—follow the strongest pheromone trail, say, or save the queen at all costs when under attack—arises a classic example of emergence: the ant colony. The colony exhibits an extraordinary ability to explore and exploit its surroundings. It is aware of and reacts to food sources, floods, enemies, and other phenomena, over a substantial piece of ground. Each ant dies after days or months, but the colony survives for years, becoming more stable and organized over time" (Nova, 2007).

Ants provide an example of emergent behavior.

Jung's concept of synchronicity represents an application of the idea of self-organizing systems to psychology. Synchronicity incorporates emergent properties of personal experience, brain, fields, and environment (Hogenson, 2004). Jungian researcher Joseph Cambray says that "Emergent phenomena, especially in the human realm, can appear to ordinary, individual consciousness as meaningful, if inexplicable, coincidences. . . . Synchronicities can be explored as a form of emergence of the Self and have a central role in individuation or psychological maturation" (Cambray, 2002).

Members of the Santa Fe Institute argue that self-organizing systems may be as important in evolution as natural selection: "Life and its evolution have always depended on the mutual embrace of spontaneous order and [natural] selection's crafting of that order" (Kaufman, 1993).

In 1959, Jung wrote a letter to his friend Erich Neumann, observing, "In this chaos of chance, synchronistic phenomena were probably at work, operating both with and against the known laws of nature to produce, in archetypal moments, syntheses which appear to us miraculous. . . . This presupposes not only an all-pervading, latent meaning which can be recognized by consciousness, but during that preconscious time, a psychological process with which a physical event meaningfully coincides" (Jung, 1975).

Cambray concludes that "Meaningful coincidences are psychological analogues that spur the evolution of both the personal and the collective psyche, organizing images and experiences into previously unimagined forms" (Cambray, 2009).

Synchronicities are part of how we grow and evolve as people, as societies, and as a species.

September 11 Synchronicities

Like most people, I remember where I was on September 11, 2001. I was living in a cottage in Guerneville, California, with my two young children. My ex-wife, knowing I don't watch TV, phoned and told me to turn it on. Horrified, I watched as the second jet crashed into the towers and they collapsed. Along with millions of others, I felt as though the world as we knew it had come crashing down too.

Estimates of those killed in the towers exceeded 6,000. That number was arrived at by reporters who calculated how many people would normally be working in the two towers at 8:46 A.M., when the first jet hit. The official estimate from the New York Police Department almost two weeks later, after the dust had settled, was 6,659 dead.

However, as the months went by and the story kept unfolding, the numbers kept dropping. The final death toll was 2,753. That's less than half the initial estimate. What explains such a huge disparity between the numbers?

Part of the answer is that the evacuation efforts were largely successful. Most of those who worked below the impact points managed to escape. Yet there were many more who were supposed to be at their desks above the impact points that morning but were not. Where were they?

According to a careful analysis of this question by *USA Today*, "Many companies did head counts after the attack. . . . Counts from more than 50 floors indicate the buildings were barely half full" (Cauchon, 2001). Where were the missing people?

There are many reasons why people weren't in the World Trade Center that morning. When talking to survivors, some describe having been warned by intuition, dreams, or precognition. Others experienced unexpected delays due to crowded trains or family problems.

Rebeka Javanshir-Wong is one of our energy psychology practitioners. Her husband is one of those who was absent when the planes hit. Here's how she tells the story:

"My husband, who worked at Tower 2, also had an out-of-routine day when he went to work later than usual and was on his way to the office when the planes crashed.

"His company had invited two of their young employees from Malaysia to come for training. They had arrived the night before, and since it was their first time in the U.S., my husband, along with other colleagues, had taken them out to dinner and helped them settle in an apartment the company had rented for them near the Twin Towers. Knowing that these two had big jet lag, they all decided to start work a little later the next morning and give them time to rest."

The delay saved all their lives.

Celebrities often make their schedules public, so their comings and goings are easy to track. There are many stories of well-known people who weren't at the World Trade Center that morning as scheduled. Among them are these:

- Sarah Ferguson, Duchess of York, was scheduled to be on the 101st floor for a charity event. She ran late and was still doing an interview in the NBC television studio at 8:46 A.M. when the first plane hit.

- With a group of friends, actor Mark Wahlberg was due to fly on American Airlines flight 11. They changed their plans and, at the last minute, chartered their own plane.

- Actor and producer Seth McFarlane was also booked on American Airlines flight 11. His travel agent gave him the wrong takeoff time and he arrived at the gate after it had closed.

- Actress Julie Stoffer had a fight with her boyfriend and missed the same plane.

- Michael Lomonaco, head chef of the restaurant at the top of the towers, Windows on the World, was heading up to his office half an hour before the first plane hit. He had a noon appointment to have his glasses fixed at the optometry store in the lobby, and he decided to go back down again to see if they could fit him in early. The half-hour delay saved his life.

- The developer who held the lease on the World Trade Center, Larry Silverstein, had a dermatology appointment that morning. He had decided to skip the appointment and go to work, but his wife persuaded him to visit the doctor instead.

- Olympic swimmer Ian Thorpe was out for a jog that he planned to end at the observation deck on the World Trade Center. He realized he'd forgotten his camera and returned to his hotel room. When he turned on his TV, he saw the north tower on fire.

- Corporate director Jim Pierce was due to attend a meeting on the 105th floor of the south tower. But by the evening before, the organizers realized that there were too many people in the group to fit in the meeting room, so they switched the venue to the Millennium Hotel across the street. Pierce later learned that 11 of the 12 people who'd been in the original conference room died in the tragedy.

- Lara Lundstrom was rollerblading down a street in lower Manhattan when she realized that the driver of a silver Mercedes SUV stopped at a light was actress Gwyneth Paltrow. Lara stopped to talk for a few minutes. This resulted in her missing her train to the south tower and her absence in her office on the 77th floor.

Sometimes small synchronicities—the forgotten camera, jet lag, the chance meeting with an actress, the eyeglasses repair—have a disproportionate effect on our lives. Big events like 9/11 seem to spawn many synchronicities—or perhaps we just notice them when they're dramatized by a global event.

SYNCHRONICITY IS SCIENCE

Synchronicity, which seems to be so mysterious when we first encounter it, turns out to have solid scientific explanations behind it. Spontaneous order arises in living systems, from the atom to the galaxy.

Our brains are attuned to the same frequencies as the planet on which we live. In altered states of consciousness such as dreams, trance, meditation, hypnosis, and epiphany, we enjoy access to a nonlocal information field that extends far beyond our local senses.

Fields permeate the cosmos, including our planet and our bodies. When resonance is established between macro and micro, such as between a Schumann and brain wave frequency, the macro and the micro can fire in coherence. Bodies entrain to fields, and two-way intercommunication occurs between them. Information flows between all levels of reality, including both mind and matter, permeating the emosphere, psychosphere, and magnetosphere. That's how all the seemingly mysterious parts of synchronous events are able to come together.

The psychosphere.

The great scientists of the early quantum age in the first part of the 20th century were aware of the great fields in which our local human minds operate. Einstein said: "Everyone who is seriously involved in the pursuit of science becomes convinced that some spirit is manifest in the laws of the universe, one that is vastly superior to that of man" (as cited in Calaprice, 2002).

Max Planck, a founding father of quantum physics, said: "All matter originates and exists only by virtue of a force which brings the particles of an atom to vibration and holds this most minute solar system of the atom together. . . . We must assume behind this force the existence of a conscious and intelligent Mind. This Mind is the matrix of all matter" (as translated in Braden, 2008). The deeper scientists delve into the workings of matter, from subatomic particles to the enormous scale of galaxies, the more they notice the synchronous coordination present in the whole.

BRAIN AS TRANSDUCER OF UNIVERSAL FIELD

The view of skeptics and materialists is that the mind is *in* the brain: "Mind is what brain does." Mind is believed to be an epiphenomenon of brain, a consequence of brain. As brains evolved, becoming larger and more complex, goes this theory, they gave rise to mind. When enough neurons fire together, they produce this artifact called consciousness. Sir Francis Crick, the co-discoverer of the double helix structure of DNA, summed up this proposition with the words: "A person's mental activities are entirely due to the behavior of nerve cells, glial cells, and the atoms, ions, and molecules that make up and influence them" (Crick & Clark, 1994).

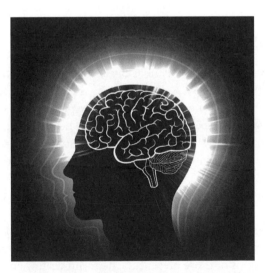

The theory that the complex brain gives rise to
consciousness is unsupported by science.

There is no proof supporting the theory that consciousness lives inside the brain. A review by the Cambridge Center for Behavioral Studies notes, "Brain-centered theories of consciousness seem to face insuperable difficulties" (Tonneau, 2004). Despite the lack of evidence at present, however, materialist skeptics assure us that science will eventually fill in the gaps.

Nobel Prize–winning neurophysiologist Sir John Eccles called this "promissory materialism." He regarded it as "a superstition without a rational foundation . . . a religious belief held by dogmatic materialists . . . who confuse their religion with their science. It has all the features of a messianic prophecy" (as cited in Dossey, 2009).

There is, on the other hand, plenty of evidence that consciousness exists outside the brain. The mind does not behave as though it is confined to the brain, and there are many experiences of nonlocal consciousness that cannot be explained by a local mind trapped inside the confines of the human skull.

CONSCIOUSNESS BEYOND THE BORDERS OF THE SENSES

In altered states, our consciousness is able to go far beyond the borders of our senses and obtain information that comes from far beyond our local minds. In the past few decades, dozens of scientific papers studying altered states such as near-death experiences (NDEs) and out-of-body experiences (OBEs) have been published (Facco & Agrillo, 2012). While people who are medically dead can experience NDEs, in 37 percent of NDE cases, the person was not close to death (Clark, 2012).

These experiences have some characteristics in common. People having OBEs and NDEs report a sense of having actually left their physical body. They have full use of their senses, which are often greatly enhanced. They have freedom of movement and a sense of well-being. They can see things that would normally not be visible to them, such as objects on top of cabinets in the operating room or on the rooftops of nearby buildings, or family members not present in the room. They may know the thoughts of those present in the room with them or report precise details of conversations that occurred when they were under general anesthesia.

Having an out-of-body or near-death experience changes people.

Once people come back from an OBE or NDE, they are changed. They are not afraid of death, and they believe in a loving and compassionate universe. They have a sense of certainty about what they perceived.

Dr. Mario Beauregard, author of *Brain Wars,* believes that the function of the brain is to act as a filter. The consciousness of each person exists in this all-knowing state of infinite perception, which is characteristic of OBEs and NDEs. That infinite mind is then filtered by the brain into a manageable experience in order to exist in a physical body (Beauregard, 2012).

Dr. Kenneth Ring and Sharon Cooper performed a study examining the NDEs of people who have been blind from birth (Ring & Cooper, 2008). The results offer particularly compelling evidence of the existence of consciousness beyond the body, because these people have never been able to see. Unlike sighted people having NDEs who are describing objects and people they have witnessed before, blind people have no such frame of reference.

The Blind Woman Who Saw

During their NDEs, blind people have been able to describe details of objects they have never seen. One such experiencer was a 45-year-old woman named Vicki Umipeg, whose optic nerve had been destroyed at birth by an overdose of oxygen. She reported, "I don't see anything, not even in my dreams, not even black."

After a car accident, she was taken to the emergency room. She found her awareness floating above her body: "I found myself in the hospital looking down at what was happening, frightened since I had never 'seen' before." Vicki was disoriented and had difficulty recognizing that the body she was staring down at was hers: "I knew that it was mine because I wasn't in mine."

Vicki was later able to describe the doctor and nurse who were working on her unconscious body, as well as their words: "They kept saying, 'We can't bring her back.' I felt very detached from my body and couldn't understand why they were upset. I went up through the ceiling hearing beautiful sounds of wind chimes. Where I was I could see trees, birds, and people but all made of light. I was overwhelmed because I couldn't imagine what light was like. It was like a place where all knowledge was. I was then sent back and into my body in excruciating pain."

Vicki was also able to describe details of objects she had never been able to see, such as the patterns on her rings: "I think I was wearing the plain gold band on my right ring finger and my father's wedding ring next to it. But my wedding ring I definitely saw. . . . That was the one I noticed the most because it's most unusual. It has orange blossoms on the corners of it." Vicki later said that this experience was "the only time I could ever relate to seeing and to what light was, because I experienced it."

Thirteen hundred years ago, the Tibetan Book of the Dead described states of nonlocal consciousness. In a place suspended between life and death called the bardo state, the bardo body is able to perceive the world without the mediation of the senses. It can move through solid objects and travel to any place in the cosmos instantly, just like the consciousness described by people having OBEs and NDEs.

Indian Vedic philosophy holds that the great nonlocal universal consciousness is reflected in each of us. The analogy is that of buckets of water in which the sun is reflected. Though there are many different buckets, it is the same sun reflecting in all of them.

Shamans were believed to move between the local and nonlocal world.

Only in recent times has the belief arisen that nonlocal consciousness is "paranormal" or "psychic" and that study of these phenomena is off-limits to conventional science. For most of the thousands of years of human history, the holy person or shaman was a special member of the tribe. Such people were believed to "travel between the worlds" of local awareness and nonlocal mind, bringing back wisdom and healing from realms beyond those of ordinary consciousness (Eliade, 1964).

Shamans were able to commune with animals and beings outside of local awareness and were often gifted with dreams and visions that conveyed meaning from the nonlocal universe. Only recently have altered states such as those experienced in dreams, mystical ecstasy, oneness with nature, NDEs, and OBEs come to be regarded as anything other than a normal part of human experience.

NDEs and OBEs can be transformative. John is a gay African American man with an advanced degree, but after being diagnosed with AIDS, he hit rock bottom. Then, while participating in a study of AIDS patients, he found himself transcending preoccupation with his own suffering and helping a drunk white man who was in distress. Right afterward, he had an OBE. Here's how he describes the experience (Church, 2013).

No One Has a Monopoly on God

"I felt like I was floating over my body, and I'll never forget this, as I was floating over my body, I looked down, it was like this shriveled-up prune, nothing but a prune, like an old dried skin. And my soul, my spirit was over my body. Everything was so separated. I was just feeling like I was in different dimensions, I felt it in my body like a gush of wind blows. I remember saying to God, 'God! I can't die now, because I haven't fulfilled my purpose,' and, just as I said that, the spirit and the body became one, it all collided, and I could feel this gush of wind and I was a whole person again.

"That was really a groundbreaking experience. Before becoming HIV-positive, my faith was so fear based. I always wanted to feel I belonged somewhere, that I fit in, or that I was loved. What helped me to overcome the fear of God and the fear of change was that I realized that no one had a monopoly on God. I was able to begin to replace a lot of destructive behavior with a sort of spiritual desire. I think also what changed [was] my desire to get close to God, to love myself, and to really embrace unconditional love."

The study of AIDS patients found that those who believed in a loving God or benevolent universe had much better health outcomes than those who believed in a punishing one (Ironson et al., 2011). It also found that a diagnosis was often followed by a crisis leading to a spiritual breakthrough.

IS THE MIND IN THE BRAIN?

The mind is not in the brain any more than the picture on your computer is inside the screen.

When you turn on your TV and watch *Comedy Central,* the show is not inside your screen. There is certainly a close correlation between your device and the show. If your screen has a crack in it, it won't display the show properly. That doesn't mean that the existence of *Comedy Central* is dependent on your screen. The show has an existence independent of your screen and its degree of functionality.

Many experts looking at the research on brain and mind have suggested that the brain functions in a similar way (Kelly, 2011; Dossey, 2013). It is a transducer of mind in the same way that your screen is a transducer of the signal that carries the show. Mind and consciousness are independent of the screen.

Research shows that consciousness is not located in the brain. Dr. Bruce Greyson, who performed a study of NDEs in a cardiac care unit, concludes, "No one physiological or psychological model by itself explains all the common features of NDE. A clear sensorium and complex perceptual processes during a period of apparent clinical death challenge the concept that consciousness is localized exclusively in the brain" (Greyson, 2003). Your consciousness extends far beyond your local self, and your brain is akin to the receiver that translates it into your everyday experience.

In ordinary waking states, consciousness is firmly anchored to local reality. When you're driving to work or watching your child's baseball game or walking your dog or filling out your tax returns, your mind is focused on local reality. What you perceive as "you" is driving the car, looking at the traffic, and noticing the surrounding vehicles. Nonlocal fields are still there, but your mind isn't tuned in to them.

In anomalous states, we're no longer bound by local reality.

During times of anomalous states, such as dreaming, trance, meditation, mystical ecstasy, or hypnosis, our consciousness is no longer tethered to local reality. We lose identification with our bodies and our local sense of self. Like souls in the bardo state, we can move instantly to distant parts of the universe, unconfined by the constraints of local reality.

Some anomalous states are unremarkable regular experiences, like our nightly dreams. Others are transcendent experiences, like the oneness with nature we might experience during a mindful moment deep in the woods or splashing our toes in the ocean. At such times, our sense of a local self falls away and we feel one with all that is. In a mystical state, the boundaries of local self dissolve, and we become one with the universe.

THE BRAIN AS BRIDGE BETWEEN LOCAL AND NONLOCAL REALITY

The brain is also capable of bridging local and nonlocal reality. As well as providing the biological anchor through which we participate in nonlocal mind, it is constantly processing information from our surroundings.

This information flow is a two-way street. If we're lost in a daydream, our consciousness far away from our body, and a car backfires outside our window, our attention is shocked immediately back into the present. If we're in the middle of a dream at night, traveling far beyond the limits of waking awareness, and we smell smoke, our brain alerts us to danger and brings us back to earth in a hurry.

Our brain takes the information from the outside world and conveys it to our mind.

The ability of the brain to engage with and interpret the outside world is key to our functioning as human beings. But if we devote all our attention to the outside world and the local thoughts that cycle through our brains, we can miss out on the ecstatic states available to us when we are connected to nonlocal mind. A human experience that is focused only on local awareness and phenomena is an impoverished one, partaking in only a tiny sliver of the consciousness available to it.

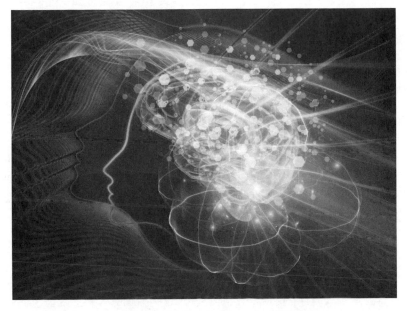

The brain bridges local and nonlocal reality.

Recent research has shown that large-scale fields exist around the planet and that they both entrain human consciousness and are affected by it (McCraty & Deyle, 2016). The human brain is a plausible biological mediator between these large-scale nonlocal fields and individual human awareness, the bridge between the local and the universal.

CHOOSING THE SIGNAL TO WHICH WE ATTUNE

We can choose the frequency to which we attune our minds. Like a streaming music service with millions of choices of stations, there are millions of competing nonlocal signals to choose from all the time.

Some of these signals are permutations of fear, while others are permutations of love. We can choose to attune the transceiver of our local mind with any one of the infinite varieties available.

We can choose magical experiences, orienting our awareness to them consciously. Rather than an occasional random fluke, they then become our default setting. We can decide to meditate when we wake up each morning, not leaving it up to chance whether or not we feel in tune with the cosmos that day. When we're stressed, we can tap, restoring equilibrium to our troubled emotions and maintaining our ability to connect with a larger perspective.

We can decide to go to our favorite spot in nature or listen to a piece of music that lifts us into a state of ecstasy. We can change the broadcast channel, turning off the news and tuning to the words and energy of an inspirational teacher instead. We can make a conscious decision to lift our attention from ordinary local reality to the sublime nonlocal signal of the universal mind.

By choosing these practices, we use our minds deliberately in order to induce transcendent states. Such states become not an inadvertent happy accident, but a lifestyle upgrade that we have deliberately installed.

The Bill on the Beach

In my dream, I am giving a speech. The auditorium is dark, but in the blackness and via live streaming, millions of people are listening intently. I'm using a PowerPoint presentation.

The next-to-last slide is one of a gateway. It has a big wooden post on either side. In the middle hangs a yellow sign with crenellation on top. It says, "The Happy Universe."

I tell the audience that every one of them deserves to live there. There's nothing stopping them. Well, almost nothing. I flip to my last slide.

It's a ticket that says, "Admit one."

I tell them that they have to pay for this ticket. The price of admission is their suffering. They can't get in if they hang on to even one atom of it. They have to give up absolutely every shred of suffering to purchase the ticket. Do that, and you're in.

The ticket only admits one person. You can't take your loved ones in there with you. They have to make the choice to buy a ticket themselves. Each person has to give up his or her suffering to get in, and you can't let go of it for someone else.

That's the end of the dream. I awake with the images embossed on my mind.

That was the dream I had the day I finished this book. Every part of the writing process was laced with synchronicities.

The previous New Year's Eve, my primary prayer for the year was that I be able to enter a deep meditative state quickly. Usually, it took me a while to shed all the mental chatter, and I wanted to be able to dive right in without spending so much time quieting my mind.

In a few weeks, this began to happen. I could invoke alignment quickly.

Two months later, taking a break from a conference at which I was speaking, I took a walk on the beach in San Diego. I was becoming obsessed with the idea of writing a book about the scientific evidence linking mind and matter. But I already had another book project half finished, too much other work, and no publisher. There were far more reasons not to proceed with the project than to go ahead.

It was a chilly winter's day, so my wife, Christine, had decided to stay in the car. I paced for a mile, wrestling with the book idea. I dodged children, dogs, and kites, all of which were out in force despite the cold weather. I could find no clarity, and I asked the universe for a clear sign.

I didn't receive any great epiphany, so I turned to walk back to the car. My eye caught something at the tide line. It was a $10 bill. There was no one around who it might belong to, and I picked it up.

The bill on the beach.

I got back in the car and showed it to Christine. Like any other bill, it said, "In God We Trust."

That seemed like an appropriate though unexceptional message. But why a $10 bill, rather than $1, $5, or $20?

Then the association hit me. In all my work, I use a rating scale from 0 to 10. If you believe something strongly, your belief is a 10 out of 10. The symbolism seemed to indicate that I could trust the universe to proceed with this project and it would be a 10 out of 10 grand slam.

A week later, the outline had written itself. Two weeks after that, I had a talk with Reid Tracy, the president of Hay House, who loved the idea. He preferred the title *Mind to Matter* to my alternative title *Thoughts to Things,* so the first option became the book title while *Thoughts to Things* became the title of my accompanying online course.

I wrote up a detailed proposal, and the day I mailed it in, a message arrived in my e-mail inbox from Mike Dooley, another Hay House author who sends daily messages to his subscribers. The subject line was "Thoughts become things and dreams come true." Another synchronicity.

I carved out several three-to-four-day blocks of time to write. Those days, I found myself wide awake at 4 A.M. I would spend an hour in meditation, getting my mind perfectly aligned, after which I would read and write obsessively for about 15 hours.

My friend David Feinstein gave me valuable feedback after I'd written the first three chapters. One morning after meditation, I had a strong urge to thank him. I decided to phone him later that morning. I hardly ever use my phone because I prefer e-mail, and I know he travels most of the year and rarely turns on his phone. So I knew I'd get his voicemail and be able to leave a warm message of appreciation.

I was surprised when, instead, David answered the phone. He told me he'd just returned the day before from a trip and turned on his cell phone a few minutes before I called. When the call came through, the phone displayed no caller ID, and he doesn't usually answer such calls. But he received an intuitive nudge to do so. Yet another synchronicity.

When I was writing this chapter on planetary-scale effects, I was struggling to understand the Schumann resonances. That month, I had also inadvertently double-booked myself to speak at two conferences the same weekend. One was in the Caribbean and the other at the opposite side of the continent in California. I had to split my time by speaking at one on Saturday, then flying back to California early Sunday morning to speak at the other.

Sunday afternoon, I was on a science panel at the second conference. Sitting next to me was HeartMath research director Rollin McCraty. He had just published a major paper on . . . you guessed it. Besides Schumann resonances, he also told me about field line resonances, which I had never even heard of before. They became a major part of the chapter. Synchronicities abounding!

Christine and I visited our friends Bob and Lynne Hoss in Arizona on the way to another conference. Bob is an expert on the neuroscience of dreaming. He had recently keynoted a conference and prepared a presentation on Carl Jung, the collective unconscious, and the double-slit experiments. His PowerPoint filled in crucial gaps in my knowledge. Synchronicity again!

On the same day, Jack Canfield, John Gray, and Rick Leskowitz all e-mailed me to say they'd endorse the book.

The June 12, 1982, peace rally.

When the publisher gave me the official publication date, June 12, a shiver ran up my spine. That date is highly significant for me. On June 12, 1982, I was in Central Park, New York, joining hundreds of thousands of people protesting against the nuclear standoff between the U.S. and the USSR. After the rally, Secretary of State George Schultz went on television to say that the rally would make absolutely no difference in U.S. policy.

A few months later, U.S. president Ronald Reagan made an astonishing U-turn. The most hawkish of presidents amazed the world by proposing the START (Strategic Arms Reduction Treaty) nuclear reduction talks. Every year, on the anniversary of June 12, I remember the day when, in a powerful collective act of group mind, we decided not to blow up the planet and ourselves along with it.

Finally, on the very last day I had available to complete the manuscript of this book, I visited a neighborhood grocery store for breakfast. Near the checkout stand, my eye was caught by the latest special from *Time* magazine, entitled "The Science of Emotions." I opened it to a random page, and saw the headline of an article on how synchronicity can be predictable and not simply a matter of chance. That piece led me to the last four studies I needed to complete the synchronicity chapter.

Each day, I begin with attunement. I know that if I begin resonating with the fields of fear and lack that are present in the psychosphere, they will absorb my attention. Instead, I deliberately align my mind with the highest possibilities for me and for the planet.

We can choose to attune to the fields of love, peace, and joy. Like selecting the stations on a radio dial, we can allow the instrument of our brain and body to play the melodies of beauty and wonder that resonate through the planetary field. When we align ourselves with these fields, they resonate through our worlds, connecting us synchronistically with the highest possibilities in our destiny.

ATTENTION BUILDS BRAINS

Research into the brains of people in elevated spiritual states tells us that they are processing information very differently from the way they function in ordinary consciousness. The ratio of delta, beta, alpha, theta, and gamma waves changes drastically as the brain functions in an entirely different way. When these patterns of neural firing are changed on a regular basis, they quickly begin to build new synaptic connections. The volume of the various parts of our brain begins to change as the matter of brain tissue reconfigures itself to match the mind of deliberate creation.

The brain then becomes more skilled at transducing these signals. With more neural connections to carry the information flow, the brain is better at picking signals up from the universal field. It's more attuned to signaling from the field, with a higher degree of the neural circuits that facilitate synchrony.

A study performed by researchers at the University of Zurich compared people who were making a choice about how generous to be. A sum of money was promised to 50 participants at the start of the experiment. Half committed to spending the money on themselves alone, and the other half committed to spending it on someone else. Both groups were then asked to make a series of decisions indicative of generous behavior.

The investigators used MRIs to measure brain activity during and after the decision-making process. They found that participants who behaved the most generously had the biggest changes in brain regions associated with happiness. The researchers were surprised that the mere intent to spend money on someone else, before the generous act occurred, was sufficient to trigger changes in neural patterns (Park et al., 2017).

**Of the choices available to us each moment,
where will we direct our awareness?**

Every moment, we're faced with choices about where to direct our consciousness. Will we focus on the agonizing suffering with which the media tries to trap our awareness? Or will we orient our attention to the eternal now? Will we get sucked into the petty dramas of the human condition or align our thoughts with the wisdom of universal mind? With each choice we make, we shape our brain. Choose consistently for months and years, and you literally create a brain in synchrony with nonlocal mind.

Sir John Eccles, who earned a Nobel Prize for his work on the brain's neural synapses, says that "We have to recognize that we are spiritual beings with souls existing in a spiritual world as well as material beings with bodies and brains existing in a material world" (Popper & Eccles, 2012). When we live as though we are spiritual beings with material bodies and orient our consciousness in that way each day, the matter we create with our minds is very different.

ENTRAINING SELF WITH SYNCHRONICITY

Does synchronicity just happen, or can we encourage it? Is it a phenomenon that appears randomly by chance or can we step into a reality in which synchronicity is common?

Rather than being just an occasional accident, synchronicity, I've found, is a state that can be cultivated. We can deliberately entrain our local minds to the nonlocal consciousness of the universe in which the spontaneous coordination of nature is ever present. With practice, living synchronously and in harmony with the unfolding patterns of the universe becomes our minds' default setting.

Since I've started writing those big S's into my journal whenever synchronicities happen, they seem to be happening more often. Because I'm observing them, I'm attuned to them. As we do when practicing any new skill, I'm building the neural pathways that carry that type of information. I'm using the observer effect consciously, collapsing the possibility wave into the probabilities that I desire.

That doesn't mean that I can magically create anything I want like a magician pulling a rabbit out of a hat. It's a process of nudging reality consistently rather than manifesting something out of nothing immediately. It's *using* the principles of nature rather than defying them.

For instance, I've wanted to learn some French to use during my frequent trips to that country. Collapsing the possibility wave doesn't mean that I can instantly speak French. I still need to buy the online course, practice my pronunciation, and learn the vocabulary.

Ordinary things then happen that support my intent. A friend mentions a book that's available. It contains stickers with French words that you place on those items in your house. Seeing the objects and French words together every day builds your vocabulary quickly.

French language stickies adorn common objects in my house.

Next, I start to notice correspondences between Spanish words I already know and French words I don't know. I meet a Frenchman at a farmer's market and exchange a few words of French. Another friend tells me you can turn on French subtitles when you watch movies or watch them dubbed in French with English subtitles. My wife and I occasionally have dinner with our tablets next to us, with a translation window open, and practice having a simple French conversation. And on and on. Once I decide to learn French, the whole universe appears to conspire to support my goal.

THOUGHT BY THOUGHT AND
NEURON BY NEURON

You cultivate synchronicity with consistently held thought. Perhaps you're making supper, and you discover that you're missing white pepper, which is essential to the recipe. The nearest convenience store is two miles away. You get in your car, leave your driveway, make the turns required, park, go in the store, and find the aisle in which white pepper is kept. You don't just go from standing in your kitchen, needing white pepper, to standing in the spice aisle. There are many steps along the way. That's the way consistently held thoughts produce things.

Researchers at New York University found that romance-minded students who believed they would get a date were significantly more likely to do so. Golfers who were told that they were playing with a lucky ball scored better during putting practice. In games of chance, optimists win more prizes than pessimists. People who see a silver lining around dark clouds, using their minds to positively reframe negative events, deactivate the amygdala, the midbrain structure that processes fear. According to psychologist Richard Wiseman, these people "expect the best outcomes, and these expectations become self-fulfilling prophecies" (Rockwood, 2017). Best-selling author Tim Ferriss says, "The most fulfilled and effective people I know—world-famous creatives, billionaires, thought leaders, and more—look at their life's journey as perhaps 25 percent *finding* themselves and 75 percent *creating* themselves" (Ferriss, 2017).

Over the course of 15 years, a team led by Dr. Robert Gramling of the University of Rochester surveyed 2,816 adults between the ages of 35 and 75. His study was aimed at identifying those at risk for heart disease. The results showed that beliefs made a huge difference in their health.

Those who believed they were at low risk of heart disease had only a third the incidence of strokes and heart attacks. The effect held even after controlling for variables such as cholesterol level, smoking, high blood pressure, family history, and other risk factors (Gramling et al., 2008). The belief in—and fear of—heart problems was associated with contracting cardiovascular disease.

That's the way mind becomes matter. Thought by thought, we're engaging neural pathways. When you have a belief about your heart, and you practice that belief in your mind year after year, you're building new neurons, neuron by neuron. It's not that you have a single negative thought about heart disease and drop dead instantly. It's not that you have a single positive thought and find yourself healed forever—just the way you don't desire white pepper and find yourself instantly in the grocery store. There are steps in between, as beliefs are rehearsed and thoughts become things and neurons shape biology. Hold a thought consistently, and you create the biological and environmental conditions that draw that thing to you.

THOUGHT FIELDS AND THE COLLECTIVE UNCONSCIOUS

In my live workshops, I've noticed that generally people seem to be effortless masters of one aspect of life. We work with five life areas:

- Work (including career and retirement)
- Love (including all close relationships)
- Money
- Health (including weight, diet, and exercise)
- Spirituality

Typically, people have no problem at all with at least one of these areas. Some, for instance, are career masters, enjoying fast-track success from their teenage years. Others effortlessly maintain a deep and abiding spiritual practice, woven into the fabric of their lives. Some, like my wife, automatically create great marriages and wonderful relationships with family and children.

One of my friends, Phil Town, is a money master. He's one of the most successful hedge fund managers in the business. He's written two best-selling books on taking charge of your own money. Money is his medium, and he talks, thinks, and acts effortlessly in this sphere of influence.

Another of my friends, Andrew Vidich, is a spiritual master. He has meditated every day of his life since his teen years. He spends over an hour in meditation every morning, and kindness and joy sparkle out of his eyes and his being. He is in the energy field of spirituality, and people feel transformed in his presence without a word being spoken. When you read his books, *Light upon Light* and *Love Is a Secret,* you share the energy field he inhabits, and you feel uplifted.

While we may be effortless masters of one of the five life areas, we may struggle with another. A friend of mine who started a hugely successful personal growth company in the late 1980s became a multi-millionaire in his 20s. He's healthy and has enjoyed all the trappings of success. Yet after two glasses of wine at a mastermind group meeting, he confided in me how desperately unhappy he was in his love life. "I just got divorced from my third wife," he said disconsolately. "I had to sell my executive jet to get the money to pay her off. I understand why she divorced me . . . I'm a jerk, and I've screwed up every relationship in my life." Being a master in one life area is no guarantee of success in another.

One of the pioneers in the use of acupressure for healing was a clinical psychologist named Roger Callahan. He developed a method called thought field therapy. The term *thought field* is striking. Callahan believed that we have habitual patterns of consciousness, which he called thought fields. When we participate in a thought field, we inhabit the energy of that field, and we perceive the material world through the lens of that field.

Thought fields can also be large scale, akin to Jung's collective unconscious. Jung believed that most of our behavior is driven by the unconscious. The part of the mind we're aware of is like the tip of an iceberg protruding from the top of the sea. We think that's all there is. In reality, our behavior is being shaped by the collective thought fields below the surface, even though we're not conscious of them.

The collective unconscious is like an iceberg. We're only aware of the tip, our conscious thought processes above the surface. Below is the collective unconscious, driving behavior.

Types of energy in the collective unconscious can form thought fields. These can be simple and innocuous, like the thought field associated with the hobby of quilting. I once attended a workshop at a big conference center that was hosting several other groups. One of these was a quilting convention.

I didn't know a thing about quilts when I walked in the door. So I sat at a table with the quilters for some of the meals. Sucked into their thought field, resonating with their enthusiasm, quilting seemed like the most fascinating activity in the world.

Those who have mastery in one of the five life areas inhabit that particular thought field. Get two investors together and they begin sharing their investing insights as they resonate together. Put two meditators together and they reinforce the thought field of meditation as they interact.

Other thought fields are not so benevolent. Spend time with drug addicts or alcoholics and you can sense the thought fields holding their habits in place. People with similar patterns resonate together. That's why it is impossible for addicts to get and stay clean if they keep the company of other addicts. They are used to resonating with that thought field, and it sucks them in when they are close.

When you are in a fearful state of mind, fear breeds fear. The thought field of fear seeks out external stimuli to be afraid of. The fearful mind precipitates fearful probabilities out of the infinite potentials in the possibility wave. You might believe that the problems are "out there" in your environment, caused by other people, corporations, the government, or random events. In reality, you are inhabiting a thought field that shapes the material space around you. Mind can produce matter in negative as well as positive ways. In the Bible, the ancient philosopher Job laments: "What I feared has come upon me."

EMBODYING THE FIELDS OF MASTERY

When you're in a meditation workshop with Andrew Vidich, meditation seems easy. In his thought field, sharing in his unwavering attunement with the field of spiritual experience, similar frequencies are activated in you. Those frequencies resonate with similar frequencies in Andrew's local field and, through him, the same frequencies in the nonlocal field. While connected in powerful resonance patterns with the field produced by meditation, you participate in that energy.

I've had a similar experience in money workshops with Phil Town. While you're in the field of money expertise Phil generates, his explanations seem clear and simple. You have breakthroughs in your understanding of stocks and financial reports as you align your consciousness with Phil's field. In a room with 200 people all entrained to the same money frequency, you condition your mind and brain in resonance.

**It's easy to meditate when resonating with
the local field of a meditation group.**

After you leave the meditation workshop or money seminar, the concepts soon become fuzzy. You start to forget what you learned and the state you attained, unless you practice. When you rehearse attunement with that thought field by reading books, watching videos, and learning more, you maintain your resonance with the field. Soon you've built the neural pathways and brain states that are characteristic of that thought field. You've moved from touching the field to embodying the field. You're on your way to mastery.

When we use our minds in this way, we condition matter. When we make a conscious choice to attain mastery in a field, we activate resonance with all the components of that field. Some may be local to us right where we are. Others may be nonlocal, distant in time or space.

Our intent, filling our consciousness, opens the doors to synchronicity. Opportunities and connections appear seemingly out of the blue. Yet they are generated by our participation in that particular thought field.

As an author and trainer, I'm fortunate to spend personal time with many transformational leaders. Individually, they generate inspiring energy fields. When they're together, the effect is enhanced. Being with them conditions my thinking and my energy as we come into resonance. Surrounding yourself with uplifting people is one of the best things you can do for both mental and physical health.

The following story, told by one of those leaders, is a remarkable story of manifestation. Who hasn't dreamed of manifesting a million dollars? This type of aspiration might seem beyond the pale of possibility. Yet as the German philosopher Goethe exclaimed (1887):

> What you can do, or dream you can, begin it,
> Boldness has genius, power, and magic in it.

Manifesting a Million Dollars

By Raymond Aaron

I lead transformational retreats, and in one exercise at the start of each event, we ask people to define what they'd most like to manifest during the course of the workshop.

As we went around the group, people chose the usual goals, like sleeping through the night, a revelation about which career path to choose, or having no conflicts with their spouse during the event.

But one man said he wanted a million dollars. He had started a company with a new technology to harvest stem cells, at the leading edge of health research. His goal was to have the financial freedom to pursue his dreams.

I didn't comment out loud, but I thought, *Wow, that's a huge goal.*

When the turn came for the next participant, he decided to copy the man who'd just spoken. He said he wanted a million dollars too!

I groaned inside. Two men who both want a million dollars to manifest during the retreat! It seemed impossible.

Three days later, the two men were bursting with excitement, and shared their news with the group. The second man's father was an investment banker. He'd told his father about the stem cell company, set up a meeting with the first man, and his father had become incredibly excited by the potential of the startup company. He'd told the first man that he'd be able to raise $100 million for him. Not $1 million, $100 million!

"And I get a one percent finder's fee!" said the second man. "That's a million dollars!"

ATTUNING YOUR MIND TO THE HIGHEST POSSIBLE STATE

Synchronicity is much more than meets the eye. It seems like a series of events that mysteriously line up to produce a significant result.

In reality, synchronicity represents the coordination of all life, from the most distant nonlocal reaches of space to the most intimate local environment of our thoughts. All are synchronized by resonant fields, and as we make choices with our minds, we set up resonance patterns that extend to infinity.

Our thoughts are profoundly creative. Once we realize this, we direct our thoughts consciously. We do what it takes to attune the functioning of our minds with the most elevated possibilities. We use our creative power deliberately. Goethe said, "We all have certain electric and magnetic powers within us and ourselves exercise an attractive and repelling force" (as cited in Jung, 1952). Understanding the creative power of our thoughts empowers us to use them wisely and deliberately, attuning to the thought fields of love, kindness, and creativity.

When I wake up in the morning, my first priority is attunement. My mind is swirling and my attention scattered, often focusing on the problems and negative aspects of the day ahead. Fragments of bad dreams and disturbing images I've seen on TV pop in and out at random.

If I were to start my day that way, I would bring that swirling, negative, scattered thought field to my material reality. I would condition my material world with the energy of that dysfunctional field.

So the first thing I do is attune my thoughts to the highest possible state. I tap away my worry and stress, and sit calmly in meditation. I know what my body feels like when I'm in that state of attunement to the infinite, with my brain producing high amplitudes of alpha, theta, and delta waves, and get in touch with that frequency. Once I'm attuned, I bask in that state for a long time. My thoughts escape from the swirl of confusion in which I woke up.

I feel happiness and optimism surging up within me like the exuberance of spring. I celebrate that wonderful feeling and tap again to anchor it in mind and body. If there's a patch of grass nearby, I walk outside, stand barefoot in the dew, and ground myself in Earth's frequencies. I might listen to an inspirational audio to give my thoughts direction. If I'm home, I look at my vision board and affirm my goals. I write in my journal, recording positive intentions for the life journey ahead. I fill my mind with gratitude for the blessings of my life. I savor the anticipation of the synchronicities that will appear to delight me in the hours ahead.

Then, centered and inspired, I walk into my day.

Making attunement the first priority each day conditions your local field.

Do this for just one month, every day, and your life will start to change. Use your mind deliberately, and matter will change. You will call synchronicity to you. Whether your challenges are with money, health, love, work, or spirituality, you'll find that you quickly move to a new level of mastery when you begin using your mind for conscious creation. Attune to those energy fields, and matter follows right along. Synchronicities line up all around you, and you live a life attuned to the music of the spheres.

Sometimes, right in the middle of an ordinary day, the beauty of life hits me like a cloudburst. I stop in my tracks, overwhelmed, tearful, too stunned to be able to take it all in. I stop what I'm doing and allow the feeling to expand. I open my heart big enough to stretch around the full extent of my blessings.

I relish those moments, savoring them as I expand my sense of self to accommodate the full measure of life's beauty and perfection. A life lived in conscious synchrony with the universe is a life well lived.

PUTTING THESE IDEAS INTO PRACTICE

Activities to practice this week:

- As you practice EcoMeditation morning and evening, hold the intention that you align your life with synchronicity.

- Notice emergence when it appears in your personal world. You might observe this in:

    Colonies of insects
    Flocks of birds
    Schools of fish
    The flow of traffic in cities

- In your journal, write down three or more big synchronous events that have happened in your life.

- Also in your journal, make a brief note of any experiences of emergence you've witnessed in the past few days.

The Extended Play version of this chapter includes:

- Video and full report of Mathias Rust's flight

- How emergence permeates our daily life

- Metronome entrainment videos

- "Hawaii Aloha" sung by IZ, on YouTube

- The extraordinary healing story of concentration camp survivor Jack Schwarz

- Ten famous people who eluded death on 9/11

To access the Extended Play version, visit:
MindToMatter.club/Chapter6

CHAPTER 7

Thinking from
Beyond Local Mind

Muir Woods National Monument is one of the loveliest places in California. It is named after conservationist John Muir. When he was 11 years old, his family emigrated from Scotland to the United States. He became an avid outdoorsman, with a wanderlust that took him all over the continent. Just before his 30th birthday, he walked from Indianapolis to the Gulf of Mexico, a distance of a thousand miles.

Muir eventually settled in California, writing an influential series of articles called Studies in the Sierra. He published 10 books expounding his philosophy of naturalism. His 1901 book *Our National Parks* brought him to the attention of president Theodore Roosevelt, who made a trip to Yosemite Valley to visit Muir in 1903. Muir's life became a tribute to connection with nature.

The forest in the park itself is primeval. Coast redwoods are the tallest living beings on the planet, reaching heights of over 100 yards or meters. The oldest trees alive were saplings when Jesus walked the earth 2,000 years ago, while some alive today were 1,000 years old when Columbus sailed the Atlantic. Fossilized examples show that the species has been around for over 200 million years.

The giant redwoods carry a powerful presence.

The land on which Muir Woods is located was purchased in 1905 by conservationists William and Elizabeth Kent. Believing the place was sacred, they wanted to protect the giant redwoods from loggers. The Kents were forced to take out a bank loan to acquire the property. Elizabeth was nervous about their financial exposure, but William responded, "If we lost all the money we have and saved these trees, it would be worthwhile, wouldn't it?" In 1908, President Theodore Roosevelt proclaimed the land the Muir Woods National Monument.

In the historic spring following World War II, delegates from all the primary nations of the world met in San Francisco to draft the charter of the United Nations. Just before he was due to open the conference, President Franklin D. Roosevelt died. On May 19, 1945, to honor him, the delegates held a ceremony in Muir Woods' Cathedral Grove. Today, around a million people a year visit Muir Woods to gape in wonder at trees that have been around longer than recorded human history.

WHEN THE UNIVERSE SIGNALS A U-TURN

One afternoon on the way to visit a friend, Christine and I drove past Muir Woods—accidentally. We'd missed a turn at an intersection a mile away.

It was the Memorial Day holiday weekend, the official start of summer in the United States. There were thousands of people at the park. Traffic was backed up before and after the entrance. All the parking lots were full to overflowing, and visitors were parked along the side of the road more than a mile away. Pedestrians were walking along both sides of the narrow road in a steady stream of coming and going.

We talked about how much we would like to visit Muir Woods but that we'd wait for a time when it wasn't so crowded.

We enjoyed our evening with our friends and decided to spend the night in their spare room. We left the following morning, heading for home. Suddenly, Christine exclaimed, "We're so close to Muir Woods, why don't we go there now?" We made a quick U-turn and drove back to the park.

It was 7:45 A.M., and the parking lot was almost empty. We walked down the path toward Cathedral Grove, the heart of the forest. We drank in the beauty of the trees, the air, and the sounds of birds, squirrels, and the stream. Christine said, "Let's treat this as a walking meditation." We walked in silence.

We walked for more than a mile, all around the most popular loop in Cathedral Grove. It took an hour. Frequently, we stopped in awe to gaze up at the grandeur of the trees.

The redwood trunks draw the eye upward.

We didn't see a single person anywhere along the way. On the return journey, we headed for the park entrance, our souls deeply nourished, feeling profoundly connected with nature, one with the great universal field.

When we got back to our starting point in the parking lot, the morning's visitors were streaming into the park. Four tour buses had arrived, disgorging hundreds of people. The crush of humanity at the entrance was so thick that we had to elbow our way out.

Yet we'd been able to enjoy the forest, all to ourselves, basking in the sacred space of nature, between the two invasions. Just following our bliss, with no fixed plan, going with the flow, we had our wish to enjoy Muir Woods without the crowds—on the most crowded weekend of the year.

BEING IN THE FLOW OF NONLOCAL MIND

Alignment with the universal flow unlocks alignment with all the synchrony, grace, beauty, and wisdom of the universe. As you, an individual human being, a local mind, move into alignment with the great nonlocal mind—the mind behind all mind, the mind that gives rise to all consciousness—as you merge and become one with that mind, your mind, your individual local mind, is no longer functioning as an isolated, separate, lonely fragment, cut off from the whole by the illusion of separateness.

Instead, the flow of nonlocal mind is now in you, and you are in the flow. You are now no longer local consciousness. You are now universal consciousness. You have stepped from the position of that which is acted on to the perspective of that which acts.

Horizons of creativity open up to you. Vistas of possibility flood your awareness. You know yourself to be one with universal wisdom, with universal power, with universal intelligence, with universal love. From that place in consciousness, you live a life of wisdom, intelligence, and love. You no longer ask for love, need love, or crave love, because you are love. You no longer pray for wisdom, because you are wisdom. You no longer seek inner peace, because your very nature is peace. Standing in that place, you have access to all the wisdom, peace, and love in the universe.

This is the transcendent state that has been experienced and described by mystics throughout the ages. It is the state of flow that elite athletes experience at times of peak performance. It is the state into which artists enter when they create their most inspired work. It is the state children naturally inhabit when they lose themselves in play.

It is the state we're meant to live our lives in all the time. It's been perceived as a special, occasional exception to the grind of daily life. Yet it's actually meant to be the way we start and end each day. Each day is meant to flow in an unfolding of synchronous possibilities.

When I meet people in my workshops and they tell the stories of their lives, I'm moved by their suffering. Yet I'm also struck by the way this suffering accumulates as they move through life. They weren't born suffering. As toddlers, they knew how to laugh, love, and play. They then have negative experiences and gradually move from the spontaneously joyful childhood state to the worried, diminished, stressed adult state.

PUTTING FLOW INTO PRACTICE

How can we reverse the process? That may be the most important question of our lives. We can learn to be proactive, doing those things in consciousness and in practice that bring us back into synchrony with the universe. We can learn to release our suffering and learn to play again.

We can rehearse the states of consciousness that we knew as children and turn our adult lives into a joyful playground of possibility.

The way to put this into practice is simple.

When you wake up every morning, simply align your consciousness with the highest possible frequency of which you are capable. Sit quietly, read the words that inspire you the most, and enter a contemplative state. Before you begin your day, before you begin to think or create, align yourself. Align yourself to the highest possible vibrational frequency that you know. Align yourself with the most elevated energy field of which you are conscious.

The first conscious act of the day is to align with the nonlocal universal field.

Use this gift called consciousness to constantly align yourself to that highest possible energy field at the start of every day. As you do this, you will feel a shift in your body. You will feel a physical sense of shifting to a new plane, of moving into an altered state.

The physical sensation of being aligned with the universal field, one with nonlocal mind, is quite different from the physical experience generated by the illusion of being a separate local mind cut off from the love, the wisdom, the brilliance, the elevated perspective of the great nonlocal intelligence.

Then, in this space you create for yourself every morning, at one with the universe, the thoughts you think will be different. The actions you take will be different. The aspirations you have will be completely different. The expectations you hold will change. The assumptions you make will be nothing like the assumptions made in a state of isolated local mind. The worldview from which you see life and creation will be expansive. The possibility fields you perceive will be infinite. Your very sense of self, who you are as a human being, will shift completely.

LIVING IN ATTUNEMENT WITH THE UNIVERSAL FIELD

A *you* living in attunement with the universal field has an entirely different sense of self than a *you* living as a self isolated in local mind. Perceiving yourself as one with this synchronized universe, you move into your day with a sense of equanimity, power, peace, joy, love, and exuberance. You align with creative genius, and you shape the world outside of yourself based on a sense of high vision drawn from the reality field of that universal mind.

Suddenly, you are no longer an isolated individual bumping into this or that problem or challenge. Instead, you are part of an orchestra of synchronized movement. One with the universe, you are one with everyone else who is one with the universe. One with the universe, you are one with every force and phenomenon in nature that is also one with the universe. One with the universe, you dance to the tune of the natural harmonics of creation.

When we're in resonance with the universal field, we're in synchrony with everyone else who is resonating with the field.

THE RESONANT SYMPHONY OF ALL MIND

When you align with the universe, your individual mind is automatically synchronized with every other mind that is also synchronized with the universe, and the only minds with whom you are out of tune are those who are themselves out of tune with the universe.

You love them, you bless them, and by your attunement, you invite them to attunement as well. You cannot help those you love by moving out of attunement and into the place of non-attunement in which they live. You can only help them by being vibrantly attuned to universal self. You are then a beacon of invitation, welcoming them to the possibility of joining you in the dance of attunement.

If they do join you, they are naturally and effortlessly attuned with you, and if they choose otherwise, you bless them on their path. You need not persuade them or induce them. They will join the dance whenever they are ready. Let them go; you will find that there are thousands of people, millions of people, billions of people, ready to dance with you in attunement with life.

This is the universe's wish for you: That you find and remain in this attunement. That you start your day calibrating yourself to the universal field. That you start each day by dropping the illusion that you are a struggling local entity and by accepting the reality that you are one with all that is. That is what the universe most wants for you.

RELINQUISHING THE ILLUSION OF LOCALITY

The universe knows that once you let go of the illusion that you are an isolated, local entity and embrace the reality that you are one with universal mind, suddenly you are part of the flow. Synchronously, you dance with every being who is part of the universal dance. Your life flows easily and organically. All of the friction, all of the static that you experience at the level of local mind falls away. Your life is easy, happy, and naturally creative. You feel one with this universal reality of oneness. The kind of life you create for yourself from that perspective is radically different from the life you create from the perspective of an isolated local self.

We move through our lives in conscious alignment with the universal field.

Making this choice day after day, this choice to align every morning, sends your life off on a completely new trajectory, one rich in possibilities. One suffused with joy. One bursting with vitality and enthusiasm.

You are at a crossroads in this moment. A choice point. The point at which you either embrace the reality of yourself as one with a benevolent universe or continue in the illusion that you are not. You face this choice this moment. You face this choice every moment.

THE MOST IMPORTANT CHOICE YOU'LL EVER MAKE

This is the most important choice you will make in your entire life: aligned or not aligned. And as you make that choice now, as you align in the next moment, and the next and the next, and the next day, the next week, the next month, as you make that choice an infinite number of times, it becomes not a choice but a fact. It becomes not a decision but a way of life. As it becomes a way of life, as it becomes the default setting for your consciousness, you begin to build the neural wiring that anchors it in matter. The matter of your body becomes the vehicle not for your local mind but for nonlocal mind.

Nonlocal mind, driving the neural circuits of your brain and body, creates a new brain and body. It builds cells. Regenerates DNA. Creates a field of connection. Generates coherence in your thoughts, words, and deeds. Opens possibilities in your sphere of influence. Co-creates with you at the level of your material reality.

The material reality you create when one with the universal mind is completely different from the material reality you create when cut off from universal mind. You think these thoughts in alignment with universal mind and they become things in alignment with universal mind. The matter of your body is shifted and changed. The matter of your material reality is shifted and changed. And after moment after moment after moment of alignment, you live in an entirely different material reality from the one you would have created had you remained locked in the prison of local mind and local self.

What will we create together in this unified field? Let's find out!

PUTTING THESE IDEAS INTO PRACTICE

Activities to practice this week:

- Take a walk in nature and practice walking slowly. Feel each footfall.

- Walk or stand barefoot on sand or wet grass for a few minutes each day.

- During your EcoMeditation practice morning and evening, consciously tune your local self to nonlocal mind.

- One day, after meditating, in your journal, draw an illustration of your local self and nonlocal reality. You don't have to be a great artist—just a simple line drawing is fine.

- Ask nonlocal mind, *What is your highest vision for me?* and write whatever pops into your head down in your journal.

The Extended Play version of this chapter includes:

- Video of fields of the human heart

- Instruction for how to ground and center yourself in Earth's fields

- Researcher Stephan Schwartz on anomalous experiences and quantum consciousness

To access the Extended Play version, visit:
MindToMatter.club/Chapter7

AFTERWORD

Where Mind Takes Us Next

I'm privileged to live among awesome creators. You and I are creating the world around us by our thoughts in this very moment. And in every moment.

We are members of a community of artists, painting our world into existence moment by moment. The visions we see in our mind's eye translate themselves, thought by thought, into the concrete reality of material form all around us. As we choose our thoughts, we are in fact choosing our material reality, whether we are consciously aware of it or not.

What sort of world will we create in the coming moments, days, months, years, and decades?

I'm convinced it will be a world of peace, of compassion, of beauty, of opportunity, of wisdom. In the past centuries, we've practiced creating survival, fear, anger, war, resentment, competition, shame, guilt, rivalry, and other forms of strife. As a species, we've had thousands of generations to experience the material circumstances that result from that type of thinking.

We have seen the suffering it produces. Now, I believe, we are ready for a new experience. We are ready to paint a new world. As we realize our ability to choose that world, we begin to select thoughts, feelings, experiences, and beliefs that facilitate its creation.

When we first make the discovery that we create with our minds, we produce our first small deliberate creations. Like a baby taking its first steps, we're tentative and uncertain.

But if you've ever watched a child learn to walk, you know that this hesitancy quickly gives way to exuberant confidence. Now free to explore the world, the child strides about enthusiastically. She goes places she has never been able to go before. Her circle of influence expands ever wider, as she ventures farther and farther from her point of origin. She quickly adjusts her mind to the new reality and assumes a degree of mobility and freedom she never knew before she took the first step.

That's us today. As a species, we have just begun to scratch the surface of our power. We have no idea yet what we are capable of. We've hardly taken even our very first step. We are only just beginning to realize what we might accomplish.

While the future is unknown, shrouded in mystery, we can look back and see clearly what has happened in the past. We see the two world wars of the 20th century, and the even bloodier conflicts of the 19th century and earlier times. We see the ignorance, poverty, starvation, injustice, and cruelty in which our species has been bred for millennia. While a millennium of progress in science and philosophy has given us the first glimmers of enlightenment, human existence has been driven by the stark requirements of survival for most of our history.

As a species, we've been there, done that, and bought the T-shirt. Now it's time for more. When we didn't know that our thoughts created our reality, we assumed that all the suffering in which we lived was a fixed and objective reality.

Now we know better. We have begun to understand the immense potential of our minds to create reality. We understand the leverage we possess over both the microscopic and the macroscopic levels of form. On the microscopic scale, we understand that our thoughts are shaping the anatomy and physiology of our cells at every moment, calling molecules into and out of existence, like a medieval alchemist's fantasy.

On the macroscopic level, our thoughts combine with those of the rest of our species to create the broad sweep of history. The history we create once we understand our power is very different from the history we created when we labored blindly under the illusion that reality was composed of random events that simply happened to us.

As conscious creators, we choose differently. When our survival needs push us to think angry and bitter thoughts, born out of the illusion of scarcity and competition, we choose not to think them. Not thinking them, we join with the millions of other people making similar choices. We find ourselves drawn into the reality fields of that new community. Multiplying the resonance of those shared fields, we shift the direction of society.

When you choose not to think that negative thought, and you replace it with a positive one instead, you aren't just shifting your own reality. You're shifting reality for the whole human species. You're adding to the sum of kindness and compassion in the world. You're reinforcing that new reality field. You're one of millions of people adding their positive energy to the new reality. You're helping transform it into an irresistible force that turns the tide of history.

While the forces of misery—people driven by survival and ignorant of the fact that they were creating the same dark world that they feared—may have been running the show for millennia, today is different. We understand our power. We make different choices. We use our power to shape first our own personal reality and then, collectively, the reality of the planet.

Having experimented with fearful thinking and its consequences, I believe that we have now embarked on a new experiment. Like that toddler taking her first steps, we are shining light into the darkness of our old conditioned thinking. That first beam of light, like that first step, gleams hesitantly. Yet the light feels good. The molecules we create in our bodies when we lighten our thinking feel good. The circumstances we create in the world around us when we enlighten our minds are infinitely more enjoyable. In a positive feedback loop, this reinforces our desire for more of the same.

Growing increasingly confident in our newfound power to create a positive world, we begin to think boldly. We imagine what a world without war, hunger, or poverty might look like. That subjective immaterial vision is the embryo of objective material reality.

This is the work we now do together. Joining with the millions of other people all over the world who have made the commitment to a positive future for themselves and humankind, we produce an irresistible field of love. The field of love we create opposes no one. We don't judge, condemn, or complain. We simply love.

As the field of love grows stronger, it bathes everything within its circumference. Out of this shared reality field of love, a new material reality is born. The material reality reflects the energy of the vibrational reality. In the new material reality, people act instinctively with kindness and compassion. Respect and altruism are the new normal in human relationships.

From the moment they are conceived, the children of the future grow up with these assumptions. Bathed in love from conception onward, children experience nothing else. They become vibrant creators, with their play, social interactions, and life expectations saturated with the certainty of love. Growing up in a world of love, they create love in their careers and families. The world changes to reflect their expectations.

I have no idea what our children, or our children's children, might create. I am certain that the types of creations produced by human beings saturated with love will be the products of happiness. I believe that their fresh creations will take science, technology, education, art, music, philosophy, religion, architecture, the environment, civilization, and society to places far beyond what our generation can conceive of.

That's the world I plan to live in for the rest of my life. That's the world I choose to create with my personal thoughts from the moment I open my eyes at the start of each new day. That's the world I invite you to join me in creating with your personal thoughts moment by moment. There is no better place to live.

Thank you for partnering with me in this journey of exploration. We have seen how the proposition that mind creates matter is not mere metaphysical speculation, but scientific fact. We have discovered that our minds create reality and become aware of the potential each of us has to create a benevolent reality using the astonishing power of thought. As we play together from this point on, I look forward to co-creating this delicious world of love and joy with you.

REFERENCES

CHAPTER 1

Baker, S. J. (1925). *Child hygiene.* New York: Harper.

Barinaga, M. (1998). New leads to brain neuron regeneration. *Science, 282*(5391), 1018–1019. doi:10.1126/science.282.5391.1018b.

Bengston, W. F. (2007). A method used to train skeptical volunteers to heal in an experimental setting. *The Journal of Alternative and Complementary Medicine, 13*(3), 329–332.

Bengston, W. F. (2010). *The energy cure: Unraveling the mystery of hands-on healing.* Boulder, CO: Sounds True.

Bengston, W. F., & Krinsley, D. (2000). The effect of the "laying on of hands" on transplanted breast cancer in mice. *Journal of Scientific Exploration, 14*(3), 353–364.

Chiesa, A., Calati, R., & Serretti, A. (2011). Does mindfulness training improve cognitive abilities? A systematic review of neuropsychological findings. *Clinical Psychology Review, 31*(3), 449–464.

Church, D. (Ed.). (2004). *The heart of healing.* Santa Rosa, CA: Elite Books.

Eden, D., & Feinstein, D. (2008). *Energy medicine: Balancing your body's energies for optimal health, joy, and vitality.* New York: Penguin.

Frey, A. H. (1993). Electromagnetic field interactions with biological systems. *FASEB Journal, 7*(2), 272–281.

Goleman, D., & Davidson, R. J. (2017). *Altered traits: Science reveals how meditation changes your mind, brain, and body.* New York: Penguin.

Hameroff, S., & Penrose, R. (1996). Orchestrated reduction of quantum coherence in brain microtubules: A model for consciousness. *Mathematics and Computers in Simulation, 40*(3–4), 453–480.

Hugo, V. (1877). *The history of a crime*. (T. H. Joyce & A. Locker, Trans.). New York: A. I. Burt.

Kandel, E. R. (1998). A new intellectual framework for psychiatry. *American Journal of Psychiatry, 155*(4), 457–469.

Kim, S., & Coulombe, P. A. (2010). Emerging role for the cytoskeleton as an organizer and regulator of translation. *Nature Reviews Molecular Cell Biology, 11*(1), 75–81.

King, C. R. (1993). *Children's health in America: A history*. New York: Bantam.

Lerner, L. J., Bianchi, A., & Dzelzkalns, M. (1966). Effect of hydroxyurea on growth of a transplantable mouse mammary adenocarcinoma. *Cancer Research, 26*(11), 2297–2300.

Malik, T. (2006, March 26). Fuel leak and fire led to falcon 1 rocket failure, SpaceX says. *Space.com*. Retrieved from www.space.com/2200-fuel-leak-fire-led-falcon-1-rocket-failure-spacex.html.

McTaggart, L. (2007). *The intention experiment: Using your thoughts to change your life and the world*. New York: Free Press.

Oschman, J. L. (2015). *Energy medicine: The scientific basis*. London: Elsevier Health Sciences.

Phillips, G. (2016). Meditation. *Catalyst*. Retrieved May 16, 2017, from www.abc.net.au/catalyst/stories/4477405.htm.

Radin, D., Schlitz, M., & Baur, C. (2015). Distant healing intention therapies: An overview of the scientific evidence. *Global Advances in Health and Medicine* 4(Suppl.):67–71. doi:10.7453/ gahmj.2015.012.suppl. Retrieved from http://deanradin.com/evidence/RadinDistantHealing2015.pdf.

Schlam, T. R., Wilson, N. L., Shoda, Y., Mischel, W., & Ayduk, O. (2013). Preschoolers' delay of gratification predicts their body mass 30 years later. *The Journal of Pediatrics, 162*(1), 90–93.

Schmidt, S., Schneider, R., Utts, J., & Walach, H. (2004). Distant intentionality and the feeling of being stared at: Two meta-analyses. *British Journal of Psychology, 95*(2), 235–247.

Schweizer, S., Grahn, J., Hampshire, A., Mobbs, D., & Dalgleish, T. (2013). Training the emotional brain: Improving affective control through emotional working memory training. *Journal of Neuroscience, 33*(12), 5301–5311.

Shealy, N., & Church, D. (2008). *Soul medicine: Awakening your inner blueprint for abundant health and energy*. Santa Rosa, CA: Energy Psychology Press.

Siegel, D. (2017). *Mind: A journey into the heart of being human*. New York: Norton.

Smith, L. (2004). Journey of a Pomo Indian medicine man. In D. Church (Ed.), *The heart of healing* (pp. 31–41). Santa Rosa, CA: Elite Books.

Stoll, G., & Müller, H. W. (1999). Nerve injury, axonal degeneration and neural regeneration: Basic insights. *Brain Pathology, 9*(2), 313–325.

Tang, Y. Y., Hölzel, B. K., & Posner, M. I. (2015). The neuroscience of mindfulness meditation. *Nature Reviews Neuroscience, 16*(4), 213–225.

CHAPTER 2

Bengston, W. (2010). *The energy cure: Unraveling the mystery of hands-on healing.* Boulder, CO: Sounds True.

Burr, H. S. (1973). *The fields of life: Our links with the universe.* New York: Ballantine.

Burr, H. S., & Mauro, A. (1949). Electrostatic fields of the sciatic nerve in the frog. *Yale Journal of Biology and Medicine, 21*(6), 455.

Church, D. (2013). *The EFT manual* (3rd ed.). Santa Rosa, CA: Energy Psychology Press.

Clarke, D., Whitney, H., Sutton, G., & Robert, D. (2013). Detection and learning of floral electric fields by bumblebees. *Science, 340*(6128), 66–69.

Czech-Damal, N. U., Liebschner, A., Miersch, L., Klauer, G., Hanke, F. D., Marshall, C., Dehnhardt, G., & Hanke, W. (2017). Electroreception in the Guiana dolphin (*sotalia guianensis*). *Proceedings of the Royal Society, Biological Sciences, 279*(1729), 663–668. doi:10.1098/rspb.2011.1127.

Grad, B. (1963). A telekinetic effect on plant growth. *International Journal of Parapsychology, 5*(2), 117–133.

Grad, B. (1967). The "laying on of hands": Implications for psychotherapy, gentling, and the placebo effect. *Journal of the American Society for Psychical Research, 61*(4), 286–305.

Kaplan, M. (2013, February 21). Bumblebees sense electric fields in flowers. *Nature News Online.* Retrieved from www.nature.com/news/bumblebees-sense-electric-fields-in-flowers-1.12480.

Kronn, Y. (2006, April 6). *Subtle energy and well-being.* Presentation at California State University, Chico, CA.

Kröplin, B., & Henschel, R. C. (2017). *Water and its memory: New astonishing results in water research.* Germany: GutesBuch Verlag.

Langman, L., & Burr, H. S. (1947). Electrometric studies in women with malignancy of cervix uteri. *Obstetrical and Gynecological Survey, 2*(5), 714.

Lu, Z. (1997). Laser raman observations on tap water, saline, glucose, and medemycine solutions under the influence of external qi. In L. Hui & D. Ming (Eds.), *Scientific qigong exploration* (pp. 325–337). Malvern, PA: Amber Leaf Press.

Radin, D., Hayssen, G., Emoto, M., & Kizu, T. (2006). Double-blind test of the effects of distant intention on water crystal formation. *Explore: The Journal of Science and Healing, 2*(5), 408–411.

Rao, M. L., Sedlmayr, S. R., Roy, R., & Kanzius, J. (2010). Polarized microwave and RF radiation effects on the structure and stability of liquid water. *Current Science, 98*(11), 1500–1504.

Schwartz, S. A., De Mattei, R. J., Brame, E. G., & Spottiswoode, S. J. P. (2015). Infrared spectra alteration in water proximate to the palms of therapeutic practitioners. *Explore: The Journal of Science and Healing, 11*(2), 143–155.

Scofield, A. M., & Hodges, R. D. (1991). Demonstration of a healing effect in the laboratory using a simple plant model. *Journal of the Society for Psychical Research, 57*(822), 321–343.

Vardalas, J. (2013, November 8). A history of the magnetic compass. Retrieved from http://theinstitute.ieee.org/tech-history/technology-history/a-history-of-the -magnetic-compass.

Wheatstone, C. (1833). On the figures obtained by strewing sand on vibrating surfaces, commonly called acoustic figures. *Philosophical Transactions of the Royal Society of London 123*, 593–633. Retrieved from http://archive.org/stream /philtrans07365800/07365800#page/n17/mode/2up.

Yan, X., Lu, F., Jiang, H., Wu, X., Cao, W., Xia, Z., . . . Zhu, R. (2002). Certain physical manifestation and effects of external qi of Yan Xin life science technology. *Journal of Scientific Exploration, 16*(3), 381–411.

CHAPTER 3

ADInstruments. (2010). *Electroencephalography.* Retrieved May 21, 2017, from web.as.uky.edu/Biology/_./Electroencephalography%20Student%20Protocol.doc

Barsade, S. G. (2002). The ripple effect: Emotional contagion and its influence on group behavior. *Administrative Science Quarterly, 47*(4), 644–675.

Bengston, W. (2010). *The energy cure: Unraveling the mystery of hands-on healing.* Boulder, CO: Sounds True.

Benor, D. J. (2004). *Consciousness, bioenergy, and healing: Self-healing and energy medicine for the 21st century* (Vol. 2). Bellmar, NJ: Wholistic Healing Publications.

Cade, M., & Coxhead, N. (1979). *The awakened mind: Biofeedback and the development of higher states of awareness.* New York: Dell.

Castro, M., Burrows, R., & Wooffitt, R. (2014). The paranormal is (still) normal: The sociological implications of a survey of paranormal experiences in Great Britain. *Sociological Research Online, 19*(3), 16.

Chapman, R., & Sisodia, R. (2015). *Everybody matters: The extraordinary power of caring for your people like family.* New York: Penguin.

Cohen, S. (2017). Science can help you reach enlightenment—but will it mess with your head? *New York Post,* February 26, 2017, retrieved at https://nypost.com/2017/02/26/science-can-help-you-reach-instant-enlightenment-but-will-it-mess-with-your-head/.

Davidson, R. J., & Lutz, A. (2008). Buddha's brain: Neuroplasticity and meditation. *IEEE Signal Processing Magazine, 25*(1), 176.

Dispenza, J. (2017). *Becoming supernatural.* Carlsbad, CA: Hay House.

Fehmi, L. G., & Robbins, J. (2007). *The open-focus brain: Harnessing the power of attention to heal mind and body.* Boston: Trumpeter Books.

Ferguson, N. (2008). *The ascent of money: A financial history of the world.* New York: Penguin.

Fowler, J. H., & Christakis, N. A. (2008). Dynamic spread of happiness in a large social network: Longitudinal analysis over 20 years in the Framingham Heart Study. *British Medical Journal, 337*, a2338.

Fredrickson, B. (2013). *Love 2.0: Finding happiness and health in moments of connection.* New York: Plume.

Goldhill, O. (2017, February 19). You're a completely different person at 14 and 77, the longest-running personality study ever has found. *Quartz Media.* Retrieved from https://qz.com/914002/youre-a-completely-different-person-at-14-and -77-the-longest-running-personality-study-ever-has-found.

Goleman, D. (1987, June 9). Personality: Major traits found stable through life. *New York Times.* Retrieved from www.nytimes.com/1987/06/09/science /personality-major-traits-found-stable-through-life.html.

Greeley, A. M. (1975). *The sociology of the paranormal: A reconnaissance.* Beverly Hills, CA: Sage Publications.

Groesbeck, G., Bach, D., Stapleton, P., Banton, S., Blickheuser, K., & Church, D. (2016, October 12). *The interrelated physiological and psychological effects of EcoMeditation: A pilot study.* Presented at Omega Institute for Holistic Studies, Rhinebeck, NY.

Gruzelier, J. (2009). A theory of alpha/theta neurofeedback, creative performance enhancement, long distance functional connectivity and psychological integration. *Cognitive Processing, 10*(Suppl. 1), S101–109.

Harris, M. A., Brett, C. E., Johnson, W., & Deary, I. J. (2016). Personality stability from age 14 to age 77 years. *Psychology and Aging, 31*(8), 862.

Hatfield, E., Cacioppo, J. T., & Rapson, R. L. (1994). *Emotional contagion.* New York: Cambridge University Press.

Hendricks, L., Bengston, W. F., & Gunkelman, J. (2010). The healing connection: EEG harmonics, entrainment, and Schumann's Resonances. *Journal of Scientific Exploration, 24*(4), 655.

Hoyland, J. S. (1932). *An Indian peasant mystic: Translations from Tukaram.* London: Allenson.

Hughes, J. R. (1964). Responses from the visual cortex of unanesthetized monkeys. In C. C. Pfeiffer & J. R. Smythies (Eds.), *International review of neurobiology 7* (pp. 99–153). New York: Academic Press.

Kotler, S., & Wheal, J. (2017). *Stealing fire: How silicon valley, the navy SEALs, and maverick scientists are revolutionizing the way we live and work.* New York: HarperCollins.

Johnson, M. L. (2011). Relationship of alpha-theta amplitude crossover during neurofeedback to emergence of spontaneous imagery and biographical memory. Doctoral dissertation, University of North Texas. Retrieved from http://citeseerx .ist.psu.edu/viewdoc/download?doi=10.1.1.842.2019&rep=rep1&type=pdf.

Kershaw, C. J., & Wade, J. W. (2012). *Brain change therapy: Clinical interventions for self-transformation.* New York: W. W. Norton.

Kramer, A. D., Guillory, J. E., & Hancock, J. T. (2014). Experimental evidence of massive-scale emotional contagion through social networks. *Proceedings of the National Academy of Sciences, 111*(24), 8788–8790.

LeDoux, J. (2002). *Synaptic self: How our brains become who we are.* New York: Penguin.

Lehmann, D., Faber, P. L., Tei, S., Pascual-Marqui, R. D., Milz, P., & Kochi, K. (2012). Reduced functional connectivity between cortical sources in five meditation traditions detected with lagged coherence using EEG tomography. *Neuroimage, 60*(2), 1574–1586.

Leskowitz, E. (2007). The influence of group heart rhythm on target subject physiology: Case report of a laboratory demonstration, and suggestions for further research. *Subtle Energies and Energy Medicine Journal, 18*(3), 1–12.

Liu, Y., Piazza, E. A., Simony, E., Shewokis, P. A., Onaral, B., Hasson, U., & Ayaz, H. (2017). Measuring speaker-listener neural coupling with functional near infrared spectroscopy. *Scientific Reports, 7,* 43293.

Llinás, R. R. (2014). Intrinsic electrical properties of mammalian neurons and CNS function: A historical perspective. *Frontiers in Cellular Neuroscience, 8,* 320.

Millett, D. (2001). Hans Berger: From psychic energy to the EEG. *Perspectives in Biology and Medicine, 44*(4), 522–542.

Morris, S. M. (2010). Achieving collective coherence: Group effects on heart rate variability coherence and heart rhythm synchronization. *Alternative Therapies in Health and Medicine, 16*(4), 62–72.

Nunez, P. L., & Srinivasan, R. (2006). *Electric fields of the brain: The neurophysics of EEG.* New York: Oxford University Press.

Osborn, J., & Derbyshire, S. W. (2010). Pain sensation evoked by observing injury in others. *Pain, 148*(2), 268–274.

Pennington, J. (in press). The brainwaves of creativity, insight and healing: How to transform your mind and life. *Energy Psychology: Theory, Research, and Treatment.*

Reece, A. G., & Danforth, C. M. (2017). Instagram photos reveal predictive markers of depression. *EPJ Data Science, 6*(1), 15.

Restak, R. M. (2001). *The secret life of the brain.* New York: Joseph Henry Press.

Schaefer, M., Heinze, H. J., & Rotte, M. (2012). Embodied empathy for tactile events: Interindividual differences and vicarious somatosensory responses during touch observation. *Neuroimage, 60*(2), 952–957.

Shiller, R. J. (2015). *Irrational exuberance* (3rd ed.). Princeton, NJ: Princeton University Press.

Shirer, W. (1941). *Berlin diary: The journal of a foreign correspondent, 1934–1941.* New York: Alfred A. Knopf.

Schwartz, J. M., & Begley, S. (2009). *The mind and the brain.* New York: Springer Science & Business Media.

Schwartz, J. M., Stapp, H. P., & Beauregard, M. (2005). Quantum physics in neuroscience and psychology: A neurophysical model of mind-brain interaction. *Philosophical Transactions of the Royal Society of London B: Biological Sciences, 360*(1458), 1309–1327.

Smith, H. (2009). *The world's religions* (50th anniv. ed.). San Francisco: HarperOne.

Thatcher, R. W. (1998). EEG normative databases and EEG biofeedback. *Journal of Neurotherapy, 2*(4), 8–39.

Tononi, G., & Koch, C. (2015). Consciousness: Here, there and everywhere? *Philosophical Transactions of the Royal Society of London B: Biological Sciences, 370*(1668), 20140167, 1–17.

Wright, R. (2017). *Why Buddhism is true: The science and philosophy of meditation and enlightenment.* New York: Simon and Schuster.

Zahn-Waxler, C., Radke-Yarrow, M., Wagner, E., & Chapman, M. (1992). Development of concern for others. *Developmental Psychology, 28*(1), 126.

CHAPTER 4

Ahmed, Z., & Wieraszko, A. (2008). The mechanism of magnetic field-induced increase of excitability in hippocampal neurons. *Brain Research, 1221,* 30–40.

Akarsu, E., Korkmaz, H., Balci, S. O., Borazan, E., Korkmaz, S., & Tarakcioglu, M. (2016). Subcutaneous adipose tissue type II deiodinase gene expression reduced in obese individuals with metabolic syndrome. *Experimental and Clinical Endocrinology and Diabetes, 124*(1), 11–15.

Ardeshirylajimi, A., & Soleimani, M. (2015). Enhanced growth and osteogenic differentiation of induced pluripotent stem cells by extremely low-frequency electromagnetic field. *Cellular and Molecular Biology, 61*(1), 36–41.

Azevedo, F. A., Carvalho, L. R., Grinberg, L. T., Farfel, J. M., Ferretti, R. E., Leite, R. E., . . . Herculano-Houzel, S. (2009). Equal numbers of neuronal and nonneuronal cells make the human brain an isometrically scaled-up primate brain. *Journal of Comparative Neurology, 513*(5), 532–541.

Becker, R. O. (1990). The machine brain and properties of the mind. *Subtle Energies and Energy Medicine Journal Archives, 1*(2).

Bengston, W. (2010). *The energy cure: Unraveling the mystery of hands-on healing.* Boulder, CO: Sounds True.

Bianconi, E., Piovesan, A., Facchin, F., Beraudi, A., Casadei, R., Frabetti, F., . . . Perez-Amodio, S. (2013). An estimation of the number of cells in the human body. *Annals of Human Biology, 40*(6), 463–471.

Boyd, W. (1966). *Spontaneous regression of cancer.* Springfield, Il: Thomas.

Boyers, L. M. (1953). Letter to the editor. *JAMA, 152,* 986–988.

Cantagrel, V., Lefeber, D. J., Ng, B. G., Guan, Z., Silhavy, J. L., Bielas, S. L., . . . De Brouwer, A. P. (2010). SRD5A3 is required for the conversion of polyprenol to dolichol, essential for N-linked protein glycosylation. *Cell, 142*(2), 203.

Church, D., Geronilla, L., & Dinter, I. (2009). Psychological symptom change in veterans after six sessions of Emotional Freedom Techniques (EFT): An observational study. *International Journal of Healing and Caring, 9*(1), 1–14.

Church, D., Hawk, C., Brooks, A., Toukolehto, O., Wren, M., Dinter, I., & Stein, P. (2013). Psychological trauma symptom improvement in veterans using Emotional Freedom Techniques: A randomized controlled trial. *Journal of Nervous and Mental Disease, 201*(2), 153–160. doi:10.1097/NMD.0b013e31827f6351.

Church, D., Yang, A., Fannin, J., & Blickheuser, K. (2016, October 14). *The biological dimensions of transcendent states: A randomized controlled trial.* Presented at Omega Institute for Holistic Studies, Rhinebeck, New York. Submitted for publication.

Church, D., Yount, G., Rachlin, K., Fox, L., & Nelms, J. (2016). Epigenetic effects of PTSD remediation in veterans using clinical Emotional Freedom Techniques: A randomized controlled pilot study. *American Journal of Health Promotion,* 1–11. doi:10.1177/0890117116661154.

Cosic, I., Cosic, D., & Lazar, K. (2015). Is it possible to predict electromagnetic resonances in proteins, DNA and RNA? *EPJ Nonlinear Biomedical Physics, 3*(1), 5.

De Girolamo, L., Stanco, D., Galliera, E., Viganò, M., Colombini, A., Setti, S., . . . Sansone, V. (2013). Low frequency pulsed electromagnetic field affects proliferation, tissue-specific gene expression, and cytokines release of human tendon cells. *Cell Biochemistry and Biophysics, 66*(3), 697.

Destexhe, A., McCormick, D. A., & Sejnowski, T. J. (1993). A model for 8–10 Hz spindling in interconnected thalamic relay and reticularis neurons. *Biophysical Journal, 65*(6), 2473–2477.

Deutsch, D., Leiser, Y., Shay, B., Fermon, E., Taylor, A., Rosenfeld, E., . . . Mao, Z. (2002). The human tuftelin gene and the expression of tuftelin in mineralizing and nonmineralizing tissues. *Connective Tissue Research, 43*(2–3), 425–434.

Foletti, A., Ledda, M., D'Emilia, E., Grimaldi, S., & Lisi, A. (2011). Differentiation of human LAN-5 neuroblastoma cells induced by extremely low frequency electronically transmitted retinoic acid. *Journal of Alternative and Complementary Medicine, 17*(8), 701–704. doi:10.1089/acm.2010.0439.

Frenkel, M., Ari, S. L., Engebretson, J., Peterson, N., Maimon, Y., Cohen, L., & Kacen, L. (2011). Activism among exceptional patients with cancer. *Supportive Care in Cancer, 19*(8), 1125–1132.

Fumoto, M., Sato-Suzuki, I., Seki, Y., Mohri, Y., & Arita, H. (2004). Appearance of high-frequency alpha band with disappearance of low-frequency alpha band in EEG is produced during voluntary abdominal breathing in an eyes-closed condition. *Neuroscience Research, 50*(3), 307–317.

Fumoto, M., Oshima, T., Kamiya, K., Kikuchi, H., Seki, Y., Nakatani, Y., . . . Arita, H. (2010). Ventral prefrontal cortex and serotonergic system activation during pedaling exercise induces negative mood improvement and increased alpha band in EEG. *Behavioural Brain Research, 213*(1), 1–9.

Geesink, H. J., & Meijer, D. K. (2016). Quantum wave information of life revealed: An algorithm for electromagnetic frequencies that create stability of biological order, with implications for brain function and consciousness. *Neuro-Quantology, 14*(1).

Geronilla, L., Minewiser, L., Mollon, P., McWilliams, M., & Clond, M. (2016). EFT (Emotional Freedom Techniques) remediates PTSD and psychological symptoms in veterans: A randomized controlled replication trial. *Energy Psychology: Theory, Research, and Treatment, 8*(2), 29–41. doi:10.9769/EPJ.2016.8.2.LG.

Gray, C. M. (1997). Synchronous oscillations in neuronal systems: Mechanisms and functions. *Pattern Formation in the Physical and Biological Sciences, 5,* 93.

Groesbeck, G., Bach, D., Stapleton, P., Banton, S., Blickheuser, K., & Church, D. (2016, October 15). *The interrelated physiological and psychological effects of EcoMeditation: A pilot study.* Presented at Omega Institute for Holistic Studies, Rhinebeck, New York.

Gronfier, C., Luthringer, R., Follenius, M., Schaltenbrand, N., Macher, J. P., Muzet, A., & Brandenberger, G. (1996). A quantitative evaluation of the relationships between growth hormone secretion and delta wave electroencephalographic activity during normal sleep and after enrichment in delta waves. *Sleep, 19*(10), 817–824.

Hall-Glenn, F., & Lyons, K. M. (2011). Roles for CCN2 in normal physiological processes. *Cellular and Molecular Life Sciences, 68*(19), 3209–3217.

Hong, Y., Ho, K. S., Eu, K. W., & Cheah, P. Y. (2007). A susceptibility gene set for early onset colorectal cancer that integrates diverse signaling pathways: Implication for tumorigenesis. *Clinical Cancer Research, 13*(4), 1107–1114.

Iaccarino, H. F., Singer, A. C., Martorell, A. J., Rudenko, A., Gao, F., Gillingham, T. Z., . . . Adaikkan, C. (2016). Gamma frequency entrainment attenuates amyloid load and modifies microglia. *Nature, 540*(7632), 230–235.

Jacobs, T. L., Epel, E. S., Lin, J., Blackburn, E. H., Wolkowitz, O. M., Bridwell, D. A., . . . King, B. G. (2011). Intensive meditation training, immune cell telomerase activity, and psychological mediators. *Psychoneuroendocrinology, 36*(5), 664–681.

Kang, J. E., Lim, M. M., Bateman, R. J., Lee, J. J., Smyth, L. P., Cirrito, J. R., . . . Holtzman, D. M. (2009). Amyloid-β dynamics are regulated by orexin and the sleep-wake cycle. *Science, 326*(5955), 1005–1007.

Kelly, R. (2011). *The human hologram: Living your life in harmony with the unified field.* Santa Rosa, CA: Elite Books.

Kim, D. K., Rhee, J. H., & Kang, S. W. (2013). Reorganization of the brain and heart rhythm during autogenic meditation. *Frontiers in Integrative Neuroscience, 7,* 109. doi:10.3389/fnint.2013.00109.

Krikorian, J. G., Portlock, C. S., Cooney, D. P., & Rosenberg, S. A. (1980). Spontaneous regression of non-Hodgkin's lymphoma: A report of nine cases. *Cancer, 46*(9), 2093–2099.

Laflamme, M. A., & Murry, C. E. (2011). Heart regeneration. *Nature, 473*(7347), 326–335.

Lee, P. B., Kim, Y. C., Lim, Y. J., Lee, C. J., Choi, S. S., Park, S. H., . . . Lee, S. C. (2006). Efficacy of pulsed electromagnetic therapy for chronic lower back pain: A randomized, double-blind, placebo-controlled study. *Journal of International Medical Research, 34*(2), 160–167.

Lee, D. J., Schönleben, F., Banuchi, V. E., Qiu, W., Close, L. G., Assaad, A. M., & Su, G. H. (2010). Multiple tumor-suppressor genes on chromosome 3p contribute to head and neck squamous cell carcinoma tumorigenesis. *Cancer Biology and Therapy, 10*(7), 689–693.

Lim, L. (2014, July 21). The potential of treating Alzheimer's disease with intranasal light therapy. *Mediclights Research*. Retrieved from www.mediclights.com/the -potential-of-treating-alzheimers-disease-with-intranasal-light-therapy.

Lim, L. (2017). *Inventor's notes for Vielight "Neuro Alpha" and "Neuro Gamma."* Retrieved September 4, 2017, from http://vielight.com/wp-content/uploads/2017/02 /Vielight-Inventors-Notes-for-Neuro-Alpha-and-Neuro-Gamma.pdf.

Lin, H., Goodman, R., & Shirley-Henderson, A. (1994). Specific region of the c-myc promoter is responsive to electric and magnetic fields. *Journal of Cellular Biochemistry, 54*(3), 281–288.

Lomas, T., Ivtzan, I., & Fu, C. H. (2015). A systematic review of the neurophysiology of mindfulness on EEG oscillations. *Neuroscience and Biobehavioral Reviews, 57,* 401–410. doi:10.1016/j.neubiorev.2015.09.018.

Maharaj, M. E. (2016). Differential gene expression after Emotional Freedom Techniques (EFT) treatment: A novel pilot protocol for salivary mRNA assessment. *Energy Psychology: Theory, Research, and Treatment, 8*(1), 17–32. doi:10.9769 /EPJ.2016.8.1.MM.

Nadalin, S., Testa, G., Malagó, M., Beste, M., Frilling, A., Schroeder, T., . . . Broelsch, C. E. (2004). Volumetric and functional recovery of the liver after right hepatectomy for living donation. *Liver Transplantation, 10*(8), 1024–1029.

Omary, M. B., Ku, N. O., Strnad, P., & Hanada, S. (2009). Toward unraveling the complexity of simple epithelial keratins in human disease. *Journal of Clinical Investigation, 119*(7), 1794–1805. doi:10.1172/JCI37762.

O'Regan, B., & Hirshberg, C. (1993). *Spontaneous remission: An annotated bibliography.* Novato, CA: Institute of Noetic Sciences.

Park, E. J., Grabińska, K. A., Guan, Z., & Sessa, W. C. (2016). NgBR is essential for endothelial cell glycosylation and vascular development. *EMBO Reports, 17*(2), 167–177.

Razavi, S., Salimi, M., Shahbazi-Gahrouei, D., Karbasi, S., & Kermani, S. (2014). Extremely low-frequency electromagnetic field influences the survival and proliferation effect of human adipose derived stem cells. *Advanced Biomedical Research, 3,* 25–30.

Sakai, A., Suzuki, K., Nakamura, T., Norimura, T., & Tsuchiya, T. (1991). Effects of pulsing electromagnetic fields on cultured cartilage cells. *International Orthopaedics, 15*(4), 341–346.

Saltmarche, A. E., Naeser, M. A., Ho, K. F., Hamblin, M. R., & Lim, L. (2017). Significant improvement in cognition in mild to moderately severe dementia cases treated with transcranial plus intranasal photobiomodulation: Case series report. *Photomedicine and Laser Surgery, 35*(8): 432–441.

Salvatore, D., Tu, H., Harney, J. W., & Larsen, P. R. (1996). Type 2 iodothyronine deiodinase is highly expressed in human thyroid. *Journal of Clinical Investigation, 98*(4), 962.

Sastry, K. S., Karpova, Y., Prokopovich, S., Smith, A. J., Essau, B., Gersappe, A., . . . Penn, R. B. (2007). Epinephrine protects cancer cells from apoptosis via activation of cAMP-dependent protein kinase and BAD phosphorylation. *Journal of Biological Chemistry, 282*(19), 14094–14100.

Sisken, B. F., Midkiff, P., Tweheus, A., & Markov, M. (2007). Influence of static magnetic fields on nerve regeneration in vitro. *Environmentalist, 27*(4), 477–481.

Sood, A. K., Armaiz-Pena, G. N., Halder, J., Nick, A. M., Stone, R. L., Hu, W., . . . Han, L. Y. (2010). Adrenergic modulation of focal adhesion kinase protects human ovarian cancer cells from anoikis. *Journal of Clinical Investigation, 120*(5), 1515.

Sukel, K. (2011, March 15). The synapse—a primer. *Dana Foundation*. Retrieved from www.dana.org/News/Details.aspx?id=43512.

Takahashi, K., Kaneko, I., Date, M., & Fukada, E. (1986). Effect of pulsing electromagnetic fields on DNA synthesis in mammalian cells in culture. *Experientia, 42*(2), 185–186.

Tang, Y. P., Shimizu, E., Dube, G. R., Rampon, C., Kerchner, G. A., Zhuo, M., . . . Tsien, J. Z. (1999). Genetic enhancement of learning and memory in mice. *Nature, 401*(6748), 63–69.

Tekutskaya, E. E., & Barishev, M. G. (2013). Studying of influence of the low-frequency electromagnetic field on DNA molecules in water solutions. *Odessa Astronomical Publications, 26*(2), 303–304.

Tekutskaya, E. E., Barishev, M. G., & Ilchenko, G. P. (2015). The effect of a low-frequency electromagnetic field on DNA molecules in aqueous solutions. *Biophysics, 60*(6), 913.

Van Cauter, E., Leproult, R., & Plat, L. (2000). Age-related changes in slow wave sleep and REM sleep and relationship with growth hormone and cortisol levels in healthy men. *JAMA, 284*(7), 861–868.

Ventegodt, S., Morad, M., Hyam, E., & Merrick, J. (2004). Clinical holistic medicine: Induction of spontaneous remission of cancer by recovery of the human character and the purpose of life (the life mission). *Scientific World Journal, 4*, 362–377.

Wahlestedt, M., Erlandsson, E., Kristiansen, T., Lu, R., Brakebusch, C., Weissman, I. L., . . . Bryder, D. (2017). Clonal reversal of ageing-associated stem cell lineage bias via a pluripotent intermediate. *Nature Communications, 8*, 14533.

Walløe, S., Pakkenberg, B., & Fabricius, K. (2014). Stereological estimation of total cell numbers in the human cerebral and cerebellar cortex. *Frontiers in Human Neuroscience, 8.*

Wei, G., Luo, H., Sun, Y., Li, J., Tian, L., Liu, W., . . . Chen, R. (2015). Transcriptome profiling of esophageal squamous cell carcinoma reveals a long noncoding RNA acting as a tumor suppressor. *Oncotarget, 6*(19), 17065–17080.

Wu, M., Pastor-Pareja, J. C., & Xu, T. (2010). Interaction between RasV12 and scribbled clones induces tumour growth and invasion. *Nature, 463*(7280), 545–548.

Xiang, G., Yi, Y., Weiwei, H., & Weiming, W. (2016). RND1 is up-regulated in esophageal squamous cell carcinoma and promotes the growth and migration of cancer cells. *Tumor Biology, 37*(1), 773.

Ying, L., Hong, L., Zhicheng, G., Xiauwei, H. & Guoping, C. (2000). Effects of pulsed electric fields on DNA synthesis in an osteoblast-like cell line (UMR-106). *Tsinghua Science and Technology, 5*(4), 439–442.

Yong, E. (2016, Dec 7). Beating Alzheimer's with brain waves. *Atlantic.* Retrieved from www.theatlantic.com/science/archive/2016/12/beating-alzheimers-with -brain-waves/509846.

Yu, X., Fumoto, M., Nakatani, Y., Sekiyama, T., Kikuchi, H., Seki, Y., . . . Arita, H. (2011). Activation of the anterior prefrontal cortex and serotonergic system is associated with improvements in mood and EEG changes induced by Zen meditation practice in novices. *International Journal of Psychophysiology, 80*(2), 103–111.

Zahl, P. H., Mæhlen, J., & Welch, H. G. (2008). The natural history of invasive breast cancers detected by screening mammography. *Archives of Internal Medicine, 168*(21), 2311–2316.

CHAPTER 5

Bach, D., Groesbeck, G., Stapleton, P., Banton, S., Blickheuser, K., & Church, D. (2016, October 15). *Clinical EFT (Emotional Freedom Techniques) improves multiple physiological markers of health.* Presented at Omega Institute for Holistic Studies, Rhinebeck, New York.

Baker, M. (2016). 1,500 scientists lift the lid on reproducibility. *Nature, 533*(7604), 452–454.

Begley, C. G., & Ellis, L. M. (2012). Drug development: Raise standards for pre-clinical cancer research. *Nature, 483*(7391), 531–533.

Bem, D. J. (2011). Feeling the future: Experimental evidence for anomalous retroactive influences on cognition and affect. *Journal of Personality and Social Psychology, 100*(3), 407.

Bem, D., Tressoldi, P., Rabeyron, T., & Duggan, M. (2015). Feeling the future: A meta-analysis of 90 experiments on the anomalous anticipation of random future events. *F1000Research, 4,* 1188.

Bem, D. J., Utts, J., & Johnson, W. O. (2011). Must psychologists change the way they analyze their data? *Journal of Personality and Social Psychology, 101*(4), 716–719.

Bengston, W. (2010). *The energy cure: Unraveling the mystery of hands-on healing.* Boulder, CO: Sounds True.

Blake, W. (1968). *The portable Blake.* New York: Viking.

Born, M., (Ed.). (1971). *The Born–Einstein letters: Correspondence between Albert Einstein and Max and Hedwig Born from 1916–1955* (I. Born, Trans.). New York: Macmillan.

Chambless, D., & Hollon, S. D. (1998). Defining empirically supported therapies. *Journal of Consulting and Clinical Psychology, 66,* 7–18.

Church, D. (2013). Clinical EFT (Emotional Freedom Techniques) as single session therapy: Cases, research, indications, and cautions. In M. Hoyt & M. Talmon (Eds.), *Capture the moment: Single session therapy and walk-in service.* Bethel, CT: Crown House.

Church, D., & Brooks, A. J. (2010). The effect of a brief EFT (Emotional Freedom Techniques) self-intervention on anxiety, depression, pain and cravings in healthcare workers. *Integrative Medicine: A Clinician's Journal, 9*(5), 40–44.

Church, D., Yount, G., & Brooks, A. J. (2012). The effect of Emotional Freedom Techniques on stress biochemistry: A randomized controlled trial. *Journal of Nervous and Mental Disease, 200*(10), 891–896. doi:10.1097/NMD.0b013e31826b9fc1.

Cooper, H., DeNeve, K., & Charlton, K. (1997). Finding the missing science: The fate of studies submitted for review by a human subjects committee. *Psychological Methods, 2*(4), 447.

Davidson, R. J. (2003). Affective neuroscience and psychophysiology: Toward a synthesis. *Psychophysiology, 40*(5), 655–665.

Diener, E., & Chan, M. Y. (2011). Happy people live longer: Subjective well-being contributes to health and longevity. *Applied Psychology: Health and Well-Being, 3*(1), 1–43.

eLife. (2017). Reproducibility in cancer biology: The challenges of replication. *eLife, 6,* e23693. doi: 10.7554/eLife.23693.

Feynman, R. P., Leighton, R. B., & Sands, M. (1965). The Feynman lectures on physics (Vol. 1). *American Journal of Physics, 33*(9), 750–752.

Fickler, R., Krenn, M., Lapkiewicz, R., Ramelow, S., & Zeilinger, A. (2013). Real-time imaging of quantum entanglement. *Nature–Scientific Reports,* 3, 2914.

Gane, S., Georganakis, D., Maniati, K., Vamvakias, M., Ragoussis, N., Skoulakis, E. M., & Turin, L. (2013). Molecular vibration-sensing component in human olfaction. *PLoS one, 8*(1), e55780.

Giltay, E. J., Geleijnse, J. M., Zitman, F. G., Hoekstra, T., & Schouten, E. G. (2004). Dispositional optimism and all-cause and cardiovascular mortality in a prospective cohort of elderly Dutch men and women. *Archives of General Psychiatry, 61*(11), 1126–1135.

Goswami, A. (2004). *Quantum doctor: A physicist's guide to health and healing.* Hampton Roads, VA: Hampton Roads Publishing.

Grinberg-Zylberbaum, J., Delaflor, M., Attie, L., & Goswami, A. (1994). The Einstein-Podolsky-Rosen paradox in the brain: The transferred potential. *Physics Essays, 7*, 422.

Hammerschlag, R., Marx, B. L., & Aickin, M. (2014). Nontouch biofield therapy: A systematic review of human randomized controlled trials reporting use of only nonphysical contact treatment. *The Journal of Alternative and Complementary Medicine, 20*(12), 881–892.

Hanson, R. (2013). *Hardwiring happiness: The practical science of reshaping your brain—and your life.* New York: Random House.

Heisenberg, W. (1962). *Physics and philosophy: the revolution in modern science.* New York: Harper & Row.

Hensen, B., Bernien, H., Dréau, A. E., Reiserer, A., Kalb, N., Blok, M. S., . . . Amaya, W. (2015). Loophole-free Bell inequality violation using electron spins separated by 1.3 kilometres. *Nature, 526*(7575), 682–686.

Hoss, R. (2016, June 12). *Consciousness after the body dies.* Presentation at the International Association for the Study of Dreams, Kerkrade, Netherlands.

Ironson, G., Stuetzle, R., Ironson, D., Balbin, E., Kremer, H., George, A., . . . Fletcher, M. A. (2011). View of God as benevolent and forgiving or punishing and judgmental predicts HIV disease progression. *Journal of Behavioral Medicine, 34*(6), 414–425.

Joergensen, A., Broedbaek, K., Weimann, A., Semba, R. D., Ferrucci, L., Joergensen, M. B., & Poulsen, H. E. (2011). Association between urinary excretion of cortisol and markers of oxidatively damaged DNA and RNA in humans. *PLoS ONE, 6*(6), e20795. doi:10.1371/journal.pone.0020795

Jung, C. G. (1952). The structure of the psyche. In *Collected works, vol. 8: The structure and dynamics of the psyche.* London: Routledge & Kegan Paul.

Kaiser, J. (2017, January 18). Rigorous replication effort succeeds for just two of five cancer papers. *Science.* Retrieved from www.sciencemag.org/news/2017/01/rigorous-replication-effort-succeeds-just-two-five-cancer-papers.

Kamp, J. (2016). It is so not simple: Russian physicist Yury Kronn and the subtle energy that fills 96 percent of our existence but cannot be seen or measured. *Optimist,* Spring, 40–47.

Klinger, E. (1996). The contents of thoughts: Interference as the downside of adaptive normal mechanisms in thought flow. In I. G. Sarason, G. R. Pierce, & B. R. Sarason (Eds.), *Cognitive interference: Theories, methods, and findings* (pp. 3–23). Hillsdale, NJ: Lawrence Erlbaum.

Kronn, Y., & Jones, J. (2011). Experiments on the effects of subtle energy on the electro-magnetic field: Is subtle energy the 5th force of the universe? *Energy Tools International.* Retrieved July 5, 2017, from www.saveyourbrain.net/pdf/testreport .pdf.

LeDoux, J. (2003). The emotional brain, fear, and the amygdala. *Cellular and Molecular Neurobiology, 23*(4), 727–738.

Lee, K. C., Sprague, M. R., Sussman, B. J., Nunn, J., Langford, N. K., Jin, X. M., . . . Jaksch, D. (2011). Entangling macroscopic diamonds at room temperature. *Science, 334*(6060), 1253–1256.

Leskowitz, R. (2014). The 2013 World Series: A Trojan horse for consciousness studies. *Explore: The Journal of Science and Healing, 10*(2), 125–127.

Lewis, C. S. (1970). *God in the dock: Essays on theology and ethics.* London: Eerdmans.

McCraty, R., Atkinson, M., & Tomasino, D. (2003). *Modulation of DNA conformation by heart-focused intention.* Boulder Creek, CA: HeartMath Research Center, Institute of HeartMath, Publication No. 03-008.

McCraty R. & Childre, D. (2010). Coherence: Bridging personal, social, and global health. *Alternative Therapies in Health and Medicine, 16*(4), 10.

McCraty, R., & Deyhle, A. (2016). *The science of interconnectivity.* Boulder Creek, CA: HeartMath Institute.

McMillan, P. J., Wilkinson, C. W., Greenup, L., Raskind, M. A., Peskind, E. R., & Leverenz, J. B. (2004). Chronic cortisol exposure promotes the development of a GABAergic phenotype in the primate hippocampus. *Journal of Neurochemistry, 91*(4), 843–851.

McTaggart, L. (2007). *The intention experiment: Using your thoughts to change your life and the world.* New York: Free Press.

Moga, M. M., & Bengston, W. F. (2010). Anomalous magnetic field activity during a bioenergy healing experiment. *Journal of Scientific Exploration, 24*(3), 397–410.

Moreva, E., Brida, G., Gramegna, M., Giovannetti, V., Maccone, L., & Genovese, M. (2014). Time from quantum entanglement: An experimental illustration. *Physical Review A, 89*(5), 052122–052128.

Nakamura, T. (2013, November 14). One man's quest to prove how far laser pointers reach. Retrieved from http://kotaku.com/one-mans-quest-to-prove-how -far-laser-pointers-reach-1464275649.

Nelson, R. (2015). Meaningful correlations in random data. *The Global Consciousness Project.* Retrieved August 20, 2017, from http://noosphere.princeton.edu/ results.html#alldata.

Nesse, R. M., Curtis, G. C., Thyer, B. A., McCann, D. S., Huber-Smith, M. J., & Knopf, R. F. (1985). Endocrine and cardiovascular responses during phobic anxiety. *Psychosomatic Medicine, 47*(4), 320–332.

Open Science Collaboration. (2015). Estimating the reproducibility of psychological science. *Science, 349*(6251), aac4716.

Powell, C. S. (2017, June 16). Is the universe conscious? Some of the world's most renowned scientists are questioning whether the cosmos has an inner life similar to our own. National Broadcasting Company (NBC). Retrieved from www.nbcnews.com/mach/science/universe-conscious-ncna772956.

Radin, D. I. (2011). Predicting the unpredictable: 75 years of experimental evidence. *AIP Conference Proceedings, 1408*(1), 204–217.

Radin, D., Michel, L., & Delorme, A. (2016). Psychophysical modulation of fringe visibility in a distant double-slit optical system. *Physics Essays, 29*(1), 14–22.

Ritchie, S. J., Wiseman, R., & French, C. C. (2012). Failing the future: Three unsuccessful attempts to replicate Bem's 'Retroactive Facilitation of Recall' Effect. *PLoS ONE, 7*(3), e33423.

Romero, E., Augulis, R., Novoderezhkin, V. I., Ferretti, M., Thieme, J., Zigmantas, D., & Van Grondelle, R. (2014). Quantum coherence in photosynthesis for efficient solar-energy conversion. *Nature Physics, 10*(9), 676–682.

Rosenthal, R., & Fode, K. (1963). The effect of experimenter bias on performance of the albino rat. *Behavioral Science, 8,* 183–189.

Rosenthal, R., &. Jacobson, L. (1963). Teachers' expectancies: Determinants of pupils' IQ gains. *Psychological Reports, 19,* 115–118.

Russ, T. C., Stamatakis, E., Hamer, M., Starr, J. M., Kivimäki, M., & Batty, G. D. (2012). Association between psychological distress and mortality: Individual participant pooled analysis of 10 prospective cohort studies. *British Medical Journal, 345,* e4933.

Sapolsky, R. M., Uno, H., Rebert, C. S., & Finch, C. E. (1990). Hippocampal damage associated with prolonged glucocorticoid exposure in primates. *Journal of Neuroscience, 10*(9), 2897–2902.

Sheldrake, R. (1999). How widely is blind assessment used in scientific research? *Alternative Therapies in Health and Medicine, 5*(3), 88.

Sheldrake, R. (2012). *Science set free: 10 paths to new discovery.* New York: Deepak Chopra Books.

Shelus, P. J., Veillet, C., Whipple, A. L., Wiant, J. R., Williams, J. G., & Yoder, C. F. (1994). Lunar laser ranging: A continuing legacy of the Apollo program. *Science, 265,* 482.

Standish, L. J., Kozak, L., Johnson, L. C., & Richards, T. (2004). Electroencephalographic evidence of correlated event-related signals between the brains of spatially and sensory isolated human subjects. *Journal of Alternative and Complementary Medicine, 10*(2), 307–314.

Tchijevsky, A. L. (1971). Physical factors of the historical process. *Cycles, 22,* 11–27.

Thiagarajan, T. C., Lebedev, M. A., Nicolelis, M. A., & Plenz, D. (2010). Coherence potentials: Loss-less, all-or-none network events in the cortex. *PLoS Biology, 8*(1), e1000278.

Tiller, W. A. (1997). *Science and human transformation: Subtle energies, intentionality and consciousness.* Walnut Creek, CA: Pavior Publishing.

Wagenmakers, E. J., Wetzels, R., Borsboom, D., & Van Der Maas, H. L. (2011). Why psychologists must change the way they analyze their data: The case of psi: Comment on Bem (2011). *Journal of Personality and Social Psychology, 100*(3), 426–432.

Ward, M. M., Mefford, I. N., Parker, S. D., Chesney, M. A., Taylor, B. C., Keegan, D. L., & Barchas, J. D. (1983). Epinephrine and norepinephrine responses in continuously collected human plasma to a series of stressors. *Psychosomatic Medicine, 45*(6), 471–486.

Watt, C., & Nagtegaal, M. (2004). Reporting of blind methods: An interdisciplinary survey. *Journal of the Society for Psychical Research, 68,* 105–116.

Wolf, F. A. (2001). *Mind into matter: A new alchemy of science and spirit.* Newburyport, MA: Red Wheel/Weiser.

Yan, X., Lu, F., Jiang, H., Wu, X., Cao, W., Xia, Z., . . . Zhu, R. (2002). Certain physical manifestation and effects of external qi of Yan Xin life science technology. *Journal of Scientific Exploration, 16*(3), 381–411.

Yan, X., Shen, H., Jiang, H., Zhang, C., Hu, D., Wang, J., & Wu, X. (2006). External Qi of Yan Xin Qigong differentially regulates the Akt and extracellular signal-regulated kinase pathways and is cytotoxic to cancer cells but not to normal cells. *International Journal of Biochemistry and Cell Biology, 38*(12), 2102–2113.

CHAPTER 6

Anderson, B. J., Engebretson, M. J., Rounds, S. P., Zanetti, L. J., & Potemra, T. A. (1990). A statistical study of Pc 3–5 pulsations observed by the AMPTE/CCE Magnetic Fields Experiment. *Journal of Geophysical Research: Space Physics, 95*(A7), 10495–10523.

Beauregard, M. (2012). *Brain wars: The scientific battle over the existence of the mind and the proof that will change the way we live our lives.* San Francisco: HarperOne.

Bem, D. J. (2011). Feeling the future: Experimental evidence for anomalous retroactive influences on cognition and affect. *Journal of Personality and Social Psychology, 100*(3), 407.

Bem, D., Tressoldi, P., Rabeyron, T., & Duggan, M. (2015). Feeling the future: A meta-analysis of 90 experiments on the anomalous anticipation of random future events. *F1000Research, 4,* 1188.

Bengston, W. (2010). *The energy cure: Unraveling the mystery of hands-on healing.* Boulder, CO: Sounds True.

Braden, G. (2008). *The spontaneous healing of belief: Shattering the paradigm of false limits.* Carlsbad, CA: Hay House.

Brown, E. N., & Czeisler, C. A. (1992). The statistical analysis of circadian phase and amplitude in constant-routine core-temperature data. *Journal of Biological Rhythms, 7*(3), 177–202.

Burch, W. (2003). *She who dreams: A journey into healing through dreamwork.* San Rafael, CA: New World Library.

Burk, L. (2015, October 13). Dreams that warn of breast cancer. *Huffington Post blog.* Retrieved from www.huffingtonpost.com/larry-burk-md/dreams-that-warn -of-breas_b_8167758.html.

Calaprice, A. (Ed.). (2002*). Dear Professor Einstein: Albert Einstein's letters to and from children.* Amherst, NY: Prometheus.

Calaprice, A. (Ed.). (2011). *The ultimate quotable Einstein.* Princeton, NJ: Princeton University Press.

Cambray, J. (2002). Synchronicity and emergence. *American Imago,* 59(4), 409–434.

Cambray, J. (2009). *Synchronicity: Nature and psyche in an interconnected universe* (Vol. 15). College Station: Texas A&M University Press.

Cauchon, D. (2001, December 20). For many on Sept. 11, survival was no acci-dent. *USA Today.* Retrieved from http://usatoday30.usatoday.com/news /sept11/2001/12/19/usatcov-wtcsurvival.htm.

Church, D. (2013). *The genie in your genes: Epigenetic medicine and the new biology of intention.* Santa Rosa, CA: Energy Psychology Press.

Clark, N. (2012). *Divine moments.* Fairfield, IA: First World Publishing.

Corning, P. A. (2002). The re-emergence of "emergence": A venerable concept in search of a theory. *Complexity, 7*(6), 18–30. doi:10.1002/cplx.10043.

Crick, F., & Clark, J. (1994). The astonishing hypothesis. *Journal of Consciousness Studies, 1*(1), 10–16.

Dossey, L. (2009). *The science of premonitions: How knowing the future can help us avoid danger, maximize opportunities, and create a better life.* New York: Plume.

Dossey, L. (2013). *One mind: How our individual mind is part of a greater conscious-ness and why it matters.* Carlsbad, CA: Hay House.

Dowling, S. (2017, May 26). The audacious pilot who landed in Red Square. *BBC Future.* Retrieved from www.bbc.com/future/story/20170526-the-audacious-pilot -who-landed-in-red-square.

Eliade, M. (1964). *Shamanism: Archaic techniques of ecstasy.* London: Routledge & Kegan Paul.

Facco, E., & Agrillo, C. (2012). Near-death experiences between science and prejudice. *Frontiers in Human Neuroscience, 6,* 209.

Ferriss, T. (2017). *Tribe of mentors: Short life advice from the best in the world.* New York: Houghton Mifflin Harcourt.

Geesink, H. J., & Meijer, D. K. (2016). Quantum wave information of life revealed: An algorithm for electromagnetic frequencies that create stability of biological order, with implications for brain function and consciousness. *NeuroQuantology, 14*(1).

Goethe, J. W. (1887). *The first part of Goethe's Faust* (J. Anster, Trans.). London: George Routledge & Sons.

Gramling, R., Klein, W., Roberts, M., Waring, M. E., Gramling, D., & Eaton, C. B. (2008). Self-rated cardiovascular risk and 15-year cardiovascular mortality. *Annals of Family Medicine, 6*(4), 302 306.

Greyson, B. (2003). Incidence and correlates of near-death experiences in a cardiac care unit. *General Hospital Psychiatry, 25*(4), 269–276.

Halberg, F., Cornélissen, G., McCraty, R., Czaplicki, J., & Al-Abdulgader, A. A. (2011). Time structures (chronomes) of the blood circulation, populations' health, human affairs and space weather. *World Heart Journal, 3*(1), 73.

Halberg, F., Tong, Y. L., & Johnson, E. A. (1967). Circadian system phase—an aspect of temporal morphology; procedures and illustrative examples. In H. von Mayersbach (Ed.), *The cellular aspects of biorhythms* (pp. 20–48). New York: Springer-Verlag.

HeartMath Institute. (n.d.). Global coherence research: The science of interconnectivity. Retrieved August 6, 2017, from www.heartmath.org/research/global-coherence.

Ho, M. W. (2008). *The rainbow and the worm: The physics of organisms.* London: World Scientific.

Hogenson, G. B. (2004). Archetypes: Emergence and the psyche's deep structure. In J. Cambray & L. Carter (Eds.), *Analytical psychology: Contemporary perspectives in Jungian analysis.* London: Routledge.

Hoss, R. J., & Gongloff, R. P. (2017). *Dreams that change our lives.* Asheville, NC: Chiron.

Ironson, G., Stuetzle, R., Ironson, D., Balbin, E., Kremer, H., George, A., . . . Fletcher, M. A. (2011). View of God as benevolent and forgiving or punishing and judgmental predicts HIV disease progression. *Journal of Behavioral Medicine, 34*(6), 414–425.

Jacobs, J. A., Kato, Y., Matsushita, S., & Troitskaya, V. A. (1964). Classification of geomagnetic micropulsations. *Journal of Geophysical Research, 69*(1), 180–181.

Johnson, S. (2002). *Emergence: The connected lives of ants, brains, cities, and software.* New York: Simon & Schuster.

Jung, C. G. (1952). Synchronicity: An acausal connecting principle. In *Collected works, vol. 8: The structure and dynamics of the psyche*. London: Routledge & Kegan Paul.

Jung, C. G. (1975). *Letters, vol. 2: 1951–1961*. G. Adler & A. Jaffé (Eds.). Princeton, NJ: Princeton University Press.

Kaufman, S. A. (1993). *The origins of order: Self-organization and selection in evolution*. Oxford: Oxford University Press.

Kelly, R. (2011). *The human hologram: Living your life in harmony with the unified field*. Santa Rosa, CA: Elite Books.

McClenon, J. (1993). Surveys of anomalous experience in Chinese, Japanese, and American samples. *Sociology of Religion, 54*(3), 295–302.

McCraty, R. (2015). Could the energy of our hearts change the world? *GOOP*. Retrieved from http://goop.com/could-the-energy-of-our-hearts-change-the-world.

McCraty, R. & Deyle, (2016). *The science of interconnectivity*. Boulder Creek, CA: HeartMath Institute.

Nova. (2007, July 10). Emergence. *NOVA*. Retrieved from www.pbs.org/wgbh/nova/nature/emergence.html.

Oschman, J. L. (1997). What is healing energy? Part 3: Silent pulses. *Journal of Bodywork and Movement Therapies, 1*(3), 179–189.

Oschman, J. L. (2015). *Energy medicine: The scientific basis*. London: Elsevier Health Sciences.

Park, S. Q., Kahnt, T., Dogan, A., Strang, S., Fehr, E., & Tobler, P. N. (2017). A neural link between generosity and happiness. *Nature Communications, 8*.

Popper, K. R., & Eccles, J. C. (2012). *The self and its brain*. New York: Springer Science & Business Media.

Ring, K., & Cooper, S. (2008). *Mindsight: Near-death and out-of-body experiences in the blind* (2nd ed.). iUniverse.

Radin, D. I. (2011). Predicting the unpredictable: 75 years of experimental evidence. In *AIP Conference Proceedings 1408*(1), 204–217.

Rockwood, K. (2017). *Think positive, get lucky*. In Gibbs, N. (Ed.), *The science of emotions* (pp. 62–65). New York: Time.

Selmaoui, B., & Touitou, Y. (2003). Reproducibility of the circadian rhythms of serum cortisol and melatonin in healthy subjects: A study of three different 24-h cycles over six weeks. *Life Sciences, 73*(26), 3339–3349.

Shermer, M. (2014, October 1). Anomalous events that can shake one's skepticism to the core. *Scientific American*. Retrieved from www.scientificamerican.com/article/anomalous-events-that-can-shake-one-s-skepticism-to-the-core.

Strogatz, S. H. (2012). *Sync: How order emerges from chaos in the universe, nature, and daily life*. London: Hachette.

Tonneau, F. (2004). Consciousness outside the head. *Behavior and Philosophy, 32*(1), 97–123.

INDEX

ACKNOWLEDGMENTS

It takes a village to create a book of this magnitude, and I am deeply grateful to all the people who have played a part in making it possible.

Sir Isaac Newton said that we stand on the shoulders of giants. No scientist creates alone. We build on the discoveries of others. I am so grateful to the hundreds of visionary researchers whose work is cited in these pages, and upon whose foundations I have built. Wherever I looked for evidence, I usually found it, and the breadth of mind and imagination I discovered in the work of my colleagues often humbled and astounded me.

Everyone in the healing field, especially me, owes a debt of gratitude to clinical psychologist David Feinstein. His intellectual rigor, brilliant academic writing skills, and ethical awareness have shaped the work of an entire generation of energy healing professionals. He provided detailed feedback on the first few chapters and helped shape this book.

Many other professionals read sections dealing with their areas of expertise and corrected errors and misunderstandings. EEG expert Gary Groesbeck gave me detailed feedback on the brain wave chapters, while his colleague Judith Pennington provided clear explanations of the Awakened Mind and Evolved Mind patterns. Psychiatrist Ron Ruden alerted me to the importance of delta brain waves and the many ways we can increase them.

Rollin McCraty of the Institute of HeartMath gave me clear and explicit explanations of Schumann resonances and field line resonances, as well as conducting primary research on the topic. Dean Radin of the Institute for Noetic Sciences helped me understand the statistical basis of the research on premonition and maintains the most current website listing scientific publications of extraordinary human experiences. His remarkable experiments have provided a sound scientific basis for this work.

My close friend Bob Hoss is a brilliant polymath whose mind knows no boundaries. He's an expert on the neuroscience of dreaming and how the brain uses symbolism to solve problems. He provided the pillars for the passages on Carl Jung, the collective unconscious, the emotional brain, and quantum phenomena.

I'm grateful to Lissa Rankin for fascinating conversations that led to clearer insights into how mind becomes matter. Also to Bill Bengston for his provocative work on using energy to heal cancer and for helping me understand both the animal and human dimensions of this research.

I'm grateful to all the institutes and conferences that sponsor my live workshops, like Esalen, Kripalu, Omega, and the New York Open Center. At these modern gathering places of mind and spirit, I meet a variety of fascinating teachers whose insights enrich my understanding.

I'm privileged to interact with many other like-minded people who are members of the Transformational Leadership Council. Thank you, Jack Canfield, for founding and fostering this remarkable group of visionaries. Many of those who endorsed this book are fellow members.

I'm also grateful to the skeptics. There are many professional naysayers who claim that humans are beings of matter rather than energy. Their attacks on the field of energy healing, especially in the entries in Wikipedia that they control, and their denial of the science described in this book serve a useful purpose. Many of these experiments have been designed to rebut their arguments. The relentless barrage of skeptical criticism is indirectly responsible for the thousands of studies of energy healing published in peer-reviewed journals.

I'm especially grateful to my friend and Hay House president Reid Tracy. This book was born in a conversation with him, and he suggested the title. His entire team at Hay House, including publisher Patty Gift, editor Anne Barthel, and marketing director Richelle Fredson, has been a joy to work with, on both a personal and a professional level.

I've had an amazing professional relationship with my friend and editor Stephanie Marohn for over a decade, and I'm so thankful for her keen eye and warm encouragement. Karin Kinsey's expert eye is responsible for the illustrations and typesetting, and she's given me enthusiastic support all along. I'm also grateful for the inspired editorial guidance of Hay House editor Anne Barthel and the eagle eye of copyeditor Rachel Shields.

I cannot even begin to express how much the genius of Heather Montgomery, General Manager of my organization Energy Psychology Group, makes in my life. Heather manages a complex organization with wisdom and humor. Her hand-picked team, including Seth Buffum, Marion Allen, Kendra Heath, Jackie Viramontez, and Mack Diesel, maintain high professional standards and make work fun even under pressure. There are many more laughs in the office than tears!

I'm also grateful for the board members and volunteers of the National Institute for Integrative Healthcare, the nonprofit I founded. We've now conducted or helped catalyze over 100 scientific studies and treated more than 20,000 veterans with PTSD. Giving back is a cornerstone of my life and I'm inspired by the hundreds of NIIH volunteers who do the same.

Many of my fellow transformational entrepreneurs supported the launch of this book, and I'm grateful to Nick Ortner, Mastin Kipp, Lissa Rankin, Joe Dispenza, Natalie Ledwell, Joe Mercola, Dave Asprey, and many others who shared it with their communities.

During the wildfire that consumed my home and office in October 2017, a committed group of people came together to help us recover. I traveled for most of the month while my wife, Christine, navigated our family's next steps at home. Her daughters, Julia and Jessie, as well as my children, Rexana and Lionel, together with Julia's husband, Tyler, formed an impromptu committee to take care of hundreds of details, from finding us emergency shelter to making lists of destroyed items. This huge disruption could have derailed the book, but thanks to their efforts it did not.

I'm blessed with a large extended family. Tens of thousands of people visit my EFT Universe website each month, and thousands train with us every year. The depth of emotional intimacy and heart sharing we experience both in person and in our social networking sites makes it impossible to ever feel alone. We know we're part of a huge global movement.

My wife, Christine, makes magic with her beautiful energy. Just being near her feels like being enfolded in a warm, soft blanket of love. She provides me with an energy environment that is filled with goodwill and happiness. It was Christine who encouraged me to work with Reid Tracy and Hay House and who every day creates the beautiful home environment and energy ecology in which this book was written.

ABOUT THE AUTHOR

Dawson Church, Ph.D., is an award-winning author whose best-selling book, *The Genie in Your Genes* (www.YourGeniusGene.com), has been hailed by reviewers as a breakthrough in our understanding of the link between emotion and genetics. He founded the National Institute for Integrative Healthcare (www.NIIH.org) to study and implement promising evidence-based psychological and medical techniques. His groundbreaking research has been published in prestigious scientific journals. He shares how to apply the breakthroughs of energy psychology to health and athletic performance through EFT Universe (www.EFTUniverse.com), one of the largest alternative medicine sites on the web. Websites: www.EFTUniverse.com, www.MindToMatter.com.

IMAGE CREDITS

CHAPTER 1

CHAPTER 2

CHAPTER 3

Page 69. Douglas Myers/CC-By-SA-3.0

Page 105. Bundesarchiv, Bild 102-04062A/CC-By-SA-3.0

CHAPTER 4

Page 125. US Department of Energy Human Genome Program

Page 133. © 2011 Michael Bonert / /CC SA 3.0 U

CHAPTER 5

Page 167. © NASA

Page 178 & 179. Courtesy of HeartMath® Institute

Page 185. Jordgette / CC BY-SA 3.0

Page 187. Mark Garlick/Science Photo Library / Alamy Stock Photo

Page 188. McMillan / Nature / Fickler et al., 2013 / CC 3.0 U

Page 192. Eric Fisk / CC-By-SA- 3.0 U

CHAPTER 6

Page 224. Naturefriends/CC-By-SA-4.0

Page 229. © NASA

Page 231. iStock.com/Agsandrew

Page 236. RonnyNB / CC-By-SA-3.0 U

Page 246. iStock.com/MariaArefyeva

Page 255. iStock.com/Agsandrew

Page 247. iStock.com/ValeryBrozhinsky

Page 259. Getty Images

Page 266. iStock.com/Niyazz

Hay House Titles of Related Interest

YOU CAN HEAL YOUR LIFE, the movie, starring Louise Hay & Friends
(available as a 1-DVD program, an expanded 2-DVD set,
and an online streaming video)
Learn more at www.hayhouse.com/louise-movie

THE SHIFT, the movie, starring Dr. Wayne W. Dyer
(available as a 1-DVD program, an expanded 2-DVD set,
and an online streaming video)
Learn more at www.hayhouse.com/the-shift-movie

———

*BECOMING SUPERNATURAL: How Common People
Are Doing the Uncommon,* by Dr. Joe Dispenza

*THE BIOLOGY OF BELIEF 10th ANNIVERSARY EDITION:
Unleashing the Power of Consciousness, Matter & Miracles,*
by Bruce Lipton, Ph.D.

*MIND OVER MEDICINE: Scientific Proof That
You Can Heal Yourself,* by Lissa Rankin, M.D.

*RESILIENCE FROM THE HEART: The Power to Thrive
in Life's Extremes,* by Gregg Braden

All of the above are available at your local bookstore,
or may be ordered by contacting Hay House (see next page).

We hope you enjoyed this Hay House book. If you'd like to receive our online catalog featuring additional information on Hay House books and products, or if you'd like to find out more about the Hay Foundation, please contact:

Hay House, Inc., P.O. Box 5100, Carlsbad, CA 92018-5100
(760) 431-7695 or (800) 654-5126
(760) 431-6948 (fax) or (800) 650-5115 (fax)
www.hayhouse.com® • www.hayfoundation.org

———

Published in Australia by: Hay House Australia Pty. Ltd.,
18/36 Ralph St., Alexandria NSW 2015
Phone: 612-9669-4299 • *Fax:* 612-9669-4144
www.hayhouse.com.au

Published in the United Kingdom by: Hay House UK, Ltd.,
The Sixth Floor, Watson House, 54 Baker Street, London W1U 7BU
Phone: +44 (0)20 3927 7290 • *Fax:* +44 (0)20 3927 7291
www.hayhouse.co.uk

Published in India by: Hay House Publishers India,
Muskaan Complex, Plot No. 3, B-2, Vasant Kunj, New Delhi 110 070
Phone: 91-11-4176-1620 • *Fax:* 91-11-4176-1630
www.hayhouse.co.in

———

Access New Knowledge.
Anytime. Anywhere.

Learn and evolve at your own pace
with the world's leading experts.

www.hayhouseU.com